The Twa Miss Dawsons

Margaret M. Robertson

Alpha Editions

This edition published in 2024

ISBN : 9789362511300

Design and Setting By
Alpha Editions
www.alphaedis.com
Email - info@alphaedis.com

Contents

Chapter One.

"Auld Miss Jean."

Saughleas was not a large estate, nor were the Dawsons gentlefolks, in the sense generally accepted in the countryside.

It was acknowledged that both the mother and the wife of the new laird had had good blood in their veins; but George Dawson himself, had been, and, in a sense, still was, a merchant in the High-street of Portie. He was banker and ship-owner as well, and valued the reputation which he had acquired as a business man, far more than he would ever be likely to value any honour paid to him as the Laird of Saughleas.

He had gotten his land honestly, as he had gotten all else that he possessed. He had taken no advantage of the necessities of the last owner, who had been in his power, in a certain sense, but had paid him the full value of the place; and not a landed proprietor among them all had more pride in the name and fame of his ancestry, than he had in the fact that he had been the maker of his own fortune, and that no man, speaking truth, could accuse him, in the making of it, of doing a single mean or dishonest deed.

His mother "had come o' gentle bluid," but his father had been first a common sailor and then the mate of a whaling ship that sailed many a time from the little Scottish east coast harbour of Portie, and which at last sailed away never more to return.

His widow lived through years of heart-sickness that must have killed her sooner than it did, but that her two fatherless bairns needed her care. They were but bairns when she died, with no one to look after them but a neighbour who had been always kind to them. The usual lot awaited them, it was thought. The laddie must take to the sea, as most of the laddies in Portie did, and the lassie must get "bit and sup" here and there among the neighbours, till she should be able to do for herself as a servant in some house in the town.

But it happened quite otherwise. Whatever the Dawsons had been in old times, there was good stuff in them now, it was said. For "Wee Jean Dawson," as she was called, with few words spoken, made it clear that she was to make her own way in the world. She was barely fifteen at that time, and her brother was two years younger, and if she had told her plans and wishes, she would have been laughed at, and possibly effectually hindered from trying to carry them out. But she said nothing.

The rent of the two rooms which the children and their mother had occupied, was paid to the end of the year, and the little stock of pins and needles, and small wares generally, by the sale of which the mother had helped out the "white seam," her chief dependence, was not exhausted, and Jean, declining the invitation of their neighbour to take up their abode with her in the mean time, quietly declared her intention of "biding where she was for a while," and no one had the right to say her nay. Before the time to pay another quarter's rent came round, it was ready, and Jean had proved her right to make her own plans, having shown herself capable of carrying them out when they were made.

How she managed, the neighbours could not tell, and they watched her with doubtful wonder. But it was not so surprising as it seemed to them. She was doing little more than she had been doing during the last two years of her mother's life under her mother's guidance. She had bought and sold, she had toiled late and early at the white seam, when her mother was past doing much, and had made herself busy with various trifles in cotton and wool, with crochet-needle and knitting-pins, when white seam failed them, and that was just what she was doing now.

And she went on bravely. She accepted offered favours gratefully, but sooner or later, she always repaid them. If Bell Ray, the fishwife, left a fresh haddock at the door as she passed, she was sure to carry with her some other day a pair of little socks, or a plaything for the bairnie at home. And if Mrs Sims, next door, kindly took the heaviest part of the girl's washing into her hands, she got in return her Sunday "mutch" starched and ironed and its broad borders set up in a way that excited the admiring wonder of all.

The two rooms were models of neatness as they had always been. George was comfortably clothed, at least he was never ragged, he very rarely went hungry, and he went to the school as regularly, and to as good purpose, as the banker's son, or the minister's son, and was as obedient to Jean as he had been to his mother in the old days. Jean was neat, and more than neat in her black print frock and holland apron—it cannot be said of the first half year that she was never hungry. For many a time the portion set aside for the dinner of two was only enough for one, and it cost Jean less pain to go without her share than to let the growing laddie be stinted of his needed food. But after the first half year, they had enough, and some to spare to those who had less, and much as Jean sometimes needed money to add to her stock in trade, she had been too wisely taught by her mother, not to know that a sufficient quantity of simple and wholesome food was absolutely necessary for health of body and of mind, and therefore necessary for success in life.

Of course she was successful. In after years, when she used to go back to this time in her thoughts and in her talk, she attributed her success in business, chiefly to two things—her silence, and her determination never to fall into debt. To the talk which "neebour folk" fell into in her little shop, she listened, but she rarely added her word; and she so ordered matters that it never became, as it very easily might have been, a centre of gossip and a cause of trouble in the neighbourhood. As to falling into debt, her determination against it hindered her for a while; but when the "big" merchants of Portie came to know her and her ways, they gave her the benefit of the lowest prices in sales, so trifling to them, but so important to her. They helped her with advice, and put some advantages as to fashions and fabrics in her way; and best of all, when Geordie's schooling was supposed to be at an end, one of them took him into his employment in a humble capacity indeed, but his rise to the place of honour behind the counter, and then to the book-keeper's desk, was more rapid than generally happens in such a case as his.

Before Jean was seven and twenty years of age, she and her brother were equal partners in a fairly prosperous business established by her in the High-street. After this fortune was secure in the course of time.

They were equal partners for a good many years, but gradually, as their resources increased, and new ways of employing energy and capital were open to the brother, this was changed. With her usual prudence, Jean refused to engage in risks which she had not sufficient knowledge to guide or strength to control, and a change was made in their business relations, and each continued to prosper in the chosen way.

As time went on, Jean ruled well her brother's home and helped him in many ways; but she did not, as had been predicted of her, grow into a mere hard business woman—seeing nothing so clearly as the main chance, and loving money itself better than the comfort that money may bring. It was they who knew her least, or who knew her only in her capacity of business woman, who feared this for her. The people who had watched and wondered at her early efforts and success, the neighbours, and the fisher wives who had exchanged kindly gifts with her in these days, did not fear it, nor the "puir bodies" in the back streets and lanes of Portie, who enjoyed the pickles o' tea and snuff, and the bits of flannel that found their way to them from her hands, nor the mothers of fatherless bairns who "won through sair straits," and got the better in many a "sair fecht" with poverty and trouble by her help.

Her silence and reserve, even to her friends—and she had many—looked to those who were not specially her friends, like the coldness and hardness that strengthens with the years. It was by deeds rather than words that her strong and tender nature found expression, and those who needed her help most, knew her best and trusted her most fully, and even in the busiest time of her life, she saw enough of other people's cares and sorrows, to remind her that there was something more needed in life than money, or the good things that money could bring.

And, when she ought to have been past "the like o' that," as she said to herself, for she was not far from thirty, the wonderful gift of love was given to her. And then, through her love, came the gift which God is sure, sooner or later, to give to His own,—the gift of sanctified trouble.

There came to Portie in one of the ships in which her brother had an interest, a lad—he looked scarcely more than a lad—sick with fever. Accident brought him to George Dawson's house for a night, and in the morning he was too ill to leave it. Through long weeks of suffering and delirium, Jean nursed him, and cared for him, and saved him from death. He was not a good young man. The wild words uttered in his wanderings, proved this to Jean, only too clearly, and if he had gone away as soon as he rose from his bed, he would have taken her interest and her good will with him, and nothing more. But his convalescence was long and tedious, and whatever his sins against himself and others might have been, he was of a sweet and kindly nature, and a handsome and manly lad withal.

And of course it was the fairest side of his character that he showed to Jean in these days. Not that he tried to hide his past follies and even his sins from her. But it was his sorrow for them that he showed her, and his longing to live a better life by her help; and what with his penitence and his gentleness and his winning English ways, he wiled the heart out of her breast before she was aware. And the love was mutual. But whether he ever could have given to her all that she gave to him, was doubtful to the only one who knew what had befallen her.

To say that her brother was amazed at her love for a man so much younger and mentally and morally so much beneath her, is to say little. He was utterly dismayed. But he knew her strong and steadfast nature too well to try to move her from her purpose. He only stipulated that there should be time given to prove the young man's love, and to prove also the firmness of his determination to live a new life. It was not a severe test that he insisted on. One voyage the young man was to make, and coming home with the good word of his captain and shipmates, no difficulty should be put in the way of the marriage, strange as he confessed the idea of such a marriage to be. It was to be a six months' voyage only, and though Jean did not feel that such a sacrifice need be made, she was yet willing to make it at the will of the brother whom she loved. And so they parted.

But six months passed, and then six more, and when three more had worn away tidings came. Through these months of waiting Jean went in silence, and when the captain's son came home—the only survivor of the crew of the ship that had carried her heart and her hope away—and told the story of their wreck on wintry seas, no one knew that she listened and suffered as no widow of them all suffered for her cruel and utter loss.

Her lover's name was spoken with the rest, and it was told how brave he had been and kindly, and how he had kept up the courage of the rest and cheered them all to the last, and how the hardest and most careless of the crew had planned together to beguile him into taking more than his share of the food they had, because he was not strong like the rest, and because they loved him. And Jean listened to it all, and never uttered a word. Nor afterward did she open her lips even to her brother. He tried to speak to her some vague words of comfort, as to its being God's will, and all for the best, but she only put forth her hand to bid him cease, and when he still would fain have spoken a word of his own sorrow for her trouble she rose and went away, and it was many years before either of them returned to the sorrow of that time. She lived through her trouble, and she did not grow hard or bitter under it, as she might have done if he had lived and forgotten her; and comfort came to her as the years went on.

It came to her in a strange way, her brother thought, and though he was glad of its coming, it cost him some pain. The first, indeed the only, danger of estrangement that ever came between the brother and sister grew out of this. Not that there was any real danger even then; for Jean was, in her silent and determined way, so soft and gentle and unprovokable in the new manner of thought and life into which she fell at this time, that though her brother was both angry and ashamed, and suffered both shame and anger to appear to her and to others, it made no real breach between them.

And he had cause for neither shame nor anger. It was only that weary of herself and the drowsy ministrations of the parish kirk, Jean had strayed one stormy Sabbath night into "a little kirkie" lately built in a back street by "a queer kin' o' folk ca'ed missioners," and had there heard words such as she had never heard before, and had found in them more than comfort.

Not that the words were altogether new, nor the thoughts,—they were in her Bible, every one of them—she told her brother afterwards; but, for one thing, they were earnestly spoken by one who believed them, and then they came to one ready for them and waiting, though she knew it not.

Ah! well, that does not explain it altogether. It was the Lord Himself who spoke to her by the voice of His servant revealing Himself to her, through His own familiar Word in a new way. After that she could say of Him, "Whose I am and whom I serve," and her life took a new meaning. It was His who "had bought her with a price." All that she had done hitherto for pity's sake, she did now *for His sake.* "To one of the least of these," He had said. The world was full of "these little ones" of His, and there were some of them in Portie even, and henceforth they were to be her care.

Her outward life did not change much however. Except that at first she "whiles" went to "the little kirkie," and afterwards went there altogether, there was no difference that could be named by her little world generally. Her brother saw a difference, and so did the poor folk who shared her care and kindness. Her eye was brighter and her step lighter, and the look of suffering she had lately worn was giving place to a look of patient even cheerful peacefulness that was good to see. She had more words, too, at her command. Not for her brother—at least not for him at first. But the impulse which her new love for her Master had given her, was strong enough to overcome the silence natural to her, and "good words" gently and yet strongly spoken went with her gifts now, and sometimes they were received as gladly as her gifts. But that she should cast in her lot with the handful of "newfangled folk" in Stott's Lane was a pain and a humiliation to her brother which it took years to outlive.

Their outward life went on as it had done before for a good while, and then her brother married. His wife was of a family which had had a name and a place in the countryside for generations; but George Dawson found her earning her bread as a teacher in a school in Aberdeen, and married her "for pure love," Portie folk said; and some who had known him best, expected no such thing of George Dawson.

It was doubtful whether his love for her or his pride in her was strongest. He did not take her to the house above the shop where he and his sister had lived so long, but to a fine house at the head of the High-street in a far pleasanter part of the town, and there they began their married life together. Jean did not go with them, though they both wished it. It was better for them to be alone, she said, and as well for her. So she staid still in the house above the shop, making a home for the young men employed in the business, keeping a wise and watchful eye on them and on the business also. After a few years, when her sister-in-law became delicate, and there were little children needing her care, she, with greater self-denial than any guessed, gave up her independent life and went home to them for a while, and lightened the mother's care for them and for the home as well, and found her reward in knowing that her work was not vain.

But when more years had passed, and her brother, a richer man than she knew, bought the small estate of Saughleas, and took his family there, she did not go with them. She was getting on in years, she was too old to begin a new life in new circumstances, and the bairns were getting beyond the need of her care. So she went to a home of her own that looked out upon the sea, and set herself with wisdom and patience and loving kindness to the work which her Master had given her to do.

Chapter Two.

The Brother's Sorrow.

George Dawson had been very successful in life. He was not an old man when he took possession of his estate of Saughleas. He had many years before him in which to enjoy the fruit of his labours, he told himself, and he exulted in the thought.

What happy years the first years there were! His children were good and bonny and strong; his wife was—not very strong—but oh! so sweet and dear! What lady among them all could compare with her, so good and true, so fair and stately, and yet so kindly and so well-beloved?

"I will grow a better man to deserve her better," he said to himself with a vague presentiment of change upon him—a fear that such happiness could not last. For who was he, that he should have so much more than other men had? So he walked softly, and did justly, and dealt mercifully in many a case where he might have been severe with justice on his side, and strove honestly and wisely to make himself worthy of the woman who had been growing dearer day by day.

Growing dearer? Yes—but who was slipping away from him, slowly, but surely, day by day. He strove to shut his eyes to that which others clearly saw, but deep down in his heart was the certain knowledge that he must lose her. But not yet. Not for a long time yet. With care in a warmer climate, under sunnier skies, she might live for years yet—many years. So he set himself to the task of so arranging his affairs, that he might take her away for the winter at least, away from the bleak sea winds to one of the many places where he had heard that health and healing had come to many a one far more ill than she was.

And if he could have got her away in time, who knows but so it might have been. But illness came in amongst the children, and she would not leave them even to the wise and loving care of their aunt; and when first one, and then another little life went out, her husband could see with a sinking heart, that she longed to follow where they had gone.

When the other children grew better he took her away for a little while. But the drawing of those little graves, and the longing to die at home among those who were still left, brought them back to Saughleas—only just in time. He did not lay her in the bleak kirkyard of Portie. He *could* not do it. It was a foolish thing to do, it was said, but in the quietest, bonniest spot in Saughleas, in a little wood that lay in sight of the house, he laid her down, when he could keep her no longer, and by and by he lifted her bonny little bairns and laid them down beside her. And then it seemed for a while that to him life was ended.

But life was not ended. He had more to do, and more to suffer yet, and indeed had to become a changed man altogether before he could be ready and worthy to look again upon the face that he so longed to see.

Oh, the length of the days! the weariness of all things! He used to wonder at the sickness that lay heavy on his heart all day—at the anguish that made the night terrible to him. He was growing an old man, he said to himself, and he had thought it was only the young who strove and suffered, and could not yield themselves to the misery of loss and pain. But then—who, old or young, of all the men he had ever known, had lost what he had lost? No wonder that he suffered and could find no comfort.

"Ay! No wonder that you suffer," said his sister to him once. "But take tent lest ye add rebellion to the sin of overmuch sorrow. Have you ever truly submitted to God's will all your life, think ye, George, man? Things had mostly gone well and easily with ye. But now this has come upon you, and take ye thought of it. For ye're no' out of God's hand yet, and 'whom He loveth He chasteneth.'"

She did not speak often to him, but he heard her and made no answer. That was Jean's way of looking at things, he thought; and because she had had sore troubles of her own, he did not answer her roughly, as he felt inclined to do. There was nothing to be said.

He sent his two daughters away to be educated, first to Edinburgh and afterwards to London, and after that, the house of Saughleas, except a room or two, was shut up for a time. The father and son left it early and returned to it late, and the father spent his days in working as hard as ever he had done in the days when he was making his own way in the world. The winter was hard to bear, but the coming of the spring-time was even worse. Every bonny flower looked up at him with the eyes of her he had lost; every bird, and breeze, and trembling leaf spoke to him with her voice. The sunlight lying on her grave, the still, soft air, the sweetness of the season,—all brought back on him like a flood, the longing for her presence; and he must have gone away or broken down altogether, if it had not been for his son George, his only son.

He was a handsome, kindly lad, more like his mother than any of his bairns, and dearer than any of them to his father, because he was her firstborn. George had mourned his mother deeply and truly, but her name had never been spoken between them till on one of the first sunny days of spring, the father found the son lying on his face among the long withered grass that covered her grave. Sitting there then, lips and hearts were opened to each other, and it was never so bad to either after that.

By and by hope sprang up in the father's heart, in the presence of the son who was so like his mother, and so the weight of his heavy sorrow was lightened.

But there were folk in Portie, and his sister Jean was one of them, who doubted whether the father was doing the best that could be done for his son. He held a situation in the Portie Bank, and his father's intention was, that he should there, and elsewhere, when the right time came, acquire such a knowledge of business, as should enable him, if not to make money for himself, at least to make a wise use of the money already made for him.

But his work was made easy to the lad, as was natural enough, by others besides his father, and his comings and goings were not so carefully noted, as if he had not been his father's son. He had time and money at his disposal; not so very much of either, but more than any of his companions had, and certainly more than was good for him. Not that he fell into ill ways at this time, though that was said of him. That only came afterwards; and it might have been helped, if his father had been as wise then as he was determined with him afterwards.

But that which raised his father's anger, was almost worse, to his thought, than falling into ill ways, in the common acceptation of the term, would have been. He might have spent money freely, even foolishly, and his name might have been spoken with the names of men whose society his father would have shunned or scorned, and he might have been reproved and then forgiven. But that he should love and be determined to marry a girl in humble life, the daughter of a sailor's widow, and he not one and twenty, seemed to his father worse than folly and even worse than sin. The father had never given a thought to any woman except his sister, till he was thirty-five, and that his son, a mere lad, should wish to marry any one, was a folly not to be tolerated.

He blamed his sister in the matter, for bonny Elsie Calderwood was the daughter of the man who had brought home to her the bitter tidings that her lover was lost, and Jean had cared for and comforted his widow and orphans when their turn came to weep for one who returned no more. But he was wrong in this, for she had known nothing of the young man's wishes, certainly she had never abetted him in his folly, as was said. Indeed she had taken no thought of danger for him. "They were just a' bairns thegither," she had said, "and had kenned one another all their lives."

For the Calderwood bairns had been the chosen companions of Geordie and his sisters in the days when, openly scorning the attendance of nursemaids, they had clambered over the rocks, and waded in the shallows along the shore, and gathered dulse and birds' eggs with the rest of the bairns of the town. When his sisters went away, after their mother's death, the intimacy was naturally enough continued by George, and all the more closely that he missed his sisters, and was oppressed by the dreariness of the life at home. It was natural enough, though the father could not see it so, and he spoke angrily and unwisely to his son.

But Mrs Calderwood was as proud in her way as Mr Dawson was in his, and she scorned the thought of keeping the rich man's son to the promise he had made without leave asked of her. She was also as hard in her way as he was in his, and forbade the young man to enter her house, and gave him no chance to disobey her. But in a place like Portie young folks can meet elsewhere than at home, and one or other of them must be sent away.

So with Miss Jean's advice and help Elsie was sent to get a year at a boarding-school, as was wise and right, all her friends in Portie were given to understand. But she went away without giving back her promise for all that her mother could say. She went cheerfully enough, "to make herself fitter to be his wife," she said. But she never returned; a slow strong fever seized her where she was, and first her mother went to her, and then Miss Jean, whose heart was sore for them all.

And then Miss Jean did what the mother never would have done. When she saw that the end was drawing near, she wrote one letter to her nephew telling him to come and take farewell of his love, and another to his father telling him that so she had done. All this mattered little however. For it was doubtful whether the dying girl recognised the lover who called so wildly on her name. But she died in his arms, and he went home with her mother and his aunt to Portie and laid her down in the bleak kirkyard; and then he went away speaking no word to his father, in his youthful despair and anger, indeed never looking on his face.

There had been something said, before all this came to pass between them, of the lad's being sent to London for a while, to learn how business was done in a great banking-house, one of the partners of which was a friend of his father; and after a time he was heard of there. But he did not write to his father directly, and he never drew a shilling of the money that his father had deposited in his name.

He did not stay long in his place in the London bank, but went away, leaving no trace behind him, and was lost to them all; and it was long before his name was spoken by his father again. Even Miss Jean, having no words of comfort to put with it, never named to him the name of his son, for whom she knew he was grieving with anger and pain unspeakable. It was to be doubted, Jean thought, whether these days were not longer, and drearier, and "waur to thole" than even the days that had followed the death of the mother of the lad.

But they had to be borne, and he left himself in these days little time for brooding over his troubles. He devoted himself to business, with all his old earnestness, and wealth flowed in upon him, and the fear was strong in his sister's heart, that he was beginning, in the desolation that had fallen upon him, to love it for its own sake. He added to Saughleas a few fields on one side, and a farm or two on the other, which the necessities of the owners had put into the market, at this time; but it was more to oblige these needy men, than because he wanted their land. He had the money in hand, he said indifferently to his sister, and the land would ay bring its price. But he took little pleasure in Saughleas for a while.

When Geordie had been gone a year and more, his sisters came home from school. They had been away long, and their father had, as he said, to make their acquaintance over again. They had changed from merry girls of fifteen and sixteen, into grown up young ladies,—"fine ladies" their father called them to their aunt, and a good many people in Portie, called them "fine ladies" also, for a while. They looked to be fine ladies, with their London dresses, and London manners, and some folk added, their "London pride." They held their heads high, and carried themselves erect and firmly as they walked, and spoke softly and in "high English," which looked like pride to some of their old friends, who were more than half afraid of the young ladies of Saughleas, they said. But it soon came to be known that what looked like pride was more than half shyness, and as for the "high English," the kindly Scotch fell very readily from their lips on occasion.

It cannot be said that they made themselves very happy in Saughleas for a time. They came home in November, and that is a dreary month on the east coast, indeed all the winter is dreary there. There were gay doings in the best houses in Portie to welcome them home, and they enjoyed them well. For they had only been school-girls in London, and the gayeties they had been permitted to mingle in there, had been mostly of the kind which are supposed to blend improvement of some sort with the pleasure to be enjoyed, and though they doubtless valued such opportunities and made good use of them, both for pleasure and improvement, the gayeties of Portie were quite different and more to their taste. They were young and pretty and gay, and the kindness and the admiration so freely bestowed on them were very pleasant to them both. But they would have preferred the house in the High-street, where they had all been born, in these first days, for their home.

Saughleas was dull and dreary in the short winter days, and oh! how they missed their mother! It was like losing her again, to come home to the great empty house, which their father left almost before the sun rose for weeks together, not to return again till the lamps had been lighted for hours in the wide hall.

And Geordie! When they had been at Saughleas a month or more, their father had never spoken his name, and when Jean, the eldest and bravest of the sisters, putting great force upon herself, asked him when her brother was coming home, he answered so coldly, and with words so hard and bitter, that her heart sank as she heard. They had known for some time that something had gone wrong between them. Geordie had told them that, when he had gone to see them in London; but the sad story of poor Elsie Calderwood they had never heard. They mourned for their brother, and longed for his coming home, thinking that the happy days that were gone would come again with him.

Though the estate of Saughleas was small, the house was both large and stately. The last owner had put into the house, the money which should have been given to enrich the land, and make a beginning of the prosperity of the family which he had hoped to found. So it was like a castle almost, but it was little like a home.

The two or three great landed proprietors in the countryside were great people in their own esteem, and in the general esteem also; and George Dawson, notwithstanding Saughleas, was just the merchant and banker of the High-street to them—a man much respected in his own place, and he was not out of place on occasion, at the table of any of them all. But an interchange of civilities on equal terms between the ladies of the families was not likely to take place, nor was this greatly to be desired. It might have been different if their mother had lived, they said to one another; for in their remembrance of her, she was superior in every way to any lady of them all. But they were quite content with the society of Portie, and would have been content with the house in the High-street as well.

Mr Dawson asked his sister to come and live in his house when his daughters came home, but she declined to do so. They did not need her as mistress of the house, and she believed that her influence over them would be more decided and salutary should she remain in her own house. They were good bairns, she said, who meant to do right, and though they might whiles need a word of advice, or a restraining touch, it must be their own guidance that their father must lippen to, and not hers. And Auntie Jean was right.

They were good bairns on the whole, as their aunt said, and they were "bonnie lassies" as well. The first idea that most people had on seeing them, was that in person, mind, and manners, they were very much alike. Even their father thought this at first. But it was not long before he discovered that in most respects they were very different May, the youngest, was like her mother, "though *nothing like* so bonny," he told himself with a sigh. Jean was like her aunt, it was said, but Auntie Jean herself, and the two or three others who remembered Auntie Jean's mother as she was before her husband's ship went down, said that the elder sister was like her grandmother, who had been a far bonnier woman than ever her daughter had been.

In form and features there was a resemblance between the sisters; May was the fairer and slighter of the two, and was often called the prettier. But as time went on the resemblance did not increase. Jean was the strongest in person and in mind, and the better able of the two to profit by the discipline, which time and circumstances brought to them both, and of this difference in character her face gave token to those who had eyes to see.

They loved each other, and were patient and forbearing with each other when they did not quite agree as to the course which either wished to pursue. But when it came about that one must yield her will to the other, it was May who was made to yield when her will would have led her into wrong or doubtful paths. But if pleasure were to be given up, or a distasteful duty done, or if some painful self-denial had to be borne by one so that the other might escape, such things generally fell to the lot of Jean.

Chapter Three.

A Dreary Day.

The folk looking out of their windows in Portie might well wonder what could be bringing the young ladies of Saughleas into the town on such a dismal day. Though April was come in, it might have been the wintriest month of the year; for the wind that met them was dashing the wet sleet in their faces, and tangling their bright brown curls about their eyes, till laughing and breathless they were fain to turn their backs upon it before they were half down the High-street. They were in shelter for a little while as they crossed through a side street, but the wind met them again as they went round a corner, and came close upon the sea. They were going to their aunt's house and a few steps brought them to the door; but for all the wind and the sleet, they did not seem in haste to enter. They lingered, taking off their dripping cloaks and overshoes.

"Auntie will wonder to see us on such a day."

"She'll wonder to see you. She kens that I am not afraid of wind or rain."

As they lingered the door opened.

"Eh! Miss Dawson and Miss May. Is it you on sic a day? Wha would ha'e expected to see you—and on your ain feet too. Wet enough they must be."

"We'll go to the kitchen, Nannie, and no' wet the carpet," said May; and they staid there chatting with the maid for a minute or two. The expected greeting met them at the parlour door.

"Eh! bairns! Here on such a day!"

"Papa had to come to the town," said Jean.

"And so we thought we might as well come with him," said May.

"Weel, ye're welcome anyway, and ye're neither sugar nor salt to be harmed by a drop of rain. But come in by to the fire."

But their tussle with the wind had made the fire unnecessary.

"It's a good thing that your curls are no' of a kind that the rain does ill with, May, my dear. But you might as well go up the stair and put them in order now."

"Oh! I needna care. We have only a minute to stay, and it's hardly worth my while."

"Papa went straight to the inn with the dog-cart, and we only walked down the High-street. It *is* a dreary day."

"And we'll need to go to the inn and wait for him. For he said nothing of coming here," said May.

"But it's likely he'll come for all that. He maistly ay looks in. It's a pity he came out on sic a day, and him no weel. But I suppose he had to come. The 'John Seaton' sails the day," said their aunt.

The sisters gave a sudden involuntary glance at each other. May reddened and laughed a little. Her sister grew pale. Their aunt looked from one to the other, thinking her own thoughts, but she did not let this appear.

"She mayna sail the day. They have lost some of their men, it is said, and that may hinder them."

"And the wind and the waves are fearsome," said the elder sister with a shiver.

"Ay, but the wind is in the richt airt. That wouldna hinder them," said her aunt; and then she added in a little.

"Willie Calderwood goes as her first mate. That's a rise for him. I hope he may show discretion. He's no' an ill laddie."

"And he's on a fair way to be a captain now," said May. "So he told me—in awhile."

"Ay, in a while," said her aunt dryly. "But he has a long and dangerous voyage before him, and it's no' likely that all who sail awa' the day will ever come hame again."

The eldest sister was standing with her face touching the window.

"The sea looks fearsome over yonder," said she.

"Ay. But they'll ha'e room enough when once they are outside the harbour bar, and then the wind will drive them off the rocks and out to sea; and they are in God's hands."

"Auntie Jean," said the girl turning a pale face toward her, "why do you say the like of that to-day?"

"It's true the day as it's true ilka day. Why should I no' say it? My dear, the thought of it is a consolation to many a puir body in Portie the day."

"But it sounds almost like a prophecy of evil to—to the 'John Seaton,' as you said it. And the sea is fearsome," repeated she, turning her face to the window again.

"Lassie, come in by to the fire. Ye're trembling with cold, and I dare say ye're feet are no' so dry as they should be. Come in by and put them to the fire."

"But we havena long to bide."

However she came at her aunt's bidding, and sat down on a stool, shading her face with a paper that she took from the table.

"Auntie Jean," said May, "I have seen just such a picture in a book, as you would make if you were painted just as you are, with your hands folded on your lap, and your stocking and your ball of worsted beside you, and your glasses lying on the open book. Look, Jeannie, look at auntie. Is she not like a picture as she sits now?"

"What's the lassie at now, with her picturing and her nonsense?" said her aunt, not sure whether she should be pleased with all this. "I'm just as usual, and so is the room. No more like a picture than on other days."

She was in full dress—according to her ideas of full dress—and she was that every day of the year. She had on a gown of some soft black stuff, the skirt of which was partly covered by a wide black silk apron. A snowy kerchief was pinned across her breast, and fastened at her neck with a plain gold brooch, showing a braid of hair of mingled black and grey. Her cap was made in the fashion worn by the humblest of her countrywomen, but it was made of the finest and clearest lawn, and the full "set up" borders were edged with the daintiest of "thread" lace, and so were the wide strings tied beneath her chin. Not a spot nor a speck was visible upon it, or upon any part of her dress, nor indeed on any article which the room contained. She and her room together would have made a picture homely and commonplace enough, but it would have been a pleasing picture, with a certain quaint beauty of its own.

"It is that you are so peaceful in here always, and untroubled. That is what May means when she says it is like a picture in a book. And after the wind, and the sleet, and the stormy sea, it is quieting and restful to look in upon you."

"Weel, maybe. But it is the same picture ilka day o' the year, and I weary of it whiles. And the oftener you look in upon it, the better it will be for me. What ails the lassie? Canna ye bide still by the fire?"

For Jean had risen from her low seat, and was over at the window again.

"The clouds are breaking away. It is going to be fair, I think. We'll need to be going, May, or we may be late. I'll come over to-morrow, auntie, and good-bye for to-day."

"But, lassie, what's a' your haste? Your father will be sure to come for you. Bide still where you are."

"I think I'll bide still, anyway," said May. "I am no' going, Jeannie. I'm no' caring to go."

"Yes, you are coming with me," said her sister sharply. "You must come. I want to speak to you—and—yes, come away."

May pouted and protested, but she followed her sister to the kitchen where they had left their cloaks, and they went away together. They kept for a while in the shelter of the houses nearest the sea, but they did not speak till they were beyond these. The wind was still high, but neither rain nor sleet was falling, and they paused a minute to take breath before they turned to meet it again.

"The 'John Seaton' sails the day," said May, turning her laughing face toward her sister. Jean did not laugh. "As though that werena the very thing that brought us both out as well as papa, though we said nothing about it before we came. To the high rocks? But it would be more sensible like to go to the pier head, and then we might get a chance to shake his hand and say God bless him. And it's not too late yet."

"No, I'm no' going. It would do no good and it would anger my father."

But May persisted.

"Why shouldna we be there as well as half the town? Papa mightna like it, but he couldna help it, if we were once there. And ye ken ye never said good-bye to Willie Calderwood."

"May," said her sister, "when did you see Willie? I mean, when did he tell you that he was to be first mate of the 'John Seaton,' and maybe captain by and by?"

"Oh! I heard that long ago, and I saw him last night. He came a bit of the way home with me. He would have come all the way to say good-bye to you, but he had something to do, that couldna be put off. And I'm sure he'll expect to see you at the pier to-day."

"But I canna go."

And then she added—"Well, and what more did he say?"

"Oh! what should he say? He said many a thing. He told me if I would stand on the high rocks above the Tangle Stanes and wave my scarlet scarf when the 'John Seaton' was sailing by, he would take it as a sign of good luck, and that he would come safe home again, and get his heart's wish."

"And we are going there."

"Oh! I dinna ken. It's cold, and the ship mayna sail, and we might have to wait. I'm not going."

"Did he say that to you? Yes, you are going. Do you mean that you would let him be disappointed at the very last, and him taking it for a sign?"

"But the mist is rising, and it's all nonsense—and he winna see."

"Where is your scarlet shawl? Did you no' bring it?"

"Oh! yes. I brought it fast enough," said May, laughing and lifting her dress, under which the shawl was fastened. "As we were going to Auntie Jean's I thought it as well to keep it out of sight. But, Jean, it is wet and cold, and he was only half in earnest."

"How could he speak out all that he wanted to say, kenning my father! But you must go."

"Go yourself. He'll never ken the difference."

"No, he'll never ken the difference. But when he comes home—what will you say to him then? And besides it was your being there that was to be the sign of his safe coming home—and—his getting his heart's wish. You are coming."

They turned their steps northward, in the direction of a high ledge of rocks, that half a mile above the harbour jutted out into the sea. It was this point both had been thinking of when they left home, for they well knew that the young ladies from Saughleas could not, on such a day, go to loiter on the pier with all the town, just to see a whaling ship set sail for northern seas. If the day had been fine, they might have gone with a chance companion or two to see what was to be seen, and to while away an hour. Even in the wind and sleet Jean might have gone with her father, if the ship had not been the "John Seaton," or if Willie Calderwood had not been on board. But as it was, she could not even name such a thing to her father. He would have been angry, and it would have done no good.

So it was to the rocks above the Tangle Stanes they must go. If the day had been fine, there would have been other folk there, and many a signal would have been given as the ship went by. But they had the high desolate rocks to themselves when they had clambered up at last, and it was all they could do to keep their footing upon it, for the wind which had met them so fiercely even on the level, raged here with tenfold violence.

And there was no sign of the ship. There was nothing but great wild waves rising and falling as far as they could see, and masses of white foam here and there, where they broke themselves on half hidden rocks beneath.

There was no sign of life except that now and then a solitary sea-gull shrieked sadly through the blast.

"Eh! but it's dreary and cold," said May with a shudder.

"Go down to yon sheltered nook and bide there till I tell you that she is coming."

"But it's a' nonsense, Jean. She mayna come at all, as auntie said."

"Since we're here, we'll bide a while:" So May went down to the sheltered nook, and wrapping her cloak about her, she took from her pocket a biscuit or two with which she had providently supplied herself, and prepared to wait with what patience she could till her sister chose to go. And Jean, unable to stand still in the bitter wind, struggled up and down the narrow limits of the ledge,—not thinking—hardly feeling—for she needed all her power to keep her footing on the slippery rock—only waiting for the ship.

She came in sight at last, but, driven by the wind, as soon as she was beyond the harbour bar, she drifted so far to the eastward, that it was doubtful whether any signal from those on shore could be seen on board.

"Are you coming, May? Haste you," cried Jean, and while her sister lingered, she let the long shawl float its full length on the wind. At the moment the clouds parted, and a sudden gleam of sunshine lighted the rock and the girlish figure, and the waving signal which she held. It was but for a moment. Before May had clambered to her side, the clouds met again, and dimness and dreariness were over all.

"Take it, May. It is you he is thinking of now when he sees it. He must have seen it when the sun shone out. Take it, and hold it fast."

"It is easy said, hold it fast, and it's all nonsense," said May pettishly, and from her uncertain fingers the wind caught the scarlet signal, and carried it out to sea.

"My shawl!" gasped May. "My bonny scarlet shawl?"

"It's an ill omen, I doubt," said Jean in a whisper. "But never mind the shawl; you shall have my bonny blue one instead. And now we may go home."

"It is all folly from first to last," said May. "And what I am to say about my shawl, I canna tell."

"Say nothing. Who has a right to ask? And, May, I think I'll walk home— to warm myself, for I am cold." She looked cold and could not keep herself from trembling. "Go back to Auntie Jean's. My father will be sure to seek us there, and I'll be home before you."

May was not sure of the wisdom of consenting to meet her father without her sister, lest he might ask any questions as to how they had spent the afternoon. But hoping that she might get to her aunt's house before him, she hurried away, scarcely remembering till she sat beside her aunt's pleasant fire, that she had left her sister standing there on the desolate wind-swept height.

And there she stood while the ship went slowly on its northern way, "carrying her life with it," she said to herself, in vague wonder at the utter faintness of heart, and weariness of body which had fallen upon her.

"What has come to me?" she muttered. "What is Willie Calderwood to me, but a friend? He has ay been that, and ay will be, and if he is more to my bonny May—why that makes him more to me—and not less, surely. And friends must part. There is many a sair heart in Portie the night—and folk man just thole whatever is sent, and say nothing. And oh! if Geordie would but come home?"

Again the clouds parted, and a gleam of sunshine touched the water, giving her one more glimpse of the white sails of the ship before she went down to the north, and then there was but "the fearsome waves of the sea," from which she could scarcely turn her dazed eyes. But she had to take her way down the steep rocks, and through the wet fields, the near way home. She lingered and walked wearily, and it was growing dark when she went in at the gate.

"Is it you, Miss Dawson?" said a voice in the darkness. "Has any thing happened? Are ye your lane?"

"Nothing has happened. I preferred to walk. Are they not come yet?"

"Nobody has come yet, Miss Dawson, and there has been nobody here but Robbie Saugster, wantin' a book that you promised him—or Miss May maybe it was," said Phemie. "You were hardly awa' ere he was here, and he said he'd come back the morn."

Jean sat down wearily in the hall.

"I am wet and tired," said she.

"I was sure you would be that," said Phemie, "and I made a bit fire in your ain room, and I'll bring warm water and bathe your feet in a jiffy. No wonder you are tired."

"That was well done. They cannot be long now in coming. I'll go and make myself ready, and have the tea made at once."

Phemie was up with the warm water almost as soon as her mistress.

"Eh! Miss Dawson, but you are white and spent looking. It's the heat, I dare say, after being in the cold."

She knelt and took off her shoes and stockings, and bathed her weary feet with kindly care, and Jean let her do as she would, saying nothing for a while.

"I'm better now. Yes, it must have been coming into the warm room after the cold of the afternoon. Thank you, Phemie, that is comfortable. I will be down in a minute now."

She was sitting behind the urn with a book in her hand when her father came in.

"You are late, papa."

"Yes—too late—too late," said he, and then he sat down by the fire without taking off his greatcoat or the heavy plaid which was on his shoulders above it.

"Something has happened," said Jean to herself. But she knew he would not in his present mood answer her questions. She rose and took the plaid and his hat, and carried them away. Then she helped him to take off his coat. He did not resist her, but he did not speak, and by the time he was seated at the table, May came down. Her sister met her at the door, asking softly,—

"What has happened to my father?"

"Has any thing happened? I do not know. I waited at auntie's till I was weary, and then I went to Jamieson's, and waited there. He came at last, but he has not opened his lips all the way home."

And he did not open his lips during the meal. He ate and drank as usual, and as usual took his notebook from his pocket when he was done, and turned the leaves and wrote a word or two. He was scarcely more silent than was his wont, but there was a look on his face that Jean had seen only once or twice upon it—a look at once grieved and angry, of which she had learned to be afraid. She longed to ask him if any new trouble had befallen him, but she did not dare to ask, and she sat in silence with her work in her hands till Phemie appeared at the door.

"If you please, Miss Dawson, will you speak here a minute. It's Robbie Saugster again."

Jean rose and went out of the room, conscious that her father's eye followed her, with something of suspicion in its glance. She went into the room where her father's books and papers were kept, and in a minute Phemie ushered in a boy who looked as though he had had the benefit of all the wind and the rain that had fallen through the day. He waited till Phemie had shut the door, and then he said:

"It is this I was bidden give you, Miss Jean. I cam' afore, and then I looked for ye on the pier and a' way, but I couldna see ye, and I doubt it's ower late for an answer new."

He offered her a soiled and crumpled note, which she read at a glance and put in her pocket.

"What is this about a book that I promised you, Robbie?" she asked.

"Oh! ay, Miss Dawson. I had to tell Phemie something. And I'll be glad o' an orra book or two, as I'm goin' to the school—a count-book or maybe a Latin grammar. But I'll come back for it again."

"Wait a minute, Robbie," said Jean. She went into the parlour again where her father was sitting.

"May, what is this about a book for Robbie Saugster? Did you promise him one? He says he is going to the school."

"A book? I dinna mind. Maybe I did. What kind of a book was it? I canna look it out to-night, I am too tired."

The father's eyes had gone from one to the other with eager scrutiny.

"There are old school books enough, and I'll tell him that you'll look them out to-morrow."

"You should have had them ready, no' to keep the laddie coming back again," said her father sharply.

"I didna mind about it, and I dare say Jean promised as well as me," she answered pettishly.

"Mind next time then; and, Jean, tell Phemie to give the laddie his supper before he goes home."

"Yes, papa," said Jean as she shut the door.

"Something has happened and he was watching. It is about poor Geordie, and I'm not sure whether I should tell him or not I must think about it first."

Robbie got his supper, and the promise of the books, and then Jean came in and sat down with her work at her father's side, working quietly and busily as usual, but all the time putting a strong restraint upon her thoughts lest she should betray herself unawares by look or sign. May, weary with the exertion of the afternoon, by and by fell asleep in her chair.

"Bid them come ben to worship, and let the lassie go to her bed," said her father.

When worship was over, Jean folded her work, saying she was weary too. "Unless you may want any thing, papa," said she turning before she reached the door.

He looked at her a moment as if in doubt, and then he said shortly, "I want nothing," and Jean went away to let herself think over it all.

"No answer!" said she as she took the note from her pocket again. A leaf torn from an account-book it seemed to be. She spread it before her on the table; there were only a few words written on it.

"Miss Dawson,—

"If it is possible, come to the pier head before the 'John Seaton' sails. Maybe the sight of you will do what no persuasion of mine can do. But no ill shall come to Geordie that I can keep from him. Come at all risks.

"Your humble servant,—

"W.C."

"And I might have been there, if I had but known. What will he think of me? And can it be that Geordie has sailed on the 'John Seaton'? No wonder that my heart grew sick as the ship went out of sight. And oh how can I ever tell my father?"

Chapter Four.

Saughleas.

Saughleas with the June sunshine felling on it was a very different place from Saughleas under the "drip, drip" of winter rain and sleet, with the wind moaning or roaring through the bare boughs of its sheltering beeches.

The house was plain and heavy looking. It stood too near the road for so large a house, it was said, and it was so high that it made all the trees—except the few great beeches—look smaller than they would have looked elsewhere. But it was built of the cheerful looking reddish granite of the neighbourhood, and with its green adornment of honeysuckle and climbing roses and its low French windows opening on the little terrace above the lawn, it looked in summer-time a handsome and homelike dwelling.

There were many trees about it—fruit trees, elms, and poplars, Norway spruces, and Scotch firs; but most of them had been planted within the last fifteen years, and trees on this east coast—like the children in the song—"take long to grow." The beeches, seven in number, were both old and beautiful—so beautiful and so stately amid the dwarfs around them that they, and not the wavering line of Saughs or willows that followed the margin of the burn running through the long low fields, it was sometimes said, should have given a name to the place.

There was a narrow belt of wood behind the house which had been planted long ago, and even in it the trees were not very large. But it was a very pretty spot, a real wood, where up through the undisturbed dead leaves of autumn came snowdrops and violets and primroses in the spring. Between this wood and the house was a field of grass, which was not cut smoothly every day or two like the lawn in front, but was allowed to grow tall and strong till the right time came to cut it down for hay. Through this field a gravelled walk led down to "The Well"; a clear, unfailing spring at the edge of the wood, and to a moss-covered stone seat beside it.

Beyond this a narrower path led through the grass and the last year's dead leaves into the heart of the wood, where, in a circular space, large enough to let the sunlight in though the trees had been higher, lay "Mary Keith, beloved and honoured wife of George Dawson," with her little children at her side. Here the turf was soft and green, but there was no adornment of shrub or flower on the grave or near it, only a simple headstone of grey granite and near it a turf seat, over which the slender boughs of a "weeping birch" hung sadly down.

Beyond the wood were the low fields through which the Saugh burn ran. Parks they were called, but they were just long grassy fields, with rough stone walls round them, and cows and sheep feeding in them. There was no "Park," in the grand sense of the term, about Saughleas as yet. There was no space for one without appropriating some of the best fields from the leased farms, and if things had gone right with him, that might have been done in time, Mr Dawson sometimes said to himself with a sigh.

But things had not gone right with him of late. Any thing but that—if one might judge from the look of care and pain, that had become almost habitual to him now.

"George, man, is it worth your while to wear your life away gathering gear that ye dinna need, when ye might be enjoying what ye have in this bonny place?"

"It *is* a bonny place," was all he said in reply.

They were sitting, not on the lawn, but on the other side of the drive, where the sunshine was softened by the fluttering beech leaves overhead. At least, Miss Jean was sitting there. Her brother was "daundering" up and down the walk with his hands clasped behind him, as his way was, lingering a little, now at the gate and now at his sister's side. He had forgotten her for the moment, as he stood looking out toward the distant sea, and the look which his daughter had come to know well, but which his sister was seldom suffered to see, came to his face and rested on it still when he turned along the walk again. And so he spoke.

"It *is* a bonny place," he answered, and then he walked away. But though he let his eyes wander over the gardens and the wood, and the fields beyond, there came to his face no glad look of possession or self-gratulation, and his head drooped lower and his step lagged as he drew near her again. He stood silent at her side, as though he expected her to say more, but she said nothing.

"It *is* a bonny place," said he again, "though it has given me but little pleasure as yet, and whiles I think that I am near done with it—and—there's none to come after me."

"George, man! that's an ill thing to say."

"But it's true for a' that God knows I was thinking little of myself when I put the winnings of my whole life into the land. And what is likely to come of it? Ye might weel say, Jean, that God's blessing hasna been upon it."

"No, I would never say that."

He took his way down the walk again, and went quite round the broad lawn, and she had time for a good many troubled thoughts before he came back.

"I doubt ye're overworking yourself, George," said she. She put out her hand to draw forward a garden chair that stood beyond her, and he did not refuse it, as she was afraid he might, but sat down beside her. "Where are the girls?" asked he. "They are busy up the stair—about May's dress, I think. But there is nothing to hinder them coming, if ye're wanting them."

"No. I'm no' wanting them. I have something to say to you, and I shall find no better time. I am going to make a new will."

"Well?"

"I have waited long, but if any thing were to happen to me, there would be endless trouble—if—unless—" He paused a moment and then added, "I know not well what to do."

"Need ye do any thing at once?"

"I think I should. Life is uncertain, though mine may be no more so than that of other men. But no man should put off settling his affairs, for the sake of those that are to come after him. I wish to do justly, but I will not divide the land, and I will not burden it."

"No, it wouldna be weel to divide the land nor to burden it," said Miss Jean.

There was a long silence and then Mr Dawson said gravely, felling into the Scottish tongue as he and the rest of them were apt to do when much moved.

"Gin ony stranger were to go through Portie the day and speir at ane and anither up and doon the street, as to who had been the successful man o' these pairts for the last five and twenty years or mair, there's little doubt whose name would be given them. And yet—my life looks and feels to me the day—awfully like a failure."

The shock which his unexpected words gave his sister was not all pain. She had thought him only too well content with his life and with what he had done in it. He was going down the hill now. It was well that he should acknowledge—that he should even be made sharply to feel, that all that he had—though it were ten times more—was not enough for a portion. But the bitter sadness of his look smote her painfully.

"God help him!" she said in her heart, but to him she said nothing. He did not take her silence for want of sympathy. He was too well acquainted with her ways for that, and in a little he added,—

"Like other folk I have heard o', I have gotten my wish, but all that made it worth the having has been taken from me. Gin she had lived—"

His sister did not speak. She just laid her hand on his for a moment, and looked at him with grave, wet eyes.

"If she had lived," he went on, not yielding to the weakness that had come upon, him, "if she had lived, the rest might have been hindered."

"God knows," said Miss Jean softly, taking up her knitting again.

"Ay, He knows, but I dinna seem to be able to tak' the good o' that that some folk do. But good or no good, I man submit—like the lave."

"Here are the bairns," said Miss Jean softly as the two sisters came through one of the open windows to the terrace about the lawn—"a sight worth seeing" the father in the midst of his painful thoughts acknowledged. They lingered a moment in the terrace raised a little above the lawn, the one stooping over a bonny bush of wee Scotch roses at her feet, the other standing on tiptoe trying to entangle a wandering spray of honeysuckle that it might find support. The eyes of father and aunt could not but rest on them with pleasure.

"I wonder that I ever could have thought them so much alike," said their father, in a little.

"They're like and they're no' like," said Miss Jean.

They were even less alike than they had been that day when they had startled her coming in on her out of the storm. Their dress had something to do with it doubtless. May wore something white and fluffy, with frills and flounces and blue ribbons, and her brown curls were bound back by a snood of blue. She was in her simple finery as fair and sweet a picture of a young maiden as one could wish to see.

Jean was different. Her dress was made of some dim stuff that looked in the distance like brown holland. A seafaring friend of her father's had brought it to her from India, her aunt remembered, and it came into her mind that perhaps there had not been enough of it, to make the frills and flounces, that young people were so pleased with nowadays. It was severely simple in contrast with her sister's, and her hair was gathered in one heavy braid at the back of her head. She had not her sister's fair and smiling loveliness, but there was something in her face that went far beyond it, her aunt thought, as she watched them standing there looking over the lawn to some one approaching along the road. Her face was bright and her air cheerful enough at the moment, but for all that there was a look of thoughtfulness and gravity upon it—a silent look—which reminded her father of his sister's look at her age. Only she was more beautiful. She was like a young princess, he thought, in his pride in her.

"Is it her gown?" asked he; "or is it the way that Jean puts her hair? What has 'come o' a' her curls this while back?"

The question was not to be answered. The opening of a little gate at the side of the lawn made them turn, and then Mr Dawson rose to greet a stranger who was coming up the walk. He was not quite a stranger to him. He knew his name and that he was a visitor at Blackford House, a gentleman's seat seven miles away. It was at this gentleman the girls had been looking, and at the lady who was in the carriage with him, as they passed slowly along the highway.

He was a tall fair man—young and good looking—very handsome indeed. He was a little too much inclined to stoutness perhaps, and rather languid in his movements, it might have been thought, as he came up the walk; but no fault could be found with his graceful and friendly greeting.

It was Miss Jean Dawson that he wished to see. It had been suggested to his sister, Mrs Eastwood, that Miss Dawson would be able to tell her what she wished to hear of a poor woman in whom she took an interest. She had been at Miss Dawson's house in Portie, and hearing she was at Saughleas, had called on her way to Blackford, to save another journey. She was in her carriage at the gate, and could Miss Dawson send her a message? Or perhaps—

The gate was hidden by a clump of firs. Miss Jean gave a glance in that direction and then laid her hand on her staff. Then she beckoned to her nieces who were still on the terrace. Jean came quickly toward her, and May followed more slowly. It was worth a body's while, Phemie told her fellow servants afterwards, just to see the way the gentleman took off his hat and bowed as Miss Dawson came near. Phemie saw it all from her young lady's window upstairs, and she would have liked well to hear also.

"It is about Mrs Cairnie, Jean, my dear. Ye ken her daughter Annie went south last year, and her mistress promised to see her mother, when she came north, and would like to hear o' her. I might maybe get to the gate with your help?"

"Certainly not. You are not able to walk so far. If a message will not do, it must wait."

Miss Jean shook her head with a slight smile. She had seen "Miss Dawson's grand air" before, and so had May, but her father looked at her amazed. It was not her words that startled him so much as her manner. She looked at the stranger who stood with his hat in his hand, as though he were at an immense distance from her. But in a minute she added more gently:

"I will take a message, aunt, if you wish. Or, I could—"

"Pray do not think of such a thing. I could not think of troubling you," said the young man confusedly.

"Or I could write a note," said the young lady taking no notice.

"Or the lady might drive into the place. She need not leave her carriage," said Mr Dawson, not quite pleased at his daughter's manner.

"Certainly that will be much the best way," said the stranger, bowing to Miss Jean and the young ladies.

Miss Jean the elder was generally sparing of words of reproof, and even of words of advice, unless advice was asked, and she said nothing. But May exclaimed,—

"You might have been civil to him at least, Jeannie. We have not so many gentlemen coming to see us."

"To see us! It was Auntie Jean he came to see—on an errand from his sister. And I think it was a piece of impertinence on his part to expect Miss Jean Dawson to go at his bidding—and you so lame, auntie," added Jean as she saw her aunt's face.

"He couldna ken that, and I'm no' sure that he did expect me to go to the gate. And I'm no' feared for my ain dignity, Jean lassie, and I dinna think ye need be feared for it either."

"Dignity!" exclaimed May. "Why, he is one of the fine folk that are staying at Blackford House."

"And that is the very reason," said Jean hotly—"the very reason that I—"

"It's but a poor reason," said Miss Jean.

But no more could be added, for the carriage was passing round the drive toward the spot where Miss Jean was sitting. The lady was driving her own ponies, and very nice she looked in her fresh muslins and simple straw hat. She was not very young, judging from her lace, which was thin and rather dark, but she had a youthful air, and a sweet smile, and seemed altogether a pleasing person. Even Jean could find no fault with her manner, as she addressed her aunt. There was respect, even deference, in every tone of her voice, and in every bend of her graceful head.

There was not very much to be said between them however. Miss Jean told the lady where Mrs Cairnie lived. Any body in Portie could have told her that. Then there was something said about the poor old lady's wants and ways, and the chief thing was that the daughter had sent some money and other things, which were to be left in Miss Jean Dawson's hands, for a reason which the lady could not explain. But explanation was unnecessary, for Miss Jean knew more of poor Tibby Cairnie's troubles and temptations than even her own daughter did.

It was all arranged easily enough, but still the lady seemed in no hurry to go. She could hardly have gone at once, for Mr Dawson had taken Captain Harefield round among the trees, and they were out of sight at the moment May admired the ponies, and Jean stood with her hand on her aunt's chair looking straight before her.

"A striking face and graceful figure, and a wonderfully intelligent look as well," thought Mrs Eastwood, and then in a pretty friendly way she seemed to include the silent girl in the talk she had been making with Miss Jean about the trees, and the views, and the fine weather they had had of late; and when Miss Jean became silent, as she generally did unless she had something to say that needed to be heard, Jean took her part in the conversation and did it well.

When the gentlemen returned, Mrs Eastwood still seemed in no haste to go. A new idea had seized her. Would Miss Dawson kindly go with her some morning soon to see Mrs Cairnie? It would be a pleasure to a faithful servant, if she could tell her on her return that she had seen her old mother; and if Miss Dawson could make it convenient to go with her, she would call some morning soon, and drive her to Portie.

No serious objection could be made to this, though in her heart Miss Jean doubted whether the absent Annie would care much to have the lady see her old mother, who was not always in a state fit for the eyes of "gentlefolk." However a day was set, and other little matters agreed upon, and then with many pleased looks and polite hopes that they might meet again, their visitors went away.

That night when they were sitting alone in the long gloaming, the sisters being not at home, Mr Dawson suddenly returned to the discussion of the subject which had been touched on in the garden.

"I couldna divide the land, but there is enough of money and other property to do fair justice to the other, and I think the land should go to Jean."

His sister said nothing.

"She is the eldest, and the strongest in every way. If she were to give her mind to it, she might, in time, hold her own in the countryside with the best of them."

He was silent for a minute.

"And she might marry, and get help in that way. And her son would have the place. And he might take my name, which is an honest one at least."

"Ye're takin' a lang look," said Miss Jean at last.

He gave an uncertain laugh.

"Oh! weel! That's atween you and me, ye ken. It might be. A lad like him that was here the day, for instance—a gentleman by birth and breeding. He is a poor man, as poverty looks to the like of him, a two or three hunder pounds or so a year. It would be wealth to most folk, but it's poverty to the like o' him. But if it should so happen—and I were to live another ten years—I might satisfy even the like o' him."

There was much which Miss Jean might have said to all this, which fell like the vainest folly on her ears, but she said nothing.

"And as for my Jean!—she needs to see the world and society, and all that, doubtless, but if there's many o' the fine London ladies that will hold a candle to her as far as looks go—it's mair than I think. She might stand before the queen herself with any of them."

And still Miss Jean said never a word.

"It might very well be, and I might live to see it. There's more land to be had too, if I'm willing to pay the price for it—and with this in view I might care to do it. I'll do nothing in haste."

He seemed to be speaking to himself, rather than to her.

"I'll do nothing in haste," he repeated. "But I could do it, and there would be some good in life—if this thing could be."

"Are ye forgetting that ye ha'e a son somewhere in the world?" said his sister gravely.

Mr Dawson uttered a sound in which pain and impatience seemed to mingle.

"Have I? It is hardly to be hoped. And if he is—living—it is hardly such a life as would fit him to take his place where—he might have been. I think, Jean, it might be as weel to act as if I had no living son."

"But yet he may be living, and he may come home." Mr Dawson rose suddenly and went and leaned against the darkening window.

"No, Jean, if he had ever been coming home, he would have come ere now. He was seen in Portie not three months since, and he never came near me. Ye think I was hard on him; but I wasna so hard as all that."

"Who saw him?" asked his sister greatly startled. "He was seen by more than one, though he was little like himself, if I can judge from what I heard."

"But he is living, George. There's comfort in that."

"If I had heard that he was living on the other side of the world, I might have taken comfort from it. But that he should have been here, and never came home—there is little comfort in that."

"But he is living and he'll come home to you yet. Do you think his mother's son will be left to go astray beyond homecoming? He'll come home again."

"Many a son of a good mother has gone down to death—And that he should have come so near her grave, without coming nearer! I would almost sooner know him to be dead than to know that of him. And when I mind—"

That was the last word spoken. Mr Dawson rose and went out into the faint light of the summer night, and though his sister sat long waiting for him after the girls had come in and had gone to bed, she saw no more of him that night.

Chapter Five.

A New Acquaintance.

Mr Dawson was just as usual the next morning. He was never so silent, nor in such haste to get through breakfast and away to the town when his sister was in the house, for he took pleasure in her company, and never failed in the most respectful courtesy toward her when she was under his roof—or indeed elsewhere. She saw traces of last night's trouble in his face, but it was not so evident as to be noticed by his daughters.

Indeed he seemed to them to be more interested than usual in the amusing discussion into which they fell concerning their yesterday's pleasure. They had been at a garden party given by Mrs Petrie, the wife of their father's partner in the bank, and had enjoyed it, and May especially had much to say about it.

"And who do you think was there, papa? Captain Harefield?"

"Captain Harefield! How came that about?"

"James Petrie asked him, it seems. But he said he came because he thought we might be there."

"But he acknowledged that it was his sister that 'put him up to it,'" said Jean.

"So the Petries may thank you for the honour of his company. That would rather spoil the honour to them, if they were to hear it," said Mr Dawson with a laugh.

"Well, very likely he may let them know it. I canna say much for his discretion," said May with a shrug. "He asked me who made my sister's gown, and you should have seen his face when I told him that she made it herself."

"And didna he admire your gown?" asked her father, to the astonishment of the two Jeans, and indeed to May's astonishment as well.

"Oh! yes. But then he said mine was just like other girls' gowns, 'very pretty and all that.' But Miss Dawson's was 'unique,'" said May with a drawl. "And he said he would tell his sister."

"And maybe she'll want me to make one for her. She looks like one who cares about her gowns," said Jean.

"She would be a queer kind o' a woman if she didna," said her father dryly.

Jean laughed.

"But there are degrees in that, as in other things. If Captain Harefield had spoken to me, I would have offered to make one for her."

"And had the Captain nothing to say to you; Jean?" asked Mr Dawson.

"He was feared at Jean," May said laughing. "He just stood and looked at her."

"He had plenty to say, if I had had the time to listen. He said his sister insisted on his coming north that he might keep out of mischief. He found Blackford House a bore rather," said Jean imitating May's drawl with indifferent success. Then she added,—

"I beg your pardon, auntie. I ken ye dinna like it, and then I don't do it well enough to make it worth my while, like May here."

"My dear, ye baith do it only ower weel. And as to my no' liking it—that's neither here nor there. But I have kenned such a power o' mockery give great pain to others, and bring great suffering sooner or later on those that had it. It canna be right, and it should be no temptation to a—Christian", was the word that was on Miss Jean's lips, but she changed it and said— "to a young gentlewoman."

May looked at her sister and blushed and hung her head. Miss Jean so seldom reproved any one, that there was power in her words when she did speak; and May had yesterday sent some of her young companions into agonies of stifled laughter, by echoing the Captain's drawl to his face.

"I'll never do it again, auntie," said she. "And besides," said her sister, "Captain Harefield is not fair game. It's not just airs and pride and folly with him, as it is with some folk we have seen; it is his natural manner."

"But that is just what makes it so irresistible," said May laughing. "To see him standing there so much at his ease—so strong and stately looking, and then to hear the things he says in his fine English words! It might be Simple Sandy himself," and she went on to repeat some of his remarks, which probably lost nothing in the process. Even her aunt could not forbear smiling as she listened.

"Well, I must say I thought well of what I saw of him," said Mr Dawson. "I would hardly call him a sharp man, but he may have good sense without much surface cleverness. I had a while's talk with him yesterday."

"And he's a good listener," said Jean archly.

Her father laughed.

"I dare say it may have been partly that. He is a fine man as far as looks go, anyway."

"Very. They all said that," said May. "And Mavis said to me, 'Eh, May, wouldna he do grand deeds if he were the same a' through?' He has the look of 'grand deeds.' But I have my doubts, and so had Mavis," added May shaking her head.

"There are few men that I have ever met, the same a' through. But who is Mavis that sets up with you to be a judge?" asked her father.

"Mavis!"—said May, hanging her head at her father's implied reproof, as he supposed. "Mavis—is wee Marion—Marion Calderwood."

"And we used—in the old days—to call her Mavis because she has a voice like a bird, and to ken her from our May, and Marion Petrie," said Jean, looking straight at her father, and as she looked the shine of tears came to her bonny eyes.

"She is but a bairn," said Miss Jean gravely.

Mr Dawson's face darkened as it always did at the mention of any name that brought back the remembrance of his son. May was not quick at noticing such signs, and she answered her aunt.

"A bairn! Yes, but 'a bairn by the common,' as Mrs Petrie's Eppie says. She is a clever little creature."

"She is a far-awa' cousin o' Mrs Petrie's, and she's learning some things from the governess of her bairns. But she might well have been spared on an occasion like yesterday, I would think," said Miss Jean.

"Oh! *all* the bairns were there, as well as Marion. And she looked as a rose looks among the rest of the flowers."

"As the violet looks in the wood, I would say," added Jean. "She'll be as bonny as her sister ever was."

There was a moment's silence, round the table, which Jean broke.

"She was asking when you would be home, aunt. She has gotten her second shirt finished, and she wants you to see it. She is very proud of it. I told her that you werena going to Portie, except on Sundays, for a month yet, and she must come here and let you see it."

"Weel, she'll maybe come. It was me that set her to shirt making. There is naething like white seam, and a good long stretch of it to steady a lassie like Marion. And if she learn to do it weel, it may stand her instead when other things fail."

"White seam!" exclaimed May. "Not she! May Calderwood is going to educate herself, and keep a fine school—in London maybe—she has heard o' such things. She's learning German and Latin, no less! And I just wish you could hear her sing."

"She markets for her mother, and does up her mother's caps," said Jean, "and she only learns Latin for the sake of helping Sandy Petrie, who is a dunce, and ay at the foot of the form."

"She's nae an ill lassie," said Miss Jean softly, and the subject was dropped.

Phemie came in and the breakfast things were removed, and the girls went their several ways. Miss Jean, who was still lame from a fall she had got in the winter, went slowly to her chair near a sunny window and sat looking out upon the lawn. Mr Dawson went here and there, gathering together some papers, in preparation for his departure to the town. He had something to say, his sister knew as well as if he had told her, and she would gladly have helped him to say it, as it did not seem to be easy for him to begin. But she did not know what he wished to speak about, or why he should hesitate to begin. At last, standing a little behind her, he said,—

"It's no' like John Petrie and his wife to do a foolish thing, but they are doing it now. And their son Jamie just the age to make a fool o' himself, for the sake o' a bonny face. 'A rose among the other flowers,' no less, said May."

"But Jean said better. 'A violet in the wood.' She is a modest little creature—though she has a strong, brave nature, and will hold her own with any Petrie o' them a'. And as good as the best o' them to my thinking."

"Well, that mayna be the father's thought, though it may be the son's."

"Dinna fash yoursel' about Jamie Petrie. He'll fall into no such trouble. It's no' in him?" added Miss Jean with a touch of scorn.

"I never saw the lad yet that hadna it in him to ken a bonny lass when she came in his way; and for the lassie's ain sake, ye should take thought for her."

"She has her mother," said Miss Jean, more hastily than was her way. "And any interference would come ill from you or me where this one is concerned. And my bonny Mavis is but a bairn," she added more gently, "and she's in no danger from James Petrie, who is a well intentioned lad, and who has been ower weel brought up, and who is ower fond of siller and gentility, to have either roses or violets in his plan o' life, unless they're growing in a fine flowerpot, in somebody's fine house. Marion Calderwood is no' for the like of him."

Her brother regarded her with anger so evidently struggling with astonishment in his face, that she expected hot words to follow. But he kept silence for a moment, and then he said quietly enough,—

"It seldom answers for ane to put his finger into another's pie. There are few men so wise as to profit by a lesson from another man's experience, and I doubt John Petrie is no' ane o' them."

"And there's few men, it's to be feared, wise enough to take the best lesson from their ain experience," said Miss Jean gravely. "And that is a sadder thing to say."

It was quite true, as Captain Harefield had said, that it was his sister who "put him up" to going on James Petrie's invitation to the garden party that afternoon. The natural desire to get him off her hands, for the rest of the day was her only motive in urging it, and a sufficient one, for it was true that he was bored by the quiet of Blackford House, and that he did not suffer alone. But it was the unwonted energy of his admiring exclamations as soon as they had passed out of the gate of Saughleas, that had suggested the idea.

By "this and by that," were they not beauties, these two girls? Who would have thought of coming upon two such without warning? Even his sister must acknowledge that they were beautiful.

She did acknowledge it, but there was something far more wonderful to her than their good looks. That two country girls—and Scotch country girls—should be found at home dressed as these two were, astonished her more than their beauty.

"They might have passed at any garden party of the season," said she.

"Passed! I should think so. I don't know about their gowns, but *they* would pass, I fancy."

"She couldn't have fallen on any thing to suit her style of face and figure better if she had made a study of it."

"Perhaps she did," said her brother, laughing. "Or perhaps they get their gowns from London."

"No, they would probably have been dressed alike, in that case, and in the height of the fashion. The white one was very much like the dresses of other girls, but the other was unique. And they seemed nice, lady-like girls."

"Did they not? And not so very Scotch."

"Well, perhaps not so *very*—but rather so. But then I like the Scotch of Scotch people better than their English as a rule. However, the few words I heard them speak were softly and prettily spoken, and quite appropriate to the place and time. How it might seem elsewhere I could not say."

"It is rather a nice place, too, isn't it? The estate is small, but he has no end of money, they tell me, and he seems a sensible old fellow enough."

"The sister is a striking looking woman—with a certain dignity of manner, too."

"Yes, and young Petrie tells me that she used to keep a little shop, in her young days. Indeed, not so very long ago."

Mrs Eastwood did not reply to this. Her mind was evidently intent on solving the problem of Jean's tasteful gown.

"And at home too! I have heard that young people of their class, get themselves up in fine style when they go out to tea. But sitting there on the grass, with the old woman in the cap—"

"But perhaps they are going out to tea.—To the garden party! 'By this and by that'—Did I tell you? Young Petrie at the bank asked me to go. I have a great mind to go."

He glanced down at the faultless grey morning suit he wore.

"I could not go all the way to Blackford House and return again, could I?"

"Hardly, and you could not improve yourself if you were to go. Yes, by all means accept the invitation. You will be sure to meet the Misses—Dawson is it? And the circumstances will be more favourable for knowing them than they were this morning."

It ended in Captain Harefield's leaving the carriage, and returning to Portie on foot. He lunched at the inn, and presented himself at Petrie Villa in company with the eldest son of the house in the course of the afternoon. It is to be supposed that he enjoyed himself, for this was by no means his last visit, and his sister was able to congratulate herself on getting him off her hands a good deal after this while they remained in the North.

Various circumstances combined, made this a pleasanter summer in Saughleas than the last had been. For one thing, Miss Jean was there more than usual. The fall which had made her almost helpless for a while, still prevented her from moving about with ease; and the Lord's "little ones," for the time, received the aid and comfort which she owed them for His sake, through the hands of others, and she had to content herself with sitting still and waiting His will.

She could have contented herself in circumstances more adverse than those in which she found herself. She knew that her presence in the house was a pleasure to her brother, and that it was not an uncomfortable restraint upon her nieces, as it might have become, even though they loved one another dearly, had she assumed any other place than that of visitor among them.

So young a mistress of a house, to which there were so many coming and going as there always were in summer, needed the help which the presence of an elder person gave, and it was all the better that the help was given and received with no words about it. Jean the younger, was glad of her aunt's stay, because she loved her, and because escaping now and then from the pleasant confusion that sometimes prevailed in the house, she found quiet and rest in her company. And though she might not have acknowledged her need of her help in any other way, she was doubtless the better of it.

It cannot be said that it was altogether a happy summer to her, but it was a very busy one. She was mistress and housekeeper, and gave her mind to her duties as she had not done at first. Indeed, it seemed that she was determined to give herself and her maidens no rest for a while, so intent was she in doing all that was to be done. And even when her maidens had necessary respite, she took none to herself. In the house or in the garden she occupied herself all the morning. She took long walks in the afternoon if there were no visitors to entertain, and if the rain, or the special need or wish of her aunt or her sister kept her in the house, she employed herself still with work of some sort, sitting at it steadily and patiently, "as if she had her bread to make by it," her father said one day when he had been watching her for some time unperceived.

"I should like to know how it would seem to do that," said Jean gravely.

"You would soon tire of it," said her father laughing.

"I dare say. I tire of most things," said she, rising and folding up the long, white garment on which she had been so busy.

Her father regarded her curiously from behind his newspaper. She did not look either well or happy at the moment, he thought.

"It is all nonsense, Jean lassie, to keep yourself at your seam, as you have been doing for the last two hours, when there are so many poor women in Portie that would be glad to do it for what you would hardly miss."

"But I like to do it, papa, for the moment, and one must do something."

"It is just a whim of hers, papa," said May laughing. "Think of her stinting herself to do so much an hour, when she might as well be amusing herself."

"It's good discipline, Auntie Jean says," said Jean laughing. "And I need, it she thinks. At any rate, every woman ought to do white seam in the very best way, and I didna like it when I was young."

"But now we have the sewing-machine, and as for the discipline, it's all nonsense."

"Well never mind, May. Now is the time to speak to papa about the children's party. Papa, May wants to give a large children's party—for the little Corbetts, ye ken. Though there must be grown people here too, and it will be great fun, I have no doubt."

Jean seemed quite as eager about it as May, her father thought, as they went on to discuss the proposed party. Of course the result of the discussion was just what the sisters knew it would be. Their father said they were to please themselves, only adding several cautions as to the care that must be taken of fruit trees and flower beds, and some doubts as to how the Portie bairns, accustomed to the freedom of rocks and sands, would care for a formal tea-drinking in the house, or even in the garden.

"The bairns' pleasure is the excuse, and no' the reason, I doubt," said he; but he laughed when he said it.

This was one of the things that made this summer pleasanter than the last had been. They had amused themselves last summer and their father had not objected; but as to his enjoying any thing of the kind, such a thought had never entered the minds of his daughters. But now he did not endure their gay doings painfully, protesting against them by his manner, if not by his words, nor did he ignore them altogether as had been most frequently his way. He looked on smiling at the enjoyment of the guests, and took evident pleasure in the success of his daughters in entertaining them. If it had been otherwise, there would have been few visitors to entertain, and few gayeties attempted. For Jean did not care enough for these things to make the effort worth her while, and May would have had to content herself with the gayeties provided by other people. But as it was, the elder sister did her part, and did it well; so well that none but her aunt suspected that her heart was not in these things quite as it used to be.

Certainly her father was far from suspecting any such thing. And sitting apart, seeing them both and watching, and musing upon all that was going on, Miss Jean could not but wonder at his blindness, and at the folly of the vague and pleasant possibilities he was beginning to see, and to rejoice over in the future.

Chapter Six.

A Proposal.

The garden party at Petrie Villa had been the first of a series. Not a very long series, indeed, for there were not many gardens in Portie equal to the requirements of such an entertainment, even according to the limited ideas of those who had never "assisted at" a garden party anywhere else. But there had been several, and the presence of Captain Harefield would have been generally declared to be the most interesting feature of nearly all of them.

He had not always been invited. That is, he had not always been invited in the formal way usually considered necessary on such occasions even in Portie. But through the kindness of James Petrie at first, and afterward of others, when he became better known, he was sure to make his appearance in the course of the entertainment, and so comported himself and so evidently enjoyed himself, that even those who were at first inclined to resent, as a liberty, his coming so unceremoniously among them, forgot to do so in his presence, and ended in being as pleased and flattered as the rest.

Of course there was a garden party at Saughleas, and of course Captain Harefield was a guest, formally and specially invited by Mr Dawson himself. But his presence was not the most interesting circumstance of the occasion, for his sister, Mrs Eastwood, was there also. Mrs Eastwood had come according to her promise and had taken Miss Jean in her carriage to visit Mrs Cairnie, and it had been a successful visit in every way. For May had given the old woman warning, and she had prepared herself to receive them. Not only had she on a clean "mutch" and apron, but her house was "redd up" in a way that would have seemed wonderful to her visitor, if she had been familiar with its aspect on other days.

Mrs Cairnie was a clever old woman, and made the most of her opportunity. She bewailed the loss of her daughter's society, and of the help and comfort she had been to her, but enlarged on her sense of the good fortune that had come to the lassie in being admitted into the service of such a kind and gracious lady. She declared herself overpowered at the condescension and kindness of the visit in terms which did not seem so very much exaggerated to the visitor; but Miss Jean knew that the bad auld wife was laughing in her sleeve at the English lady and her simplicity. However, the visit was considered a success by those chiefly concerned, and it was to be repeated before Mrs Eastwood took her departure.

On returning to leave Miss Jean at Saughleas, Mrs Eastwood expressed herself delighted to accept Mr Dawson's invitation to alight and drink a cup of tea before she set out for Blackford House. In a little the tea and all the pretty accessories were brought out to the terrace, and it was charming—every thing was charming, Mrs Eastwood declared, and "not at all Scotch"; but happily the last part of her opinion was reserved till she was relating her afternoon's adventures at Blackford House.

She herself did her utmost to charm every one, and succeeded very well on the whole, and her suggestion as to an invitation to the garden party came very naturally and gracefully in the midst of the gentle thanks addressed to Miss Jean because of the kindness shown to her brother. Captain Harefield, whom she confessed to be a little impatient of the quiet of Blackford House. Even Miss Dawson did not seem to think it strange when, in her pretty way, she begged to be allowed to accompany her brother to the garden party on the day appointed.

"It was very silly of her," Jean said afterwards. "What possible pleasure could she expect?"

"I don't see that. Why should she not take pleasure in it as well as you? She is young yet," said Mr Dawson, ready to take the lady's part.

"I should have no pleasure in going out of my own sphere," said Jean with dignity.

"Eh! Jeannie, I'm no' so sure of that. Werena you just the other day playing at 'the beds' with Mavis, and Emily Corbett, and the rest of the bairns on the sands? And didna you finish Maggie Saugster's seam to let her get away with the rest? And didna you—"

"Nonsense, May! I've played at 'the beds' all my life, and I dinna look down on Mavis and Maggie and the rest. And it was for their pleasure I played with them, and not for my own."

"Well, it may be for our pleasure that Mrs Eastwood is coming here, and as for looking down on us—" said May with a toss of her pretty head.

"Whisht, bairns," said Miss Jean gently. "I dare say she thinks lang in the country as weel as her brother,—her that's used with London life,—and she would like to come just for a pass-time, with no thought of looking down on any one."

"Her brother doesna seem to be looking down on any one," said Mr Dawson with a short, amused laugh.

"Oh! he makes no secret that it is just for a pass-time, that he favours Portie folk with his company. He finds Blackford House dull. He gets awfully bored," said May in the Captain's languid manner.

"It's a wonder he stays on then," said Mr Dawson.

"I said that to him once, and he said—" May hesitated. It would not have been easy to repeat all that had been said on the occasion alluded to; but she put the gist of his communications more clearly and directly than he had done himself, when she added,—

"It is a good place not to spend money at, and he does not seem to have much to spend."

"Weel, he's honest—as to his reasons, at any rate," said her father.

"Oh! that is what I gathered, rather than what he said. He is out of the reach of duns. That he *did* say."

"He doesna seem to me like an ill-disposed youth," said Miss Jean.

"Oh, no, auntie! He's nice and agreeable, and—all that; but he is—soft," said May laughing.

Her father looked as if he were going to say something sharp, but he did not.

"His sister is very fond of him, and very good to him, he says. And he must be a heavy handful whiles," said Jean gravely.

"In what way?" asked her father.

"Oh! just having him on her mind to keep sight of, and amuse, and keep out of mischief, as he says. Just fancy the weariness of it?"

"You seem to have gathered a good deal from him, as well as your sister," said Mr Dawson, not well pleased. "And you find him a heavy handfu', do you? I have thought whiles that you get on very well with him."

"Oh, yes, I get on very well with him! I'm not responsible for him, ye ken, and that makes all the difference."

"Marion Petrie says that Jean keeps him very much to herself, and Jamie looks as if he thought so, too, sometimes," said May laughing.

"That is one of your 'gatherings,' May, my dear," said her sister.

"Well, you must make your best of the visitor when she comes," said Mr Dawson as he went out.

And it was very easy to make the best of Mrs Eastwood. She was amiable and agreeable, and if she looked down on any one, it did not appear. She did not mingle much with the younger portion of the company, but she amused herself by observing all that was going on, and talked pleasantly with Miss Jean, and afterwards with Mr Dawson, about various things, but chiefly about her brother, whom she evidently loved dearly, and who as evidently caused her anxiety, though she had no thought of letting this appear.

Miss Jean found her soft flowing talk pleasant to listen to, and all the more that she did not need very often to reply. Mr Dawson was charmed with her, and it was not, as a general thing, his way to be charmed with strangers. But she was not altogether a stranger. Her husband's name— Eastwood, the London banker—had long been familiar to Mr Dawson. He knew him to be a "responsible" man, and that was more than could be said of all the fine English folk, who found it convenient to pass a part of the summer or autumn at Blackford House.

Mrs Eastwood herself was of high family, being the granddaughter, or at least the grand-niece, of a living earl, and though Mr Dawson would doubtless have scorned the imputation, it is possible that he found all the more pleasure in entertaining her because of that Mr Eastwood was not of high family. He was very rich however, and they got on together, pretty well, May "gathered" from Captain Harefield's conversation; that is, they never quarrelled, and were content to spare each other to enjoy the society of other people for a good part of the year.

But Mrs Eastwood made much of her husband when speaking of him to Mr Dawson, and of her brother also. Of the brother, she had much to say, and Mr Dawson listened with great interest to it all, as Miss Jean could not fail to see.

And in the mean time the young people amused themselves in the garden and in the wood, and Captain Harefield seemed to be at no loss for amusement among them. Jean certainly did not keep him to herself to-day, as Mr Dawson noticed; but then Jean was hostess, and had to occupy herself with the duties of her position, and with the party generally. It passed off very well, all things considered, and the children's party was likely to be the same thing over again, with the children added.

The little Corbetts, who were the reason, or the excuse, of the prospective gayeties, had come from their home in an English manufacturing town, in order that the sea breezes of Portie might put strength in their limbs and colour in their wan cheeks; and they had come at the special invitation of Mr Dawson. Their father, the son of the Portie parish minister of the time, had been his chief friend in the days of his youth, and they had never forgotten one another, though they had not for a long time been in frequent correspondence. During one of Mr Dawson's infrequent visits to

Liverpool, they had met by chance, and had renewed acquaintance to the pleasure of both, and Mr Dawson allowed himself to be persuaded to go and pass a few days with his friend.

Mr Corbett had not been a very successful man in the way of making money, and he had a large family, few of them able to do much for themselves. But they were cheerful, hopeful people, and made the best of things. There had been illness among them recently, which had left the younger children white and thin, and not likely to mend during the summer heat in a close city street; and when Mr Dawson asked as many of them as liked to spend a month or two among the sea breezes of Portie, the invitation was accepted gratefully. But it was doubtful whether, for economic reasons, they could have availed themselves of it, if Mr Dawson had not taken matters into his own hand, and insisted on taking some of them home at once.

So the two youngest, Polly and Dick, with an elder sister of fifteen to be responsible for their well-being and well-doing, were carried off to Saughleas, and presented unannounced to the startled, but well pleased, household. Their coming gave interest, and occupation as well, to every one, for "Mr Dawson had given mamma no time for preparation," as the pretty, anxious elder sister was fain to explain when she asked Miss Dawson's advice and assistance in the matter of shoes and stockings, and other things suitable for the perfect enjoyment of the rocks and sands of Portie. Miss Dawson made all that easy, taking the equipment of the children, and the elder sister as well, into her own hands.

And the puny city children enjoyed the sands and the sea, the running and clambering, and the free out-of-doors life, as much as their father had done in his boyish days; and their own mother would hardly have recognised their round brown faces before the first month was over.

As to their needing entertainment in the way of children's parties, that was not likely. But for the sake of their father and grandfather they had been invited to many houses in Portie, and it was but right that they should have a chance to invite their young friends in return. And so the party was decided on, and was much enjoyed, and so might be dismissed with no more words about it, except for a circumstance or two which attended it.

Mrs Eastwood was there again, but not by invitation. She had not been aware that there was to be such gay doings at Saughleas, she said, when she came into the garden, and she stayed a while at Miss Jean's request, to enjoy the sight of so many happy bairns. But she was not bright and beaming and bent on pleasing every one, as she had been the first time she was at Saughleas.

To tell the truth, she was anxious and unhappy, at a loss what to do, or whether she should do any thing, or just let events take their own course. It was her brother and his affairs that occupied her thoughts. She had been so long accustomed to think for him, and advise him, he had come to her so constantly for help in the various difficulties into which he had fallen during his life, and she had been so successful in helping him, and so happy in doing so, that she could not—though she sometimes tried—divest herself of a feeling of personal responsibility for his well-being. And now that he seemed to be at a turning point in his life, she felt all the anxiety of one who had a decision of importance to make, with no one at hand on whose judgment she could rely for guidance.

It added to her unhappiness, that she could not quite free herself from blame in regard to the matter to be decided. She need not have made herself unhappy about her own course. Nothing that she had done or left undone, had much to do with the intentions of which her brother had informed her that morning. She had been conscious of a feeling of relief for herself at the chance of his finding the means of amusing himself innocently in the country. That was the uttermost of her sin towards him. But his frequent visits to Saughleas, and his loiterings in Portie, would have been none the less frequent had he believed that his sister missed and mourned every hour of his absence.

And her present anxiety as to his next step was just as vain. She could neither help nor hinder it, and, whatever might be the result, neither praise nor blame could justly fall to her because of it. But she did not see it so, and so she had come to Saughleas with many vague thoughts as to what it might be wise to do, but with a firm determination as to one thing that was to be plainly said before she went away again.

Her first thought when she saw the pleasant confusion that the children were making on the lawn and in the gardens was, that nothing could be said to-day. But by and by, when children and young people, her brother among the rest, went away to amuse themselves with games in the field beyond the wood, the way to speak was opened to her, and she saw no reason why she should not say all that was in her mind. It was to Miss Jean she had intended to say it, and Miss Jean was sitting under the beeches with folded hands, ready to listen. And yet, looking into the grave, serene face of Miss Jean, she did hesitate. She could not tell why; for Miss Jean was only a person who had kept a shop, and counted and hoarded the pence, and who knew their value. A commonplace, good-natured woman, not easily offended, why should she not say to her all that she had to say— and say it plainly too?

And so she did. And Miss Jean listened with no offence apparently, with only a little gleam of surprise and interest in her eyes, and perhaps a little gleam of amusement also. Mrs Eastwood was not sure. She did not say much, but she said it very plainly.

Miss Jean must have noticed the frequency of Captain Harefield's visits to Saughleas, and his warm admiration of the young ladies, her nieces. It had gone beyond admiration, she had reason to think, as to one of them. Indeed her brother had intimated as much to her, and had filled her with anxiety; for her brother had no fortune. Of course if he married he would wish to leave the army. Could Miss Jean tell her whether the fortune which Mr Dawson could give his daughter would be sufficient to insure the comfort of the young people in case of a marriage?

"And did your brother send you to ask?" said Miss Jean quietly. "And why do you ask me?"

"Of course he did not I speak because of my own anxiety, and you must see that I could not speak to Mr Dawson about money until a proposal had been made."

"Weel, madam, I can give you no help and no information. I have no' sufficient knowledge of my brother's means, or of his intentions. And I could not influence him in this matter, even if I were to try. Which of them is it?"

But strangely enough Mrs Eastwood could not answer this question. The intimation she had that morning received of her brother's intention to propose to Mr Dawson for the hand of his daughter, had not been very definite or very clearly given. It had come in during a discussion of other and painful matters, with which money, or rather the want of money, had to do. And if her brother had told her which of them he intended to honour, she had failed to understand him, or she had forgotten. So her reply did not touch this question.

"I cannot say whether I approve or disapprove of his choice. Your niece is very pretty and lady-like, and she would take her husband's rank—and, my dear Miss Dawson, I trust you will not think me mercenary, but my brother can give his wife a high station, and a place in society, and to make the marriage an equal one, or in the least degree suitable, there should not only be beauty and grace, which your niece I must acknowledge has, but—money."

"And plenty of it," said Miss Jean.

"Of course. And unless there is, as you say, plenty of it, Percy should not be allowed to speak."

"But if they love one another?"

Mrs Eastwood turned and looked at Miss Jean. She had rather avoided doing so hitherto. She was not sure that the old woman was not laughing at her. Miss Jean's face was grave enough however.

"If there is not a prospect of—of—a fortune, he should not be allowed to speak. Not that I do not admire your niece. I admire her extremely. She is clever, and sensible also, and would restrain—I mean she would influence her husband. She would make a good wife to Percy, who is—who needs some one to lean on."

"A heavy handfu'," said Miss Jean, unconsciously repeating her niece's words.

There was a silence of several minutes between them, and then Mrs Eastwood continued, carrying on her own train of thought.

"Of course I knew that the foolish boy admired the young lady—fancied himself in love; but that has often happened to him before, and I thought it would pass with the month. But they are very pretty and fresh, and the tall one is clever, and she would—yes, she would make him a good wife—provided—"

Miss Jean's spirit was stirred within her, but she said nothing; and Mrs Eastwood said all the more, unconsciously betraying her belief that it would be the best thing that could happen to her brother, that he should marry and settle down with a wife clever enough to influence him. And to influence him meant, evidently, to keep him from spending too much money, and from the companionship of those who loved to lead him astray.

She did not say in plain words that his marriage with such a one would be a great relief to her and that it would be the saving of him to be kept out of London and out of harm's way for the greater part of the year; but Miss Jean saw clearly that she was more eager for his success than she was willing to acknowledge. Miss Jean listened silently and patiently. Her niece knew her own mind, doubtless, and would not be likely to allow herself to be influenced by the wishes of any one, and she had no call to reprove, or even to resent, the "ill manners" of the lady.

So she sat silent and let the softly spoken words "go in at one ear and out of the other," till she heard the tramp of a horse's feet, and knew that her brother was come home, and then she rose, and invited Mrs Eastwood into the house, hoping that she would refuse the invitation and take her departure. For at the sound of her brother's voice, Miss Jean's heart misgave her.

Chapter Seven.

A Misfortune.

Miss Jean's heart misgave her, for she knew that the thought suggested to her brother on the morning when Mrs Eastwood and Captain Harefield came to Saughleas to inquire about poor Tibbie Cairnie had returned to him more than once; and she feared that should Captain Harefield speak to-day, he might not refuse to listen, and then there would be troublous times before them.

That there was even a possibility that he should be willing to listen to him was amazing to Miss Jean. So wise and cautious and far-seeing as he had always shown himself to be, how could he think of trusting any part of the wealth which he had spent his life in gathering, to the hands of a man who had proved himself incapable of making a good use of that which had fallen to him? To say nothing of being willing to trust him with his daughter!

There was comfort here, however. Jean's welfare was in her own keeping. Miss Jean was not so much at a loss as Mrs Eastwood, as to which of her nieces Captain Harefield intended to seek. And she was glad it was Jean, for Jean could hold her own against father and lover and all. But still there was trouble before them, for, strangely enough, her brother, hard-working and practical, a thorough man of business, had taken pleasure in the comings and goings of this young man so utterly unlike himself in all essential respects. She had seen it with wonder and a little amusement at first; but she knew now, or she thought she knew, that he had been preparing disappointment for himself and vexation to her bonny Jean.

"Truly we need guidance," she said aloud, and then she rose and invited Mrs Eastwood to go in to the house and take a cup of tea, hoping all the time that she might refuse, and that she might be away before Mr Dawson came.

It was not to be so arranged however. Mr Dawson was delighted to see Mrs Eastwood, and expressed his pleasure so frankly, that Miss Jean thought it possible the lady might take courage, and make known to him as plainly as she had done to her the cause of her visit. So, instead of moving away with the help of her cane, as she had at first intended to do, she seated herself again. Not that she thought that her presence would be likely to prevent her speech, but she was curious to know how the matter, so interesting to the lady, should be presented to a new listener; and curious also to see how her brother might receive it.

There were the usual inquiries and compliments as to health, and the usual remarks about the weather and the appearance of the country, and then Mrs Eastwood spoke of the benefit she had received from her long stay, and her regret that the time of her departure was so near. Then Mr Dawson inquired with more interest than the occasion demanded, whether Captain Harefield was to leave also.

"If he take my advice about it, he will certainly do so," said Mrs Eastwood. "But that is doubtful. The interest of the season is just beginning to him, and as he has had his leave extended, he may remain."

"He is a keen sportsman, I hear," said Mr Dawson.

"Oh, yes; and the shooting here is good, they say, and does not involve very much fatigue. Yes, he will probably stay for a little; though I think he had much better go, for various reasons."

She spoke with a certain significance of tone and manner, and Mr Dawson remained silent, expecting to hear more; and possibly he might have had the pleasure of hearing of Captain Harefield's hopes and his sister's opinions, had no interruption occurred.

But at the moment a sudden outcry arose somewhere in the garden. They could see nothing where they were sitting, but they heard the sound of many voices—entreating, expostulating, scolding, and at last they heard words.

"Ye needna tell, May. Naebody will ken wha did it."

"I wouldna tell Mr Dawson—for—oh! for ony thing."

"An' naebody will ken that it was you that did it."

"It wasna me, but it was my fault; and if Sandy winna tell, I must, and just take the wyte (blame) mysel'."

"Eh! Marion! Yon's him speaking to the leddy. I wouldna be you for something."

"Something untoward has happened, I doubt," said Miss Jean. "I hope no ill has come to any of the apple-trees."

Now Mr Dawson's apple-trees were the pride of his heart. It is not easy to raise fruit trees of any kind so near to the sea; and as far as apple-trees are concerned, the fruit is not of the best, when success has crowned persevering effort. But on a few young trees, bearing for the first time, there hung several apples beautiful to behold, and they had been watched through all the season with interest by every one in the house, but above all by Mr Dawson. So when Miss Jean said "apple-trees," he rose at once to satisfy himself that they were safe.

But alas! before he had fairly turned to go, all doubt was at an end. There were many children at a little distance, and two or three were drawing near, and in the hand of one, a girl in her teens, was a broken branch, on which hung two of the half dozen apples from the best of all the trees. Mr Dawson had watched them with too great interest not to know just where the little branch belonged. He did not speak,—indeed the little maiden did not give him time.

"It was a' my wyte, Mr Dawson, and I'm very grieved," said she, holding up the branch, and looking up into his face with eager, wistful eyes.

Mr Dawson took it, but he looked not at it, but at the child, saying nothing.

"I beg your pardon. I'm very grieved," repeated she.

Mrs Eastwood whispered to Miss Jean what a pretty picture the child made, but Miss Jean was thinking of other things.

"It was Sandy," continued the little pleader. "He was taking a' wee David's sweetees, and I couldna bide that, ye ken, and I just—just tried to hinder him; an' he ran awa', and me after him. And he ran in beneath the tree, but he wouldna have gone, if I hadna been after him, and so—"

"She licket me, and she tried to rug my lugs," (pull my ears), said a voice in the distance.

The change in the girl's face was wonderful to see as she turned to the speaker. A sudden colour rose to her cheeks, and her grey eyes flashed scorn and anger.

"If I only had been able!" said she, and then she turned to Mr Dawson again.

"I'm very grieved," repeated she.

"It canna be helpit now, Maysie," said Miss Jean. "Never heed. Run awa' with the lave o' the bairns."

For Miss Jean knew that it was not the apples nor their destruction that had brought that look to her brother's face.

"Are ye angry with me, sir? And winna ye forgive me?" said Maysie, the sweet wistfulness coming back to her eyes. "I'm very grieved."

"It canna be helpit. Never heed," said Mr Dawson, repeating his sister's words. "I dinna think I mind your name," added he, not meaning to say it, but making a great effort to recover himself.

"I'm Marion Calderwood," said she, a sudden brightness, followed by a cloud as sudden, passing over her face. She lifted beseeching eyes to his face, and then she turned to Miss Jean.

"Run awa', lassie, with the lave o' the bairns," said Miss Jean.

"Maybe I should go hame?"

"Hoot, lassie! Never heed. Only run away with the lave."

Quite unconscious that he owed an apology to Mrs Eastwood for his abrupt departure, Mr Dawson turned and strode off in another direction.

"They must be precious apples," said Mrs Eastwood, looking after him with surprise not unmingled with disgust.

"It's an old trouble," said Miss Jean sorrowfully. "He'll hear none o' her fine words the night," she added to herself, conscious, amid her trouble, of some satisfaction that it should be so.

No, Mr Dawson was not likely to listen patiently to words of any kind that night. The very first look from the child's eyes smote his heart with a pang in which there was regret, as well as anger and pain. For a sudden remembrance of eyes as sweet, and with the same look of wistful appeal in them came back to him—the eyes of bonny Elsie Calderwood, who had come between him and his son.

Almost the last words which his son had spoken to him, the very last such as a son should speak to his father, had been spoken while those wistful eyes entreated him. It had been a moment of great bitterness, and as he passed down the lane that led to the fields, and then to the sea, eager to get beyond the sound of the gay voices ringing from garden and wood, the old bitterness returned, and with it came the added misery of the vain wish that he had yielded his own will that day—a longing unspeakable for all that he had lost.

His boy—the only son of his mother who had been so dear, had he lost him forever? Would he never return? Could he be dead? Should he never see his face or hear his voice again?

He had a bitter hour or two, this man, whom even his sister, who knew him best and loved him best, called hard in her secret thoughts. And the bitterness did not pass with the hour, nor the pain. Silence reigned in the house before he came home that night, and in the morning something of the old gloom seemed to have fallen upon him.

Captain Harefield did go home with his sister; at least he left Blackford House with her, and that without returning after the night of the children's party to say "Good-bye" to his friends at Saughleas. May remarked upon this with a little indignation, and Mr Dawson said it was not like the young man not to do what was polite and kind, and he also wondered at the omission of the visit. Jean said nothing; at least she said nothing to them. To her aunt she acknowledged that she had known of his intended departure, and that she had also known when he bade her good-bye that night, that she was not likely to see him again. But even to her aunt she did not acknowledge that he would have stayed longer if she had bidden him, or that even now a word from her would bring him back again.

Out of the unfortunate incident of the broken apple-tree, there rose a little talk between "the two Jeans." Miss Jean had for a long time had something on her mind to say to her niece, but it was the younger Jean who spoke first.

"Aunt, what is this they are saying about my father's anger at Marion Calderwood?"

"My dear, he wasna angry!"

"Did you see it all, auntie? Because Marion went home greeting, the other bairns say. Of course it was a pity about the tree, but it wasna Marion who broke it, and it wasna like my father to show anger to a guest, even to a bairn."

"My dear, he showed no anger."

"But, auntie, there must have been something; for I met Mrs Calderwood in the High-street this morning, and she went red and then white, and was stiff and distant, as she used to be when we first came home. She had grown quite friendly of late, and to-day she would have passed me without speaking. It must have been because of Marion."

"It might have been, but I dinna think it. Mrs Calderwood is a proud woman, Jean, my dear,—and—"

"Well?"

"Weel, ye have been consorting with fine folk lately, and maybe—"

"Auntie Jean! Dinna say more, for that is not your real thought; and that is a terrible thing to say of you."

"My dear, it is my real thought, as far as it goes. I ha'e little doubt that was present in Mrs Calderwood's mind when she met you in the High-street— with other things."

"We'll take the other things first then," said Jean, the angry colour rising in her cheeks. "You must think your friend but a poor creature, or she must think it of us."

It was the first time in all the girl's life, that her eyes with an angry light in them had rested fully on her aunt's face. Her aunt did not resent it, or notice it, except by a gentle movement of her head from side to side, and the shadow of a smile passed over her face. She looked grave enough as she answered, however.

"I am far from thinking her a poor creature, whatever she may think of us. And, Jean, my dear, I think ye maun ken something of the other things, though ye never heard them from me."

Jean's look grew soft and sad, and she came and leaned on her aunt's chair.

"Do you mean about bonny Elsie, and—our Geordie? Was it because of Elsie that Geordie went—and lost himself? Tell me about it."

"I think ye maun ken all that I could tell you—or mostly all."

"I only ken—I mean I used to think that they—cared for one another—oh long ago, before my mother died. And since we came home, I have heard a word dropped now and then, by different folk—Marion Petrie, and her mother; and once Tibbie Cairnie said something about my father's cursed pride, and his fine plans that would come to nothing. But it wasna till afterwards that I knew that it was Geordie she was thinking about Auntie Jean, I have had my thoughts, but I ken little. Was my father angry? But he must have been sorry for George when poor Elsie died. And was it because of Elsie that my brother went away?"

It was not an easy story to tell, and Miss Jean put it in as few words as possible, having her own reasons for telling it to Jean. She dwelt less upon her father's anger at his son's folly, than upon the heartbreak that his loss had brought him. But she made it clear that "poor bonny Elsie" was the cause of their estrangement, and that it would have been the same had Elsie lived and had George carried out his determination to marry her against his father's will.

"If the poor foolish lad had only waited and had patience in the mean time, much sorrow might have been spared to all concerned. Your father might have given in—though I dinna think it; or as they were little more than bairns, they might have forgotten ane anither—though I dinna think that either. But if George had won to man's estate, and had been doing a man's work and getting a man's wages, he would have had a better right to take his own way, and your father *might* have given in then. At least he must have been silent, and let the lad go his ain gait. I whiles weary myself thinking how it might have been."

Jean sat without a word, but with a face that changed many times from white to red and from red to white as she listened; and when her aunt paused, and took up the work which in her earnestness she had allowed to fall on her lap, she sat silent still, quite unconscious of the uneasy glances that fell on her from time to time.

"It has made an old man of your father," added Miss Jean in a little.

"Poor father! and poor Geordie! Ay, and poor Elsie! and nothing can change it now."

Jean rose from the stool on which she had been sitting at her aunt's feet, and walked restlessly about the room. By and by, she came and stood behind her aunt's chair, leaning upon it.

"Aunt—there is something I would like to tell you. I wonder if I ought?"

"Ye maun judge, my dear."

"If I were only sure."

Both were silent for a time.

"Would I be better able to give help or counsel to you or—to any one— if I were to hear what you could tell?"

Jean shook her head.

"Nothing can be done—at least not now," said she sadly. "Weel then, dearie, dinna speak. Whiles troubles take shape and strength in the utterance and grow persistent, that might have died out or come to little in silence. If a time should come that you are sure that speaking would do any good, tell me then."

"It would do no good now. And I am not sure that there is any thing to tell."

There was a long silence between them. Jean was thinking of the "John Seaton" sailing away with her brother to the northern seas. Miss Jean was thinking of the "John Seaton" too, and of Willie Calderwood, with a sad heart.

"They were just a' bairns thegither I thought, but I little kenned. And wae's me! for my bonny Jean, gin she has to go through all that—and wae's me! for her father as well. No' that the pain and the trouble need be feared for them, so that they are brought through—and no unfilial bitterness left to sicken my bairn's heart forever more; but I mustna speak, or let her speak. I think she hardly kens yet how it is with her, but she would ken at the first word; silence is best."

And silence it was. But by and by more was said about the story of those two "for whom life was ended," as Jean said sadly. She was not angry at her father's part in the matter, as her aunt had feared she might be. It could not have been otherwise, looking at things as he looked at them, she acknowledged, and she grieved for him all the more, knowing that there must mingle much bitterness, perhaps remorse, with his sorrow for his son.

"If my mother had but lived!" she said sadly. "Ay, lassie! But He kens best who took her hence where we'll a' soon follow. We make muckle ado about our gains and our pains, our loves and our losses, forgetting that 'our days are as a shadow, and there is no abiding.'"

"A shadow to look back upon, auntie, but a reality as we are going through with them day by day."

"Ay! that's true, my lassie, and a stern reality whiles. The comfort is that it is a' ordered for us."

Jean shook her head with a doubtful smile.

"Only it is not till afterward that we get the good of that knowledge."

"And coming afterward it comes ower late, ye think, lassie. But bide ye still and see. And indeed no one need wait till afterwards to know the blessedness o' just lying quiet in His hands. And ye needna wait a day for that, my dear bairn."

If Jean had spoken, the tears must have come; so she rose and kissed her aunt silently, and then went away.

Chapter Eight.

Willie Calderwood.

The name of Willie Calderwood had never been spoken between the sisters since the day when, standing on the high rocks above the Tangle Stanes, they had watched the "John Seaton" making out to sea. Jean was silent for one reason, and May for another; and there were reasons enough that both could see why silence was best, to prevent either of them from feeling such silence strange.

Willie Calderwood had been their companion and their brother's chief friend in the days when they all played together on the rocks and sands of Portie—in the days before George Dawson had admitted into his heart the thought, that the wealth he had won, and the estate he had made his own, gave his children a right to look higher for their friends than among their less prosperous neighbours. But his children were not of the sort that forget easily, nor were the Calderwoods the sort of friends to be easily forgotten. Willie had always been a leader among them, a handsome, fearless, kindly lad, and he became a hero to them all, when he went to sea and came home to tell of shipwreck first, and then of strange adventures among strange people; of hunger and cold and suffering, and escape at last.

A hero! There were many such heroes in Portie who had suffered all these things and more—old men and men old before their time who had passed their lives in whaling ships on the northern seas; who had been wounded or maimed in battles with northern bears and walruses, and with northern frost and snow; and even they made much of the lad who had begun his battles so early. So no wonder that he was a hero to his chosen companions and friends.

"They were jist a' bairns thegither," as Miss Jean had said; but it was during that summer, the last of his mother's life, that young George lost his heart to bonny Elsie, and it was during that summer too, that the visionary glory that rested on the name of the returned sailor carried captive the imagination of his sister Jean. She did not forget him while she was away from Portie; but when she returned they did not fall into their old friendly ways with one another.

That would have been impossible even if the sad story of George and Elsie had never been to tell; for Jean was a woman by this time, and she was Miss Dawson of Saughleas, and he was but the second mate of a whaling ship; a brave man and a good sailor, but not the equal of the rich man's daughter as times were now. So they seldom met, and when they did meet, it was not as it used to be in the old times between them. He never sought her out when they met in the houses of their mutual friends, and when the circumstances of the moment brought them together, he was polite and deferential and not at his ease. Jean would fain have been friendly and tried to show it, and not knowing then of her father's anger, because of his son's love, she could not but wonder at her ill success.

"Maybe he is like Tibbie Cairnie, and thinks you are set up with London pride," said May laughing. "If I were you, I would ask him."

But Jean never asked him, and he was not long in Portie after they returned. But when he came back again it was very much the same. He was at home the greater part of the winter before he sailed with the "John Seaton," and they met him often at other houses, though he never went to Saughleas. There were times when they seemed to be felling back into their old friendliness, and Jean, who was noted in their small circle for the coolness with which she accepted or rejected the compliments, or the graver attentions of some who seemed to seek her favour, grew gentle and winning, and even playful or teasing, when any movement in the room brought the young sailor to her side.

"She is just the Jean of the old days," poor Willie said to himself, and he could say nothing better than that. They fell back at such times into the kindly speech of their childhood "minding" one another of this or that happy day when they were "a' bairns thegither." They could say little of Elsie who was dead, or of George who was lost, in a bright room with others looking on, but the tears that stood in Jean's "bonny een" told more than words could have done of her love and sorrow for them both. If she had known all, she might have thought it wise to say nothing; but her words and her wet eyes were as drops of sweet to the lad in the midst of much bitterness. He did not always go home cheered and comforted after the sweetness; but Jean did, telling herself that at last they were friends as they used to be—till they met again, and then the chances were, that her "friend" was as silent and deferential and as little eager, apparently, to seek her company as ever; and she could only comfort herself with the thought that the fault was not hers.

So it went on strangely and sadly enough for a while, and then Jean began to see that though he shunned rather than sought her, he seemed friendly enough with her sister. He seemed to seek her out, and to have much to say to her; and why he should be friendly with May and not with her, she could not easily understand.

"Unless—and even then?" said Jean to herself with a little sinking of the heart.

She did not follow out her thought at the moment, but it came back to her afterwards, and on the high rocks as they watched the departing ship, she thought she saw it all clearly, and that she was content. He was her friend, and if he were May's lover, he would still be her friend, and all the more because of that, and time would make all things that might hinder their friendship now, clear to them both.

But she did not speak to her sister about this. It was for May to speak to her, she thought at first, and after a while it would not have been easy to speak, and on the whole, silence was best. Then as she listened to her aunt's story of their brother and Elsie, and of their father's opposition and anger, she was not sure that silence was best. How much of it May might know, she could not tell; but sooner or later she must know it all, and if there was trouble before her, it would make it none the easier to bear, but all the heavier, the longer the knowledge was kept from her. But she shrank from speaking all the same.

"I will tell her to-night," she said as she sat by her aunt's side. But she did not, nor the next, and even on the third night she sat long in the dark when the house was silent, listening to the wind among the trees, and the dull sound of the sea, and the painful beating of her own heavy heart, before she found courage to go into her sister's room.

"If she is asleep, I will not wake her."

But May was not asleep. She had been lingering over various little things that she had found to do, and had only just put out her light when her sister softly opened the door. She seemed to sleep, however, as Jean leaned over to listen, but as she turned away, May laughed softly.

"Well, what is it? I dinna think I have done any thing so very foolish to-day—not more than usual, I mean."

For, in her elder sisterly care for her, Jean thought it wise to drop a word of counsel now and then, and this was the hour she usually chose to do it. She stooped down and kissed her as she turned, a circumstance that did not very often occur between them. For though they loved one another dearly, they were—after the manner of their kin and country—shy of any expression of love or even of sympathy in the way of caresses.

"Is there any thing wrong?" said May startled. "Did any one ever tell you about—about our Geordie and Elsie Calderwood, May? Auntie Jean has been speaking about them to me lately."

It was not a very good beginning, but she did not know what better to say. May raised herself up, and looked eagerly in her sister's face.

"I have heard something. Do you mean that you only heard it the other day?"

"Tell me all you know," said Jean, leaning down on the bed beside her. "And why did you not tell me before?"

"I did not like—and I thought you must ken about it."

"Ah! yes. It is sad enough. No wonder you didna like to speak about it. But tell me now all you know."

And May did so, and it was very nearly all there was to tell. She had heard the story, not straight through from beginning to end, as Jean had heard it from her aunt, but from words dropped now and then by one and another of their friends. And Jean could not but wonder that, May having heard so much, she herself should have heard so little. But May knew little of the part her father had taken in the separation of the lovers, how angry he had been, and how determined to put an end to what he called the folly of his son. It was just this that May ought to know, and Jean told it in as few words as possible. She wondered a little at the way in which her sister seemed to take it all.

"Poor Elsie! But she might have died even if she had not been sent to the school. How little folk ken! They say in Portie that her mother sent her away that she might learn things that would fit her to be the wife of young Mr Dawson, and by and by the lady of Saughleas—and that her pride got a fall. It is a sorrowful story, Jean."

"And the saddest part of it to us is, that poor Geordie is lost and gone from us. And even if he were to come home, it might be little better."

"Is my father angry yet, Jean? Or is he sorry? Would he do the same if it were all to do over again?"

"Who can say! He has many thoughts about it, doubtless, and some of them cannot but be bitter enough. But as to his doing differently—" Jean shook her head.

"But, Jean, I canna blame my father altogether. His heart was set on his only son, and George was but a boy."

"Yes, and Aunt Jean says if he had but waited with patience my father might have yielded at last."

"Or George might have changed. He had seen no one else, and though Elsie was good, and bonny too, there was a great difference between her and—and some that we have seen,—ladies educated and accomplished as well as beautiful. And, Jean, I canna but be sorry for my father."

"Sorry! That says little. My heart is like to break for him whiles—and it might have been so different!" said Jean sadly.

"If he were living, we should have heard from him before this time."

"Who can say? Oh! he is living! I canna think he is dead. Poor papa, he must have a sore heart often."

"Jean," said her sister after a long silence, "do you think he would do it all over again? I mean—do you think he would be as hard on—you or me?"

"Do you mean—Willie?" asked Jean at last. "Well—Willie or another. It is not easy for my father to change."

"No, it is not. But, May, have patience. Things often come round in strange ways when we least expect it. If George would only come again! How long is it since the 'John Seaton' sailed?"

"A good while since."

Jean could have told her sister the days and even the hours that had passed since then, but she did not. When she asked the question, it was her brother she was thinking of; but May, who could not know that, believed that she was thinking of Willie Calderwood.

"He may be captain next voyage," said May. "But I wish he could leave the sea altogether. My father could open the way for that, if he chose."

"Leave the sea? Is it Willie you are speaking about? He would never do it. May, you must not ask it of him. It would be putting him in a false position altogether. He is a true sailor."

"Oh! I shall not ask him. It would do little good. But I wonder at you all the same. You have no ambition. He can never be more than just a sea captain—and always away."

"A sea captain!" repeated Jean. "A sailor!—And what would you have? Would you put him behind the counter in a shop? or set him to casting up figures or counting money in a bank? Would you even old Mr Petrie or James or any of them with the like of him?"

May laughed. "Oh! well, a sailor let him be. But ye needna flee at me as though I had said something horrible. And we needna vex ourselves. That will do no good."

"It must be late," said Jean rising. "She takes it quietly enough, and it is well she does. It would wear her out to be ay thinking and fearing and longing for his coming home, as I long for poor George's. She is ay light-hearted, dear child. God bless her," added Jean with a sigh.

The rest of the summer passed quietly away. The little Corbetts went home strong and brown and with a wonderful knowledge of and delight in their father's mother tongue, rejoicing over the invitation for another visit the next summer, if all should be well.

They were much missed in Saughleas, and so was Miss Jean, who, though she enjoyed a visit to her brother and her nieces now and then, liked best the quiet of her own house, and the silent secret doing of the work which she had chosen among the sinful and suffering poor creatures of which, especially in winter-time, Portie had its share. Her stay at Saughleas had done her good. She left her crutch behind her there, and she was able now to go with her staff in one hand and "help and comfort" in the other, to those who in the back sheets and lanes of the town needed her help most. At Saughleas they missed her greatly, for various reasons, and chiefly for this, that at meal times, and at other times also, Mr Dawson was ready to fall into his old habit of silence and reserve, when left alone with his daughters. This silence was good neither for them nor for himself.

"And I am going to try and have it otherwise," said Jean to herself, as she sat behind the urn, waiting for his coming the first morning they were alone.

He came in as usual with a bundle of papers in his hand, letters that had been received last night, and that must be answered this morning as soon as he reached the bank, and in the mean time he meant to look them over while he drank his coffee.

"I think," said his daughter looking straight into his face as he adjusted his spectacles, so that he might not let her remark fall as though it had been made to her sister, "I think Aunt Jean is the woman the most to be envied among all the women I know."

"Ay! Think ye that? And what new light ha'e ye gotten about her to-day?" said her father, arrested by her look rather than her words.

"No new light. Only I have been thinking about her last night and to-day. She is the best woman I know, and the happiest; and I envy her."

"Ye have but to follow in her steps, and ye'll be as good as she is,—in time," said her father dryly. "As to her happiness—I should say she perhaps makes the most of the means of happiness given to her, but otherwise I see little cause that you have to envy her. She is reasonable, and doesna let her wishes and her fancies get the better of her good sense, and so she is content."

"And if I were reasonable, would I be content, I wonder? As to being as good—that must come of higher teaching and peculiar discipline, and I doubt I shall never be good in her way."

"And what for no? Your aunt would be the first to tell you that you can get the higher teaching for the asking. And as for discipline—the chances are ye'll get your share as well as the rest of us."

"But not just in the same way. A long, patient, laborious, self-forgetting life hers has been—has it not? She is strong and she has been successful; yet she is not hard. She is good, but she is not down on wrong-doers in the way that some good folk are. If I had my choice, I think I would choose to have just such a life as she has had—if it would make me like her."

Mr Dawson looked at his daughter in some surprise. Jean was not looking at him, but over his head far away to the sea, bright for the moment, under a gleam of sunshine.

"Would that be your choice? A life of labour, and then the life of a solitary single woman! I think I see you!" said her father with something like indignation in his tones.

May laughed. Jean's eyes came back from the sea with a vague, wistful look in them that startled her father.

"I think, Jean, ye hardly ken what ye're speaking about."

"Yes. About Aunt Jean. 'A solitary single woman?' No. Not solitary. That has such a sorrowful sound. Oh! she is not solitary in an unhappy sense; even when she is quite alone in her own house by the sea."

"What I mean is, that she has neither husband nor child. She is alone in that sense. And if ye think that she hasna whiles felt—weel—as if she had missed something in life—that's no' my thought."

"Yes—and that is part of the discipline, I suppose. Missed something— yes. But then, having had these things she might have missed that which makes her different from, and better than, any one else. I ken no one like my Aunt Jean."

"Weel—ye're no' far wrong there. And if ye had kenned her in her youth, you would have said the same. There were none like her then more than now. But she's growing unco frail-like now, poor body?" added Mr Dawson with a sigh.

And then there was more said. Mr Dawson went on to tell many stories of his sister's youth, all going to prove that there were few like her for sense and goodness even then. Most of these his daughters had heard before, but they liked to listen all the same. And Mr Dawson forgot his letters, and Jean forgot that it was only to keep his eyes away from them, that she had begun to speak about her aunt, and she took courage because of her success.

Chapter Nine.

An Invitation.

She was not always so successful; still she was successful to a degree that surprised herself, in withdrawing her father from the silent and sombre musings which of late had become habitual to him. This was the work which she set herself. Her time, while he was in the house, or near it, was given to him. She disturbed him doubtless now and then when he would have been better pleased to be left to himself; but upon the whole he responded to her advances, and by and by showed in many ways that he counted upon her interest in whatever he might be doing, and on such help as she could give.

In all matters connected with the management of the estate he took especial pains to claim her attention and interest. She tramped with him over the wet autumn fields in all weathers, and listened to his plans for the improvement of the place in the way of dikes and ditches and drains, and to plans that went further than these—plans which it would take years to carry out well and wisely. Her interest was real for the moment, and soon it became eager and intelligent as well. She not only listened to him, but she discussed, and suggested, and even differed from him in various matters, and held to her own opinions in a way that certainly did not displease him.

She tired of it all sometimes, however, and though she permitted no sign of it to appear to her father, she could not always hide it from her sister.

"And what is the good of it all? You cannot surely be vain enough to think that you are doing any good, or that papa cares to have you tramping about in the wet and the wind."

"Oh, I like it! And I may as well do it as any thing else. As to papa—yes, I think he likes it. I am better than no one to speak to, and—oh yes, I like it!"

"It is all nonsense!" said May with a shrug. "As for papa, he might enjoy it, if it were Peter Stark, or John Stott, or any one that could understand him, or give him a sensible answer;—but you!—What is the use of it?—and just look at your shoes and stockings!"

Jean looked down, as she was bidden, at her feet, and her soiled petticoats.

"They *are* wet," said she, "and dirty."

"And tell me if you can, what is the good of it all?"

"It has made me hungry, and it will make me sleep, perhaps. And the best reason for it is, that I like it—as well as any thing."

She went away to change her wet things, and came back in her pretty house dress with a knot of gay ribbon at her throat, looking wonderfully bright and bonny her father thought as he came in at the hall door, and so he noticed all the more readily, perhaps, how white and changed she looked afterwards. When he also had changed his wet things, and came in to sit down, she was standing in the darkening room, looking out at the window, leaning on the ledge as though she were tired, and she did not turn round as he passed her to take his usual place at the fireside.

"The days are drawing in fast," said he, by way of saying something.

"Yes, it is already growing dark. I cannot see the sea."

"Ye needna care. It is an angry sea to-night, and the wind is rising."

"Yes, the moan of it is in among the trees already, and before morning it will be a cry—a terrible sharp cry—that will not be shut out. An ill night for those at sea."

"By no means. The folk at sea are safe enough, so that they bide away from the shore. There will be worse nights than this, and many of them, before the winter be over."

"The long, long winter! And think what it must be in Greenland seas, with the ice and the dark, and the bitter cold."

"Lassie, draw the curtains and come to the fire. What ails you at the wind and the sea to-night, more than usual? Draw the curtains, and shut out the night, and come and make the tea."

And then when Jean did his bidding and turned from the window, he saw that her face was white and her eyes strained and anxious. She came to the fire and stooped down, warming her hands at the blaze.

"One would think you were a sailor's wife, and that his ship was in danger," said her father.

"It is the book she has been reading," said her sister. "That American book about the men who sailed in search of Sir John Franklin and his crew. What pleasure there can be in poring over any thing so dismal, is more than I can tell."

"That is because you do not know. It gives one courage to know that there have been men—that there are men—so patient and so brave. Their leader was a hero," said Jean with shining eyes.

"Well, we'll have our tea now," said Mr Dawson in a tone that made May think he was ill-pleased at something, though he said nothing more. He was wondering what could have come to the lassie so to change the brightness of the face that had met him at the door. May knew that Jean must be thinking of the "John Seaton," but she knew that her father could have no such thought. Nothing was said by any of them for a while, but by the time tea was over, they had fallen into their ordinary mood again, and spoke of other things. But afterwards Jean was sorry that she had not taken courage that night to tell him how she had heard that her brother had sailed in the "John Seaton" so long ago.

For her secret knowledge burdened her sorely. That George should have been at home and then have gone away again without a word, it would be like to break his father's heart to know. The hope of seeing him when the "John Seaton" came home might be better than the uncertainty of the present. But if his anger still burned against his father, he might not come home, and such a disappointment would be worse to bear than even the present uncertainty.

She wearied herself thinking about it, but she did not know what to do. She longed to tell her aunt. She had almost done so, but her aunt had forbidden her, or so she had thought. And months must still pass before the "John Seaton" could be in port again.

Her thoughts were with her brother night and day, and she was pre-occupied and grave, and grew white and anxious-eyed; and by and by it added to her trouble, to know that her father was observing her. So when he was in the house, all her thoughts were given to the effort to be just as usual. She talked cheerfully and had visitors at the house; and when they were alone she worked busily and steadily, falling back, when her white seam failed her, on May's embroidery; and did her best to grow enthusiastic with her sister over silks and wools of brilliant hue.

She practised her music also, and took courage to sing even when her father was in the house. It needed some courage, for their mother had been one of the sweetest of singers, and their father had never heard the voices of his daughters since the days when they used to stand at their mother's side, and sing the songs she loved.

No harm came of it. Though her father made no remarks, she knew that he listened to her voice in the dark, and if it woke the old sense of pain and loss, it stirred neither anger nor rebellion, as the gentleness of his words and ways made her sure.

And so the winter wore on with the usual breaks in the way of hospitalities given and received till the days began to lengthen—and then something happened.

There came to the girls an invitation from a friend, to pass a month or two with her in London. The friend had been Miss Browning, their favourite teacher in their London school. Now she was Mrs Seldon, the wife of a young city merchant, "as happy as the day is long," she wrote, and she promised them a taste of many enjoyments, if they would come and see her as mistress of her own pretty house—free now to come and go at her own will and pleasure. Much she said to induce them to come, and much was not needed, as far as May was concerned.

Mr Dawson might have hesitated as to accepting an invitation for his daughters into an unknown household, even though he had every confidence in the good sense and discretion of the lady who invited them. But strangely enough, it happened that Mr Seldon was the son of almost the only man in London with whom he had ever had other than mere business intercourse, and the young man himself was not altogether a stranger to him. As men of business, father and son were worthy of respect, and socially occupied an unexceptionable position, and Mr Dawson was more than pleased that his daughters should see something of London, in circumstances so favourable as a residence with such people would imply. So his consent was given readily.

Jean listened and said little through all the preliminary discussion of the matter; but when it was settled that the invitation was to be at once accepted, she quietly declined to leave home.

She gave several good reasons why one should pay the visit rather than them both, and several why it should be May that should pay it. She gave several reasons also, why it would be wrong for both of them to leave home at once. Their father would be left in the house alone. Their aunt was by no means strong. Indeed if there were no other reason she would never think of leaving her alone during the spring months, which had during the last few years been so trying to her. Then there had been something said about certain changes to be made in the early spring in the grounds and gardens. These might certainly be put off till another year, as her father suggested, but it would be a pity to do so, and if they were to be made, Jean must be at home to superintend them.

"And indeed, papa, it was May who used to be Miss Browning's friend, much more than I. Mrs Seldon would enjoy May's company better than mine, and May would take ten times the pleasure that I should take. How should I have any pleasure knowing that my sister was lonely and disappointed at home. As to both going, it is out of the question. And I can go next time."

Of course Mr Dawson could not do otherwise than yield to such an array of good reasons, especially as May was as eager to go as her sister was to stay; but he had an uneasy feeling that Jean herself had needed none of these good reasons to induce her to remain. It pleased him, of course, that she should like home best, and he was glad not to be left to the trial of a silent and forsaken house during a gloomy month or two. But it did not please him that Jean should care so little for the enjoyment that her sister anticipated with such delight. It was not natural, and he wearied himself trying to imagine what it might be.

"I will see what my sister says about it," thought he.

But in the mean time he could only let her take her way; and he and May set out together on their journey, for he would not permit his daughter to travel alone.

And then for a few days Jean had the house to herself, and during these days, she became aware of one thing. She must turn her thoughts away from the constant dwelling on poor lost Geordie, and his wanderings on northern seas, or she would lose the power of thinking or caring for any one or any thing in the world besides.

It had nearly come to that already. If the wind blew, it was of him she thought, and it was the same if the sun shone, or the rain fell. Night and day her heart was heavy with fears for him. It was the shipping news she read first in the papers, about storms and wrecks of whale ships that had come home, and of some that might never come, till she grew morbid and heartsick with her doubts and her fears.

When she went to the town, or took her daily walk by the sea, she spoke with the fishermen about the signs of wind and weather, and with certain old sailors—long past sailing because of age and rheumatism—about the voyages they had made, and about the dangers of the deep, and the dreariness of Arctic seas when winter nights were long and the days "but a blink." And of late, she had come to be aware that now and then as they talked, there was a look of wondering curiosity in their dim old eyes. They took her sixpences, and her "bits o' backey" with smiles and nods of encouragement, and with assurances "that there was nothing like keeping a stout heart and a cheerful, on the shore as well as on the sea."

"And they canna ken about Geordie," she said to herself wondering.

No; they did not know about Geordie; but they saw the weary, wistful looks ever turned to the sea, and they could not but know that they must mean something, though neither kith nor kin of hers had sailed from the harbour of Portie, as far as they knew, for many a day. And thinking about their words and their looks, she told herself, that unless she meant to fall into utter uselessness and folly, she must shake herself free from this dull brooding over her fears. For the suspense must continue for months yet—perhaps for many months, and she began to be afraid for herself at the thought.

"I wonder what the sailors' wives do, and their mothers and sisters all these wintry months? Do they sit and think of the danger, and the distance, and the long suspense? No, they must live and have patience, and take the good of other things, and trust in God—as I must, if I would not go wild. *They* get through, and I must.

"But then I must never speak about him, and my fears for him, and that must make it worse to bear. Oh, if I had but told my father that first night! How can I wait on for months like this?" and Jean suffered herself to cry as she had never cried before. She might cry this once since there was no one at home to notice the traces of tears. But all the same she knew that she must make a braver stand against the trouble that oppressed her, and even amid her tears she was saying that to-morrow she would begin.

And so when to-morrow came, instead of going toward the wild sea shore above the town, she set out to go directly to her aunt. It was not an agreeable day for a walk. It was not raining, but the mud was deep on the road, and the fields which Jean liked best at such times, were in places under water; and a wide ditch here and there was so full, that she had doubts of being able to get across, since the footing on either side could not but be insecure in the prevailing wetness. So she kept the highway, warily picking her steps, and meeting the wind from the sea with a sense of refreshment—and by and by with a conscious effort to throw off the weight of care which had so long oppressed her.

When she came to the corner at which she turned into the High-street, she saw Marion Calderwood coming toward her with her music book under her arm. A pretty sight she was to see, and a welcome as she sprang forward, greeting her joyfully. But a shadow passed over the girl's face when the first words were spoken.

"Oh! yes. I am very glad to see you, and Miss Jean will be glad too. But if ye hadna come in this morning, I was going out to see what had become of you. Your aunt bade me ask my mother to let me go when my lesson was over—and—I think she would have let me."

"And she'll let you still. Run away now to your lesson, and you'll find me at Aunt Jean's, and we'll go out together."

Marion looked doubtful. "My mother would have let me go to oblige Miss Jean, but—she does not approve of my leaving my other lessons, for one thing—and besides—"

"Run away. I'll ask your mother. She'll let you go home with me, if I ask her."

Marion was not very sure, nor was Jean. For Mrs Calderwood was a very proud woman, and her pride took the form of reserve, and a determined avoidance of any thing that looked like claiming consideration or attention from those whom, from their circumstances, she might suspect of wishing to hold themselves above her.

And there were reasons of another kind, Jean well knew, why she should look with little friendliness on any one in the house of Saughleas—reasons that must prevent all renewal of the intimacy that had been so warm and pleasant during her mother's lifetime. Still she had almost always been friendly in manner with Jean when they had chanced to meet, but Jean had been but seldom in her house since she had come from school, and she was glad of the excuse which her proposed invitation to Marion gave her to go there. For it had come into her mind that she might speak to Mrs Calderwood about the trouble which she found it not easy to bear alone.

Chapter Ten.

Mrs Calderwood.

Mrs Calderwood's house faced the sea a little nearer the pier head than Miss Jean's, and Miss Dawson nodded and smiled to her aunt in the window as she passed, hardly confessing to herself that she felt a little anxious as to how she might be received.

"But she'll not be likely to put on her stiff, silent manner in her own house," said she, encouraging herself.

Mrs Calderwood was not alone. Mrs Cairnie was with her, asking advice and sympathy for "a beeled thoom," and Mrs Calderwood was in the act of applying a warm poultice to relieve the pain. In the poor old woman's eagerness to tell her troubles to a new listener, the awkwardness of the first moment was got over. Nor was Mrs Cairnie in any hurry to leave when the interesting subject was exhausted.

"So ye didna gang up to Lunnon with your father, Miss Dawson? Ye're wise to bide and let the great folk come to seek you. It's a thankless job whiles gaen after them."

This of course required no reply.

"And are ye your leafu' lane at Saughleas? But I suppose ye're used with it now—the big hoose and the few in it. It is changed times since ye used to bide in the High-street. But being an eddicated leddy, ye'll ha'e resources in yoursel', as the books say."

No, Miss Dawson did not like being "her leafu' lane" in the big empty house, and she turned to Mrs Calderwood with her request for Marion's company. But Tibbie had not yet said her say.

"Your leafu' lane! It's little ye ken what that means. Bide ye till the time come when ye lie through the lang nichts o' a hale (whole) winter, hearkening to the awfu' things that the winds and the waves are crying in at your window and doon your lum (chimney), and some o' yours far awa' on the sea—and syne ye'll ken. Oh! the weariness o't, and the dreariness o't, and nae help frae Heaven aboon nor frae earth beneath, but just to sit still and wait for their hame coming. And whiles they come, and whiles they never come—and ane canna be sure even o' their loss till years go by. Eh! woman' ye little ken, but speir ye at Mrs Calderwood."

She paused a moment in the surprise of seeing Jean's face grow pale as she listened, but went on again before any one spoke.

"I'm through wi't, for the last o' mine was lost lang syne. But she has ane yet—as far as she kens. God be gude to him! Ye've had no word o' the 'John Seaton' as yet, mem?"

"Not yet; it is not to be expected yet," said Mrs Calderwood quietly. "Martha will give you a cup of tea. You will be the better of it, as you were able to take little breakfast; and I hope your thumb is past the worst now."

Mrs Cairnie felt herself to be dismissed beyond even her power to linger.

"Many thanks to ye, mem, and ye ha'e nae occasion to be mair anxious than ordinar' as yet. And ye can just encourage ane another—and I'se awa' hame."

"Poor bodie! she has had her share of trouble in her day, and some of it she brought on herself, which makes it none the lighter, I dare say," said Mrs Calderwood as she shut the door.

"You are not growing anxious, Mrs Calderwood, are you?" said Jean. "It is not time to be anxious yet?"

"Not anxious—more than usual. Oh, no! Of course the wind and the waves have something to say to me most nights. But I can only wait."

"Yes, it is the waiting that is so terrible. And it must be for a good while yet."

"For months. We cannot say how many. We seldom see the ships home within the year."

"And the 'John Seaton' sailed on the tenth of April. It is nearly three months still till then. And to think of all who are waiting even here in Portie—wives and mothers and sisters. It makes one's heart sick to think about it."

Then she sat silent, with her eyes turned toward the window, through which was to be seen the dull grey sea, all unconscious of the uneasy glances with which Mrs Calderwood was from time to time regarding her.

"Mrs Calderwood," said she at last, "how will you ever bear it as the time draws near? The waiting and the suspense, I mean?"

"My dear, I have had worse troubles to bear."

"Ah! yes; but those will make this all the worse to bear."

"I can but trust in God and have patience. He is very merciful."

"Very merciful. But then—He lets terrible things happen whiles."

Mrs Calderwood rose and moved about the room. She was startled out of her usual quiet by the girl's changing colour and the sad eagerness of the eyes that looked out upon the sea. She was afraid of what might be said if they went on. She wished to hear no sorrowful secret from the girl's lips. She would hear none, she said to herself with a sudden sharp pang of remembrance. George Dawson's daughter could have nothing to say to which it would be right for her to listen. At last Jean left the window and came and stood near the fire.

"I came in to ask you if I might have Marion home with me for a day or two. I am 'my leafu' lane,' as Tibbie says. And I think she would like to come with me."

"There is little doubt of that," said Mrs Calderwood sitting down with a sense of relief, for she thought the danger was over.

"There is no danger of her falling behind in her lessons for a day or two, and I can help her with her music. I will take good care of her, and her company will be a great pleasure to me."

There was no sufficient reason why the child should not have this pleasure—at least there was none that could be spoken about. She had no time to make clear to herself why she would have liked to refuse, she could only say,—

"You are very kind. The child will be pleased to go," and Jean thanked her, accepting it as consent.

She was still standing with her muff in her hand as though she were about to take her leave. But she did not go. She stood, not looking at her friend, but past her, seeing nothing, with her eyes full of eagerness and anxiety, and before Mrs Calderwood, moved by a sudden fear, could find words to avert it, that which she feared had come upon her. Jean came a step nearer.

"Mrs Calderwood, may I tell you something? I have no one else, and you will at least help me to be patient. You were my mother's friend, and you have had much to bear, and will you help me?"

But there was no friendly response in Mrs Calderwood's face. She withdrew herself from the eager girl, with something like terror in her eyes, actually moving away till she touched the wall of her narrow parlour, holding up her hands entreatingly.

"No. Do not tell me. I am not the right person to receive confidences from—from any one. I am not sympathetic I do not care to hear secrets. And—you have your aunt."

Jean looked at her with surprise but with no anger in her eyes.

"My aunt! I tried to tell her once, but she said unless I were quite sure that she could help me, I should not speak. It would have grieved her—and—"

"She was quite right, I have no doubt," said Mrs Calderwood. "The least said is soonest mended, as the old saying has it. Silence is almost always best, even between friends."

Mrs Calderwood had come forward again to the table, and her hands were busy moving about various things upon it, hurriedly and heedlessly, as though she hardly knew what she was doing; while Jean looked on saying nothing for a little.

"Is silence always best? It would be such a comfort to me to be able to tell some one. I daze myself thinking about it. I am sorry now that I did not tell my father at once, though at the time it did not seem the wisest thing to do—or even possible. It was on the very day the ship sailed—the tenth, ye ken. And—"

"Whisht, lassie! I will not hear your secret," said Mrs Calderwood with a cry which told of many things. "It is to your father that you must tell it, if you have not the sense and courage to keep silence forever. As for me, I will hear no secret from the lips of your father's daughter. No good could come of it. Oh! must I go through with all that again! And my poor, foolish Willie that I thought so wise and strong!"

She hardly seemed to know what she was saying for the moment. But she made a great effort to restrain herself, and rose and came forward, holding out her hand as if the visit were at an end. But she paused, startled as she met Jean's look.

A sudden momentary wave of colour crimsoned her face and even her throat, and passing left her as white as death. Through it all she never turned her eyes from the face of her friend.

"Mrs Calderwood," said she in a voice that scarcely rose above a whisper, "I think I must tell you now—that my brother George sailed in the 'John Seaton.'"

Mrs Calderwood sat down on the sofa without a word. Of what horrible thing had she been guilty? What words had she spoken? She could not recall them, but the girl's changing colour showed that her thoughts had been understood. In her sorrow and shame she could have knelt and entreated forgiveness. But she well knew that *now* at least, silence was best. No words of hers could help the matter now. It cost her positive pain to raise her eyes to the girl's face. The colour came and went on it still, almost at every word; but Jean spoke quietly and firmly, and never turned her eyes from the face of her friend.

"You are right perhaps, and I ought to have spoken to my father at once; but since I have waited so long, it may be as well to wait till the 'John Seaton' comes in—and I must have patience—like the rest of those who wait."

"Are you sure he went? My son said nothing to me about George—poor dear Geordie?" said Mrs Calderwood, with a sudden rush of tears.

Jean sat down on the other side of the table and leaned her head on her hand.

"Did he not? Still I think he must have gone—or what can have become of him?"

"Who told you he went? It is strange that you have never spoken of it all this time. Why do you think that your brother sailed in the 'John Seaton'?"

"Is it strange? Perhaps I was quite wrong. But I did not know till afterwards. Robbie Saugster brought word that day to Saughleas, but I had gone to the town. That night he came back again, but it was too late. The ship had sailed, and we had been at the high rocks to see her pass, May and I—never thinking whom she was carrying away."

"And had Robbie seen him?"

"No. I never asked him. I don't think he knew. It was in a note that I got from—your son."

"And what did he say?" asked Mrs Calderwood in a little. "He said I was to come to the pier head before the ship sailed, and that perhaps I might be able to persuade my brother—though he could not. But he came too late. The ship had sailed."

"Well, we can only wait now till she comes home again."

"Yes, we can only wait. I am glad he went with—Willie, who will be good to him. That is all my comfort."

"Yes, Willie will stand his friend whatever happens." There was no more said, for Marion came dancing in. "Yes, Mavis dear, your mother says you may come home with me. I must go and see Aunt Jean first, and you will find me there."

"And, Miss Dawson, take a good rest, and we'll go round by the sea shore. It is so long since I had a walk with you. See the sun is coming out after all."

"Well," said Jean nodding and smiling. Then she shook hands with Mrs Calderwood, but they did not linger over their good-byes. Marion turned a wistful look to her mother's face when they were alone. But her mother would not meet it, but hastened her away.

Jean turned towards the pier head, to let the wind from the sea blow her hot cheeks cool, before she came into her aunt's sight, and as she went she was saying to herself,—

"It was May she was thinking about I could not speak, because May has never spoken to me. And after all—I dare say she is right. 'The sense and courage to keep silence.' No wonder that his mother should say that, who can never forget her poor bonny Elsie."

It was mid-day—the hour when the usual frequenters of the pier head were home at their dinners, and Jean stood alone for some time looking out to the sea, and thinking her own thoughts. They were troubled thoughts enough. "The sense and courage to keep silence." Her temptation was not to speech. It was sense and courage to speak that she needed.

Her aunt too had told her that silence was best—that foolish fancies, that might have vanished otherwise, sometimes took shape and became troubles when put into words. All at once it came into Jean's mind, that it could not have been of her brother's loss, but of something quite different that her aunt had been thinking when she said this. Could it have been of May and Willie Calderwood?

"She too must think that my father would never yield, and that it would be just the same sad story over again. But still, I am not sure that silence is best."

By and by those who worked or loitered on the pier head, came dropping back in twos and threes, and Jean knew that unless she would keep her aunt's dinner waiting she must go. Miss Jean had said to herself that the first word spoken would reveal to the girl her own sad secret. But it had not done so—or she would not acknowledge it—even though the remembrance of Mrs Calderwood's words and manner brought a sudden hot colour to her face.

"It was May she was thinking about," she repeated, as she went down the street.

She looked "bonny and bright—a sicht for sair e'en," Nannie, her aunt's maid, said, when she came in. She did not stay very long. She had intended to spend the day, but Marion Calderwood was going home with her, and she would have to come another day, she told her aunt.

Indeed Marion came in before dinner was over, and Jean was glad to have a long walk and the young girl's gay companionship, rather than an afternoon of quiet under her aunt's keen, though loving, eyes.

Chapter Eleven.

A Visitor.

Mr Dawson was longer away than he had intended to be when he left. A visit was made to the Corbetts on the way, and from thence came a letter telling Jean to prepare to receive another visitor when her father should return. Hugh, the Corbett who came next after Emily, a schoolboy of fourteen, had been so unfortunate as to hurt his knee in some of his holiday wanderings during the previous summer, and had been a prisoner in the house for months, and Mr Dawson proposed to bring him to Portie for a change.

Jean was promised no pleasure from the visit. The lad was ill, and "ill to do with," irritable and impatient of his long confinement in the house. There was little enough space in the Corbett house for those who were well, and it would do the lad good to see something else besides the four walls of the rather dim parlour where he had been a prisoner so long. He must be a prisoner even at Saughleas for a time, poor lad; but when the spring came so that he could get out, and get the good of the sea air, he would doubtless be better; and in the mean time, said her father, Jean must make the best of him.

The next letter was from London, telling of their safe arrival, and kind reception, but neither that nor the next, told the day on which Mr Dawson might be expected home. Indeed it told nothing in a very satisfactory manner; but Jean gathered that they found themselves in very favourable circumstances for seeing many of the wonderful sights of London, and the only thing they seemed to regret was, that Jean was not there to enjoy it all with them. A good many names of people and places were mentioned, but no very clear idea was conveyed with regard to them all, and Jean was advised to wait patiently for her father's return to hear more; and this she was content to do.

Her father came home the better for his trip, Jean saw at the first glimpse she got of his face. Of course the first minutes were given to care of the lame boy, who was tired and shy, but when he had got his tea, and was happily disposed of for the night, Jean sat down to hear what her father had to tell. Not that she expected to hear much at any one time. His news would come out by little and little on unexpected occasions, as was his way with news, but he answered her questions about her sister, and her friends, and gave his opinion of them and their manner of life readily enough. He had evidently enjoyed his stay among them, and acknowledged that he had known nothing of London before this visit.

Jean listened, pleased and interested; but all the time she was waiting to hear a certain name which had occurred more than once in the brief letters of her sister, and which had also been mentioned once at least by her father.

"And you went to the British Museum?" said she at last.

"Yes. I had been there before, but this was different. It is one thing to wander about, looking at things which you don't understand, till eyes and mind and body grow weary,—and never a clear idea of any thing gotten, to keep and carry away to look at afterwards—and it is quite another thing to go about in the company of one who, by two or three words, can put life and spirit into all there is to see. Mr Manners was with us that day."

And it seemed that Mr Manners had been with them other days, and on one occasion when her father had mentioned his name several times, Jean asked,—

"And who is Mr Manners? You have not told me who he is."

"He is a man with a clear head o' his ain, who will make his mark yet, or I'm much mistaken. No, he was not staying with the Seldons, though he was there often. He has rooms near the university in which he is a professor. I thought much of him."

"What is he like? Is he old or young?" asked Jean.

"Oh! he is not young. Not that he is to call old either. He is tall and thin rather, and stoops a little, and he wears glasses whiles, but not when he is reading."

Jean laughed.

"Stoops and wears glasses!"

She was laughing at herself. She had been conscious of a little discomfort, at the frequent mention of this man's name. A new interest and influence had come into her sister's life in which she had no part, and it saddened her though she acknowledged that her sadness was unreasonable. But she was a little anxious as well as sad, because, having so long watched over her sister, she feared that in the new circumstances in which she found herself, her care might be needed and missed—which was also unreasonable, since she might have gone with her had she cared to do so, and since her sister had both sense and judgment to care for herself.

And for the special danger which was in Jean's thoughts—though she would not allow that she feared it—surely May was safe from that. The child liked attention and admiration, and got them wherever she went; but her heart was not in her own keeping, as Jean believed, and so she was safe, and would come back to them as she went; and Jean acknowledged her own folly in being either anxious or sad. But all the same she laughed and was, pleased, that the new friend she had found should be "not young, though not just to call old," as her father had said, and that he should stoop a little and wear glasses. So she determined to put all unpleasant possibilities out of her thoughts, and the fact that the professor's name no longer found frequent place in her sister's letters, made it all the easier for her to do so.

Besides, she had more to occupy herself as the winter passed away, and less time to brood and vex herself; and as it was not in her nature when she was well to vex herself without sufficient occasion, her occupations helped her to a better kind of cheerfulness than that which of late she had sometimes assumed for her father's sake.

Young Corbett was her best help toward a more reasonable frame of mind with regard to all things. The journey had been too much for him, or he had in some way injured his knee again, for he suffered much pain in it for a time, and his young hostess was kept constantly busy, ministering to both mind and body. Dr Maitland, the chief Portie practitioner, took a different view of the lad's case from that which the doctor at home had taken, and he was subjected to different treatment which told to his benefit after a time. But just at first he suffered a good deal, and Jean "had her ain adoes wi' him," as Phemie, her maid, declared.

He was not an ill-tempered boy, though Mr Dawson had received that impression from what he had seen and heard in his own home. He suffered, and he was irritable, and impatient of necessary restraint. But he made an effort towards patience and submission to circumstances in the presence of strangers which he possibly would not have made at home, and the change and the quiet of the house helped his patience on to cheerfulness before very long.

"How my father and mother should have ventured to inflict such a nuisance upon you amazes me; and how you should consent to it amazes me more still," said he to Jean when he had been two days in the house, and when he was beginning to feel himself not so strange and forlorn as he had felt at first.

"But I did not consent I was not consulted," said Jean laughing.

"No," said the boy gravely. "And you could hardly refuse to have me when I was laid down at your door. But that only makes it all the more surprising that you should—take so much trouble with me."

"But then it was to my father's door you came, and he brought you himself. Don't be foolish. If I were lame and ill and needed your help, would not you be willing to give it to me?"

"But that would be quite different. And I could not help you, besides."

"Well, never mind. I am glad papa brought you here. I am going, by and by, to send you home strong and well, and fit to do a man's work in the world. And in the mean time—though I acknowledge that you are whiles a wee fractious and ill to do with—I like you. I'm glad my father brought you here, and we'll be friends always," and Jean held out her hand.

The tears started in the lad's eyes.

"It is very good of you," said he with a gasp.

After that, life went better with him. When after a little he could be taken every day and laid on the sofa in the parlour, he began to feel the good of the change. He had plenty to amuse him. He liked reading, well enough, as boys like it, but he was not a book worm; and Jean might have found him heavy on her hands during the first weeks after he came down-stairs, if he had had only books to fall back upon. But to her surprise and his own, an unfailing source of interest and pleasure presented itself to him.

Scarcely a vessel for the least ten years had come into the harbour of Portie without bringing some curious or beautiful thing to one member or another of the Dawson family, until the house was filled with them. A wonderful collection they made,—corals, shells, minerals, stuffed birds, beetles, and butterflies; and a scarcely less wonderful collection of objects of art and skill. A great trouble this accumulation became to housemaids, and even to the young mistress of the house, who could not always trust the dusting and keeping them in order to unaccustomed hands. There were many valuable and beautiful things among them, and almost all of them had some pleasant association with the giver, which made it not easy to part with them even to persons who would have valued them, or to put them out of sight. So there were a great many of them scattered up and down in the house.

In these the boy found constant interest and delight, and when he had gone over all that were within his reach, he was quite ready to begin again. And then Jean bethought herself of the quantities of things which in past years had been bestowed in out-of-the-way corners of the house, to make room for new treasures, and with some trouble to herself, but with some pleasure also, these were sought out, and brought to the lad, as he could not go to them.

Of course the result was an untidy room, and after a while, confusion so utter as not to be endured patiently. This lasted for a few days, and then a chance word from the lad, suggested the idea of proper cases being made in which all these things might be bestowed, and so arranged as that they might be more carefully preserved, and made useful as well as pleasant to look at.

"There are few things in our town museum at home so rare or so beautiful as several of these. I have been through ours scores of times. I like it."

Rather to Jean's surprise and much to her delight, her father took up the idea as a good one, and entered into the discussion of the different kinds of cases required, with interest. The cabinet-maker was sent for, and by the help of Hugh's description of the arrangements made for such things in the museum of his native town, they succeeded in settling all things in a satisfactory manner. The long hall extending from one side of the house to the other was the place to receive them. Therefore the cases must be handsome as furniture as well as convenient for the reception of the articles to be arranged in them; and in a shorter time than would have at first seemed possible, John Helvie finished the work in a way which pleased himself and his employers.

In the mean time May was written to for books about shells and minerals, and all such things; and Hugh, and even Jean, grew enthusiastic over them. And so the last months of winter passed more quickly than the first had done. May's visit was prolonged beyond the six weeks which had been at first stipulated for, and the third month was nearly at an end before any thing was said about her return. She was well and happy, and her friend was happy in her company. She was not especially needed at home, and neither her father nor her sister cared to shorten her holiday, as she called it. But if Jean had known what was to be the end of it all, the chances are that she would have been speedily recalled.

As Hugh grew better and the weather became milder, a new means of pleasure and health was presented to him by Mr Dawson in the shape of a small Shetland pony. He was one trained to gentleness and past his youth, so that there was no risk in riding, when the doctor's permission had been obtained. It could hardly be called riding for some time. It was slowly creeping along, with some one at his side, to make sure that no stumble should harm the still painful knee; but it was a source of much enjoyment to the lad who had been a prisoner so long.

Jean was most frequently his companion, and at such times their favourite course was along the sands when the tide was out, or by the path which led over the rocks. They lingered often on their way, to talk to the old sailors who remembered the lad's father and grandfather, and who had much to tell about his grandfather's goodness, and his father's wild exploits as a lad. They talked with the fishwives also in the town, and made friends with the bairns, who, as the days grew milder, came in flocks to their favourite playground, the sands above the town. All this was good for the lad, who caught a little healthy colour from the fresh sea breezes, and day by day, Mr Dawson thought, grew more like his companion and chief friend in the days when they were both young.

But it was not so good for Jean. For their talk with the old sailors, and the fishwives, and indeed their talk together, was mostly of the sea and its dangers, the treasures which it hid, and the far lands that lay beyond it. She told him tales of the sea, and repeated songs and ballads made about sea kings and naval heroes of all times, and sang them in the gloaming, with their wild refrains, which look like nonsense written down, but which sung, as Jean could sing them, deepened the pathos of the sad and sometimes terrible tales which were told; and the lad was never weary of listening.

And all this was not good for Jean. It stirred up again the old fears and doubts and questionings as to whether she had done right to keep silence about her brother, and whether she ought even now to speak. The wistful, far-away look which her father could not bear to see, came back to her eyes, now and then; and on stormy nights, when the moan of the wind was in the trees, and the sound of the sea came up like a sigh, the old restlessness, which in her father's presence she could only quiet by constant and determined devotion to work of some kind, came upon her. She could not read at such times or even listen. Her "white seam," on which her father used to remark, was her best resource. He remarked on it still, and not always pleasantly, and Jean began to be aware that his eyes now followed her movements as they had done in the first part of the winter, and that even when he occupied himself with a book, or with his papers, he listened to the talk into which she and Hugh sometimes fell. She did her best to be cheerful, and with the lad's help it was easier than it had once been; and she comforted and strengthened herself with the thought that the year was nearly over, and that it could not now be long before the "John Seaton" came home.

Chapter Twelve.

Northern Seas.

"Do ye ken what ye are doing, Jean? Ye're doing your best to mak' a sailor o' the lad; and ye'll do him an ill turn and get him into trouble if that happens. His father has other plans for him."

Her father had come in to find Jean singing songs in the gloaming. It could hardly be said that she was singing to Hugh. She would very likely have been singing at that hour, if she had been quite alone; but she would not have been singing,—

> "The Queen has built a navy of ships,
> And she has sent them to the sea,"

in a voice that rang clear and full in the darkness, and she would not have followed it with the ballad of "Sir Patrick Spens," which Mr Dawson was just in time to hear. He was not sure about all this singing of sea songs; but he said nothing at the time, and sat down to listen.

He had heard the ballad scores of times, and sung it too; but he felt himself "creep" and "thrill," as Jean—her voice now rising strong and clear, now falling into mournful tones like a wail—went through the whole seven and twenty verses. She said it rather than sung it, giving the refrain, not at every verse, but only now and then; the pathos deepening in her tones as she went on towards the end, when—

> "The lift was black, and the wind blew loud,
> And gurly grew the sea."

and there were "tears in her voice" as she ended—

> "And lang, lang may the ladies sit
> Wi' their fans into their hands,
> Before they see Sir Patrick Spens
> Come sailing to the strand!

> "And lang, lang may the maidens sit
> Wi' the gowd (gold) kames in their hair,
> Awaiting for their ain true loves,
> For them they'll see nae mair—"

and then the refrain—which cannot be written down—repeated once and again, each time more softly, till it seemed to die away and be lost in the moan of the wind among the trees. No one spoke for a minute or two.

"I think you might give us something mair cheerfu' than that, Jean, my lassie," said her father, inclined to resent his own emotion and the cause of it. "And in the gloaming too!"

"The gloaming is just the time for such ballads, papa. But I didna ken ye were come in. Shall I ring for lights now?" said Jean rising.

"There's nae haste. It's hardly dark yet."

Jean crossed the room to the window that looked out to the sea, and leaning on it, as she had a fashion of doing, softly sang the refrain of her song again.

Her father could not see her face, but he knew well the look that was on it at the moment,—a look which always pained him, and which sometimes made him angry; and the chances are he would have spoken sharply to her, if Hugh had not said after a little while, "But sailors don't go to sea now to bring home king's daughters, or even to fight battles with their foes. They go for wages, as the navvies do on railways, and the factory people in the towns. It is just the common work of the world with them as it is with others—buying and selling—fetching and carrying. There is nothing heroic in that."

"Of course—just the common work of the world. But I would not think less, but more, of the courage and endurance needed to do it, because of that," said Jean gravely, turning round to look at him. "It is just like the navvies, as you say, that they may live and bring up their families; and I think it is grand to leave their homes, and face danger, just because it is their duty, and with no thought beyond."

"They get used to the danger, and it is nothing to them, I suppose. And it must be fine to be going here and there, and seeing strange countries, and all sorts of people. I should like that I would like to have gone with Sir Humphrey Gilbert, or Sir Walter Raleigh in the old times. That must have been grand."

"Yes," repeated Jean, as she came forward and sat down by the fire. "That must have been grand—the sailing away over unknown seas to unknown lands. They had hope, but they could have had no knowledge of what was before them."

"What did they care for danger or hardship, or even death! They were opening the way to a new world."

"Yes. If they could only have had a glimpse of all that was to follow! I dare say they did too—some of them."

"Yes; Walter Raleigh looked forward to great things. It was worth a man's while to live as those men lived. It was not just for wages that they sailed the sea."

Mr Dawson laughed.

"That is the way you look at it, is it? And how many—even among their leaders—thought about much except the gold they were to find, and the wealth and glory they were to win! It was as much work for wages then as now. It is a larger world than it was in those days, but the folk in it ha'e changed less than ye think; in that respect at least."

There was a good deal more talk of the same sort, Jean putting in a word now and then, and what she said, for the most part, went to show, that in doing just the common work of the world, the buying and selling, the fetching and carrying, of which she thought Hugh had spoken a little scornfully, there were as many chances for the doing of deeds of courage and patience, as there could have been in the old times which he regretted. There were such deeds done daily, and many of them, and the men who did them were heroes, though their names and their deeds might never be known beyond the town in which they had been born.

She told of some things done by Portie men, and her father told of more, having caught the spirit of the theme from Jean's thrilling tones and shining eyes, and from one thing they went on to another, till at last Jean said,—

"I was reading a book not long since—" And when she had got thus far Hugh surprised Mr Dawson by suddenly rising from the sofa on which he had been lying all this time, and still more by hopping on one foot, without the help of crutch or cane, to the fireside and then laying himself down on the hearth-rug.

"My lad, I doubt the wisdom of that proceeding," said he gravely.

"Oh! there is no harm done. Miss Dawson is going to tell us about the book she has been reading lately, and I like to see her face when she is telling a story."

Mr Dawson laughed. He liked that himself. In her desire to withdraw her father from the silent indulgence of his own thoughts, into which he was inclined to fall, when left alone with her sister and herself, Jean, when other subjects of conversation failed them, had sometimes fallen back on the books she had been reading, and talked about them. She could give clearly and cleverly enough the outlines of a theory, or the chief points in an argument. She could tell a story graphically, using now and then effectively the gift of mimicry of which her aunt had been afraid. Mr Dawson's constant occupation had left him little time for general reading during the past, and had made the habit not easy to adopt now that he might have found leisure for it. But he enjoyed much having the "cream" of a book presented in this pleasant way by his daughter. So he also drew forward his chair, prepared to listen to what she might have to say, understanding quite well how the boy might like to see her face as she talked.

"Well," said Jean, "we need not have the lights, for I can knit quite as well in the dark. It is a sad book, rather. But I like no book that I have read for a long time, so well as this. It is about men who were willing, glad even, to take their lives in their hands, and sail away to northern seas, in hope of finding some trace of Sir John Franklin and his men.

"It was not for wages that they went, Hugh, my lad; at least it was not with most of them. It was with the hope—and it was only a hope, and not a certainty—of saving the lives of men who were strangers to them, who were not even their own countrymen. And they went, knowing that years might pass before they could see their homes again, and that some among them never might come home.

"It is a sad story, because they did not find the men, nor any trace of them. But it was worth all they suffered, and all that was sacrificed, just to show to the world that was looking on, so noble an example of courage and strength and patience as theirs. But I am beginning at the wrong end of the story."

Jean had read with intense interest the history so clearly and modestly written by the leader of the band, and she told it now with a power and pathos that made her father wonder. Of course there was much in the book on which she could not touch. She kept to the personal narrative, telling of the hope that had taken them from their homes, and that sustained them through the night of the Arctic winter, as they lay ice bound in the shelter of a mountain of ice on a desolate shore, when sickness came to most of their number, and death to more than one.

She told of long journeys made in the dimness of returning day, of the glad recognition of known landmarks, of the long, vain search for the lost men—of how hope fell back to patience, and patience to doubt and dread, as they waited for the sun and the summer winds to break the chains that bound their good ship in that world of ice, and set them free.

And then, when their doubt and dread became certainty, as the long Arctic day began to decline, and the choice lay between another winter in the ice-bound ship, and an endeavour to find their way over the frozen wastes that lay between them and the open sea, beyond which lay their homes, some of their number chose to go; but their leader would not forsake the ship, and a few of his men would not forsake him. And beside those brave souls who held their duty dearer than their thoughts of home, there were some who were sick, and some who were helpless through the bitter cold and the hardships they had borne, who had no choice but to stay and take what poor chance there might be of getting home with the ship, should the sun and the warm winds of a summer yet far before them set them free at last.

"And now," said Jean her voice falling low, "the time to test their courage had come."

She had told the story hitherto—in many more words than are written here—with eager gestures, and with eyes that challenged admiration for her heroes. But now her work fell on her lap, and her face was shaded from the firelight, and though she spoke rapidly still and eagerly, she spoke very softly, as she went on to tell how with a higher courage than had been needed yet, their leader looked the future in the face—seeing in it for himself, and for those for whom, as their commander, he was in a sense responsible, suffering from cold and hunger, from solitude and darkness, and from the wearing sickness of mind and body that these are sure to bring.

"'With God's help we may win through,' said this brave and patient spirit.

"And there were none who could turn cowardly under such a leadership as his," said Jean, with a sound that was like a sob, her father thought. "And so they all fell to doing with a will what might be done to protect themselves from the bitter cold, and to provide against some evils that were possible, and against others that were certain to come upon them. And surely they had God's help, as their leader had said; and those pain-worn men, in the darkness of that long night, saw in him what is not often seen—a glad and full obedience to our Lord's command, for the chief to become the servant of all. There was no duty of servant or nurse too mean for him to do. Not once or twice, but daily and hourly, as there was need, during all that time of waiting, when he only called himself well, because he was not utterly broken down and helpless, as almost all the others were.

"Patience, courage, cheerfulness, they saw in him, and they saw nothing else. For the souls and spirits of these men were in his hands, as well as their bodies, and if his courage and cheerfulness had failed in their sight, alas! for them.

"But they did not fail. And even in his solitary hours—in the night when he watched that they might sleep—and in his long, and toilsome, and often vain wanderings over the frozen land and sea in search of the food that began to fail before the end came—surely he was not left to even a momentary sense of desertion and discouragement, to a brave man an experience more terrible than death!

"That was known only to God and him, for strength came equal to his day, as far as they could see who leaned on him and trusted him through all. He did not fail them.

"And when, after months had gone by, the band who had left them, and turned as they believed their laces homeward, came back to the ship broken and discouraged with all they had passed through, he gave them a brother's welcome, and gladly shared with them the little that was left of food and fire and comfort, and doubled his cares and labours for their sakes.

"As time went on, death came to some, and the rest waited, hardly hoping to escape his call. But the greater number won through at last. They had to leave their good ship ice bound still, and then they took their way, through many toilsome days, over that wide desolation of ice and snow, going slowly and painfully because of the sick and the maimed among them, till at last they came to the open sea. Then trusting themselves to their boats, broken and patched, and scarcely seaworthy by this time, they sailed on for many days, making southward as the great fields of floating ice opened to let them through,—and still oh, after the sea was clear, till they came to land where Christian people received them kindly, and here they rested for a while.

"And one day they sailed out on the sea to meet a great ship that came sailing up from the south, and over this ship the flag of their country was flying; and as they drew near, one looked down on their little boat and said, 'Is this Doctor Kane?' And then, of course, their troubles were over, and soon they were safe at home."

No one spoke for a little while. Phemie brought in the lights, and then Jean laid down her knitting, and came to the table to make the tea. After that Mr Dawson went to his own room, and Hugh lay musing or dreaming on the rug till it was time for him to go to bed. It was when Jean went to say good-night to her father before she went to bed that he spoke to her.

"You will be making a sailor of the lad—with all that foolish singing and talk about heroes and sea kings. What on earth has set you off on that tack? The sea! the sea! and nothing but the sea! His father would be ill-pleased, I can tell you; for Hugh is a clever lad, and he has other views for him."

Jean had nothing to say for herself, and took her father's rebuke humbly and in silence. She had not thought for a moment of influencing the lad towards the life of a sailor; and when she had taken a minute to consider the matter, she was quite sure that no harm had been done, and so she assured her father.

"I would send the lad home, rather than run the risk," said he with some vexation.

"Yes, it would be better," said Jean. "But there is no risk. Hugh is older than his years, and he has taken his bent already, or I am much mistaken. Whether it will be according to his father's will, I cannot say; but there is no danger of his turning his thoughts to the sea. He might like to visit strange countries, if the way were open to him; and with opportunity he might become a great naturalist, for his knowledge of all natural objects and his delight in them is wonderful."

To this Mr Dawson had nothing to say. And indeed it was not about Hugh that he was at that moment troubling himself; but his trouble was not to be spoken about to Jean, and with rather a gruff good-night he let her go. But he could not put his trouble out of his thoughts. It had been there before, though he had almost forgotten it for a while.

"The sea! the sea! and ay the sea!" repeated he discontentedly. "What can have come to the lassie? She has no one on the sea to vex her heart about, unless indeed—she may fancy—that her brother is there," and the shadow that always came with thoughts of his son, fell darkly on his face. "Or—unless—but that can hardly be. There is no one, and she has sense. And yet—her brother—"

He rose, sick with the intolerable pain that a vivid remembrance of his loss always awakened, and there came to him suddenly a thought of Elsie Calderwood and her brother, the handsome mate of the "John Seaton," now almost a year at sea. He sank into his chair again, as if some one had struck him a blow.

"That would be terrible!" said he, putting the thought from him with an angry pang.

The remembrance of Captain Harefield's admiration, and the indifference with which his daughter had received it came back to him. Could there have been any thing besides the good sense for which her aunt gave her credit to account for her indifference? Could it be possible that young Calderwood could be in her thoughts?

He wearied himself thinking about it, long after the fire had gone out on the hearth, and he believed that he had convinced himself that his sudden fear was unreasonable and foolish. It could not be true.

"But true or not, I must keep my patience. It might have ended differently with—the other,—if I had taken a different way with him. I see that now.

I might have led him, though I could not drive him; and I fancy that would be true of his sister as well."

He went to his room with a heavy heart, but it grew lighter in the morning. He had been letting his fancy and his fears run away with his judgment, he thought, when he came into the breakfast-room, to find Jean and the lame boy interested and merry over a last year's birds' nest which Jean in her early walk had found in the wood. It was birds and birds' nests that made the subject of conversation this morning, and Mr Dawson might well express his wonder that a lad, born and brought up in a great town, should have so much to say about them. Jean suggested the idea of his having played truant whiles, to advance his knowledge in this direction, and the lad only answered with a shrug which was half a confession. His holidays, at least, had all been spent in the fields and woods even in the winter-time.

"And if I could have my own way, all my days should be spent—in the woods and fields," said he gravely, as if it were rather a sore subject with him.

Mr Dawson left the two considering the matter as though nothing of greater interest than birds and birds' nests existed for either of them.

"A far safer subject than the dangers of the sea," said he as he went his way.

Chapter Thirteen.

A Discovery.

In the beginning of April May came home—"bonnier than ever," as Jean told her father, as she met him at the door. He laughed when he heard her say it, but he agreed with her, and told her so when a day or two had passed.

He could hardly make it clear to himself, nor could Jean, in what she was different from her former self. It was because she was growing to be more like her mother as she grew older, he said. And Jean by and by came to the conclusion that something had happened to her sister while she was away—something to make her hopeful and happy, and at the same time graver and more thoughtful; yet she was very merry and sweet, and it was oh! so pleasant to have her home again. They made holidays of these first days of her home coming, and Jean was able to forget, or put aside, her sad and anxious thoughts for a while.

But there came a day when she well knew they would not be forgotten or put aside.

"May," said she one morning, "let us go down to the Tangle Stanes to-day. This is the tenth, ye ken."

"Well, let us go. It is a bonny day. But what about the tenth. I don't know what you mean."

"Have you forgotten? The 'John Seaton' sailed on the tenth," said Jean gravely.

May's colour changed a little. So did Jean's. But while May reddened, Jean grew pale.

"Have they heard bad news? Surely it is time that they were coming home again," said May.

"They might have been home before this time. But the voyage is often longer. I don't think there is any anxiety as yet."

"Well—we can go down to the Tangle Stanes. And will Hugh come too? I see the pony is brought round."

But they could not go at once, for Jean heard her father's voice calling her, and went to his room. As she did not return immediately, May and the lad set off together.

"Jean will come to the Tangle Stanes. I will wait for her there. And you can go on by yourself, Hugh, and meet us there afterwards." And a message to this effect was left for Miss Dawson.

Jean found her father sitting with an open letter in his hand. He made a movement as though he meant to give it to her, but withdrew it again saying,—

"I fancy it was only meant for my eye. I have a surprise for you, Jean. Mr Manners, the university professor I told you about, writes, offering a visit. He does not say when, but soon—as soon as may be."

"Mr Manners! I did not know that you had asked him, papa."

"Oh, yes! I asked him in a general way, as I did others—if he should ever be in this part of the country. But he is coming for a particular reason, it seems."

"Papa! Not for May?" said Jean sitting down suddenly.

"Well—it looks like it, though how you should have guessed it is queer enough. It never came into my mind, often as I saw them together. Is it from any thing your sister has said?"

"May has said nothing to me—nothing."

"I acknowledge that I am surprised. I should not have supposed that he was at all the man to be taken with a girl like May. If it had been you now—"

"Are you pleased, papa? Will you let him come? And would you give him May?"

"May must decide that for herself. All that he asks now is my leave to come and speak for himself. He does not wish any thing to be said to her till he says it himself."

"And will you let him come?" asked Jean gravely.

"Well, I think he has a right to be heard. Yes, I think we must let him come."

"Is Mr Manners a rich man, papa?"

"A rich man? I should say not. Indeed he tells me as much as that. He has a professional income, enough to live comfortably upon. He is a scholar and a gentleman, and money is a secondary consideration."

"Yes—if every thing else is right," said Jean a little surprised. She had not supposed that in any case, money would be a secondary consideration with her father.

"But he is a stranger, and—an Englishman."

Mr Dawson laughed.

"An Englishman! That can hardly be put as an objection, I should think. He is a stranger—in a sense—but he is a man well-known in his own circle, and beyond it—a man much respected, they tell me."

Jean knew by her father's manner that he was as much pleased as he was surprised.

"She is very young," said she in a little.

"She is old enough to know her own mind, I suppose, and there need be no haste, if it is to be. I think I must let him come."

"And I am not to speak to her?"

"Oh! as to that, I suppose he only meant that he wished to tell his own story. Still as there is no time set for his coming, it may be as well to say nothing for a day or two."

"Very well," and Jean rose and went away.

"She doesna seem to be over weel pleased at this, but she'll come round. I'm glad that it should be her sister rather than her that I maun part with. I could ill spare my Jean," said Mr Dawson to himself, as his eye followed her as she moved slowly down the walk. "Though I dare say her turn will come," he added with a sigh.

It was not that Jean was ill-pleased, but she was disturbed at the thought of trouble that might be before them.

"My father will never listen to a word about Willie Calderwood. And unless May is very firm—"

And she could not but have serious doubts of May's firmness in withstanding the will of her father.

"But at least he will not force her to many any one else. I could help her to stand out against such a thing as that. And I will too," said Jean.

But a greater surprise than her father had given her at home, awaited her at the Tangle Stanes. May sat on the lower ridge of rock where she had sheltered herself that day, while Jean watched for the "John Seaton." This was a very different day from that. There was no wind to-day and the sun shone and the air was soft and warm. The sea was calm and blue as the sky—with only here and there a touch of white where the tiny wavelets broke on the half hidden rocks beyond the Tangle Stanes. Jean stood still, and looked out upon it, pondering many things, then her eye fell on her sister.

She was singing softly to herself, as she plucked at the dried stalks of last summer's weeds that still clung to the sheltered side of the rock, or gathered the broken bits of stone, and threw them down into the sea. She was looking neither sad nor anxious, she was smiling, at her own thoughts, Jean fancied, as she stood still a minute or two looking down upon her. Then May turned and saw.

"Such a bonny day?" said she.

"Yes—a bonny day indeed. Where is Hugh?"

"He's not far away. I told him that we would wait for him here. Will you come down, or shall I come up to you?"

"I'll come to you. Some one might join us if we were to stay up in sight, and I have something to say to you. Or rather I have a question to ask you about some one."

"Well, come then. Is it about anyone in—London?" asked May smiling, while a little colour rose to her cheek.

"No," said Jean gravely. "I am going to ask you about Willie Calderwood. And indeed I think you might have spoken more plainly to me long ago."

May laughed.

"I have often wondered that you have never spoken plainly to me."

"Have you? Well, being your elder sister, perhaps I ought to have done so. I did not like to speak, since you did not."

"Just so. And I did not like to speak to you for the same reason."

"Well, we will speak now. May," said she softly, laying her hand on her sister's shoulder, "tell me just how it is between Willie and you."

"I don't understand you, Jean. There is nothing in the world between Willie and me."

"May, have you—changed your mind? Don't you care for him any longer?"

"I don't know what you mean. As to caring for him—of course I care for him—in a way. But, Jean, it is not me that Willie Calderwood cares for. He has said nothing to me that he might not have said to—almost any one in Portie."

"May, have you forgotten a year ago?—how you came here a year ago, because he asked you? Of course he could not speak, because of my father. Do you mean that he doesna care for you—more than for any one else."

"He has kept it to himself, if he does. Oh! yes, I know—my father. But if he had had any thing to say, he would have said it, or I would have guessed it. I don't know why you should have taken the like of that into your head."

"I saw him seeking you out wherever we met. He said more to you at such times than to all the rest of us put together. He followed you always. Every one saw it as well as I. And then the day he went away—"

"Oh, Jean, what nonsense! I came that day to please you. You made me come. You must mind that well enough. As for his asking me, it was more than half in jest. I am sure he did not expect me to come. And he never could have seen us, on such a day."

"And do you mean that if he were to come home to Portie and not find you here, it would be all the same to him?"

"Oh! he'll find me here when he comes, and I shall be glad to see him safe and well. But he has no right to expect a warmer welcome from me than from—any other friend, and he doesna expect it."

Jean looked at her in amazement.

"Have I been dreaming all the year?" said she.

"It would seem so. I have just as much right to ask you about Willie Calderwood, as you have to ask me."

Jean shook her head.

"He has very seldom spoken to me since—the old days."

"But that might be because of my father, ye ken," said May laughing. And then she added gravely, "We may be glad that there is nothing between him and either of us, Jean. It would only have been another heartbreak. I have fancied whiles, that *you* were thinking about him—but I am very, *very* glad for your sake that—"

"Of course I have been thinking about him—about him and you. I ought to be glad that I have been only dreaming, as you say, because of my father. But—poor Willie!—I doubt he has been dreaming too."

"No, Jean, not about me. And even if it had been as you thought, I would never have listened to him, and indeed he never would have spoken after all that's come and gone."

"It would not have been the same to my father, as George and Elsie."

"But coming after—it would have been all that over again, and worse. And Willie Calderwood is as proud and hard about some things, as my father."

"And that might have kept him from speaking," said Jean.

"And so it ought, even if he had had any thing to say, which he had not. You need not shake your head as though you didna believe me."

"I must believe you—since you say so—for yourself. But you may be mistaken about him, though he never spoke."

"Never spoke!" repeated May, mimicking her sister's voice and her grave manner. "And do you think I would have needed words to let me know if he had cared for me—in that way? You are wise about some things, Jean, but you are not just so wise as you might be about others. Wait a while."

May laughed and reddened, and then turned and climbed to the top of the rock to see if Hugh were in sight. Jean followed her slowly.

"I ought to be glad. I am glad. There is a great weight lifted from my heart. May is safe from the trouble that threatened, and so is my father. As for Willie Calderwood—well it is better for him too, that May doesna care, even if—And he'll get over it."

When Hugh came back they all took their way to Miss Jean's house by the sea. But as Hugh was not yet equal to the feat of dismounting without more help than he was willing to accept from the young ladies, May and he soon turned their faces homeward again, and Jean, who had something to do in the town, was left behind. She sat a while with her aunt, but she was quite silent, and her face was turned toward the sea. Miss Jean was silent also, giving her a glance now and then, feeling sure that she had something more than usual on her mind which perhaps she might need a little help to tell.

"Well," said she after a little, "have you any news? I think I see something in your e'en. Come awa' frae the window and say what ye ha'e to say."

Jean rose and came forward to the fire.

"Has my father been in? He will tell you himself, when there is really any thing to tell. He is sure to be in some time to-day."

"And it is nothing to vex you, dear? Are you glad about it?"

"It ought not to vex me. It is only what was sure to happen. And though I am not glad yet—I dare say I shall be glad in time."

"Is it about your sister?"

"Yes—and I think papa is glad. But he will tell you himself."

"And there is nothing else?"

Jean sat looking at her aunt for a minute or two.

"Yes, there is something else that ought to lighten my heart. It has lightened it, I think. I'm not just sure."

"And that is about May too?"

"Yes—about May."

She said no more and her aunt did not question her. By and by Miss Jean said,—

"It's a bonny day—and fine for the season. It was a different day last year when the 'John Seaton' sailed."

"Yes, I mind it well."

Jean did not look like herself, but absent and dazed like, as though her mind were full of other things. Miss Jean said nothing for a while, and Jean rose as if she were going away; but stood for a while looking out of the window.

"My dear," said her aunt, "I have thought that you have been troubled like about various matters, this while back, and about your sister among the rest. But I think ye ha'e nae occasion."

"Yes, I have been anxious."

"Because of Willie Calderwood? But, my dear, I canna think that there's any occasion."

"I seem to have been mistaken as far as she is concerned. She says so."

"And as for him—I never asked him and he never told me—but I'm no feared that he'll be the worse in the end for any such trouble. And, Jean, my lassie, we ha'e great reason for thankfulness that so it is. It would only have been anither heartbreak."

"Yes. That is what May said."

"Not but what they both would have outlived it—and had many a happy day after it. But I am glad we havena to go through all that, for all our sakes, and more especially for the sake of your father. For he is growing an old man now, and another blow like that would have been ill on him, whichever way it had ended."

"But, aunt,—ye mustna be angry at me for saying it,—but I canna think that my father was altogether wise or right in the way he took with George and Elsie."

"My dear, who is ever altogether wise and right in all they do, even to those they love best? And, my dear, ye are nae your father's judge. And do ye think that he sees now that all he did was wisest and best? and yet he might do the very same again. And even if he shouldna, it would be a misery and a lifelong pain to him all the same. My dear, I'm mair than thankful and we'll say nae mair about it."

And no more was said. But as Jean went slowly homeward, she had many thoughts of all she had heard that day. Glad! Of course she could not but be glad that all which must have brought disappointment and pain upon so many, had only been a dream of hers. How could she have been so mistaken! How much better it would have been if she had spoken plainly to her sister a year ago! Would May have answered as decidedly then?

Yes. Jean did not doubt that she would have done so. She did not doubt her sister's sincerity when she declared that she had never cared for Willie Calderwood "in that way."

"Wise about some things, but not so wise about others," said Jean with a smile, recalling her sister's words.

And might she not have been mistaken about Willie Calderwood as well as about May? May declared it, her aunt seemed to imply it. But surely Mrs Calderwood had been thinking about May that day! Jean's cheeks grew hot as she recalled her words and looks.

"Oh! I am thankful that I never named my sister's name to her. And if it was May she was thinking about, she will soon see that she was mistaken too, and that she needna have feared. And if it wasna May she was thinking about, she needna be feared?"

Jean walked more rapidly, and held her head higher as the thought passed through her mind. She believed herself to be very angry as all the scene came vividly back to her—angry with Mrs Calderwood. But for all that she went home with a lightened heart and with a face at once brighter and more peaceful than her father had seen for a while.

Chapter Fourteen.

Mr Manners.

It would not have been easy for Jean to set about any very elaborate preparations for the reception of the expected guest, without attracting the notice of her sister, who was to know nothing of his coming beforehand. Happily no special preparation was needed in her well-regulated household, for within a shorter time than seemed possible after her father's letter of invitation had been sent, he made his appearance at Saughleas.

He had reached the town at night, and presented himself at the bank in the morning before Mr Dawson had reached it. They missed each other as he took his way to Saughleas, and Jean was the only one there to receive him. The day was mild and dry, and May and young Corbett had set off immediately after breakfast, on an expedition to the Castle.

Jean was in the garden, intent on hastening the completion of certain changes that had been commenced in the arrangement of flower beds and shrubbery, indeed putting her own hands to the work of clipping and transplanting under proper direction and authority. She saw the stranger the moment he opened the gate, and stood still in her place behind a sheltering fir-tree, regarding him as he came slowly round the drive.

She saw a pleasant face, with something of the pallor of the student upon it—not handsome, but a good, true face, she thought as he came nearer. He was tall, as her father had said, and he stooped a little; but it was not a round-shouldered stoop, rather a slight inclining forward as he walked, such as short-sighted people are apt to fall into unawares. Certainly he was "not to call old."

A scholar and a gentleman, her father had said. He was all that, or his looks belied him, Jean told herself as he came slowly forward.

He stood for a moment looking up into the sky through the lovely mingling of faint colours made by the swelling buds and opening leaves in the tops of the great beeches, and Jean's impulse was to come forward at once and give him welcome. But she looked at her gloves, and at her thick shoes soiled with the garden mould, and at her linsey gown too short to hide them, and she thought of her sister, and "these fastidious English folk," and the "credit of the family," and so went swiftly round the house, and in at the back door, and up to her own room.

She did not linger over her toilette, however. By the time Phemie came to announce the stranger's arrival, the stately young mistress of the house was ready in her pretty house dress of some dim purple stuff to go down and receive him. She went with more shyness than stateliness, however, being conscious of the object of his coming, and entered so quietly, that he did not move from the window out of which he was gazing, till she had come near him. He turned quickly at the sound of her voice.

"Is it—Mr Manners?" said she, offering her hand. "You expected me then?"

"Yes. Papa told *me* you were coming."

"And you are Jean? And you will be my friend?" Jean's eyes met his frankly and very gravely for a moment, and then she said softly,—

"Yes. I think I may promise to be your friend."

If she could put any trust in the face as an index of character, she might surely promise that, she thought. She waited a moment, expecting that he would ask for her sister. He did not, but stood looking at her in a silence that must have become embarrassing if it had continued long. So she offered breakfast, which he declined. Then she expressed her regret that he should have missed her father, but she would send at once to tell him of his arrival.

This was not necessary, however. Mr Dawson having heard of Mr Manners' arrival at the bank, returned home immediately; but they were already in the dining-room, before May and young Corbett appeared. They went in the back way and passed through Beckie's kitchen.

"Eh! Miss May! What can ha'e keepit you? Miss Dawson has been muckle putten aboot. Your papa's come hame and a strange gentleman wi' him. Na, it's naebody ye need to heed. Was't Peters they ca'ed him, Phemie? It's luncheon and nae dinner—so you can just go ben as ye are. Ye couldna look better or bonnier though ye were to change your gown and tak' an hour to do it. And Miss Dawson was sair putten aboot."

So with no warning as to whom she was to see, flushed and laughing, and submitting to be made a crutch by the recovering and adventurous Hugh, May entered the dining-room.

"It was hardly fair upon her," her father thought, and Jean turned pale with vexation that it so should have happened. But she need not have been afraid. After the first startled glance, and rush of colour, May met her friend with a gentle dignity which left nothing to be desired in her sister's opinion. Mr Manners was to all appearance less self-possessed than she was, and his greetings were brief and grave.

All were for some time in a state of restrained excitement that made conversation not easy, till Hugh came to the rescue by referring to Mr Dawson the decision of some point which had fallen under discussion during the morning's ride, on which Miss May and he had disagreed. It had reference to a circle of stones in the neighbourhood, said to be of Druidical origin, and Hugh stated the difference of opinion clearly and fairly enough. Mr Dawson could give no light on the subject, however, and smiled at the idea of attaching any importance to the question.

"And besides," said May gently, but with an air of wishing to put an end to the matter, "I told you I did not hold any opinion with regard to them."

But Hugh, in his persistent way, refused to let it so end; and Jean, glad of any thing rather than silence, added her word, hoping that they might some time during the summer go to see the "Stanes."

"But, Miss May," continued Hugh, "though you said you did not know yourself, you gave authority for your opinion—at least as far as similar circles elsewhere are concerned. And was it not?—Yes, it was Mr Manners that you said had told you—"

Jean laughed. She could not help it. May grew red as a rose. Then Mr Manners took up the word, and there was no more uncomfortable silence after that; and Hugh heard more concerning this new subject of interest than he would be likely to hear again for many a day.

Before they rose from the table, Mr Dawson was called away by some one who wished to see him on business, and Hugh, with Jean for his crutch this time, betook herself to his room to rest and be out of the way. May went to the parlour with Mr Manners, intending only to show him the way and then go to her own room to change her habit for her house dress; but when Jean came back again, May was in the room still, and the door was shut.

Jean stood looking at it for a moment, with the strangest mingling of emotions—joy for her sister, sorrow for herself—a feeling as if the old familiar life were come to an end, and a new life beginning; nay, as if the very foundations of things were being removed.

"We can never be the same again—never," she said, with a sharp touch of pain at her heart. "I have lost my bonny May."

It was foolish to be grieved, it was worse than foolish to be angry, at the thought of change; but she knew that if she were to look closely into her heart, she would find both grief and anger there.

"I canna help it, but I needna yield to it," she said; and then she turned resolutely toward the kitchen, where Beckie was awaiting necessary directions with regard to dinner.

She lingered over her arrangements, and by and by put her own hands to some of them, for she found it impossible to settle quietly to any thing, though she told herself that her restlessness was foolish and not to be excused. It took her out of the house at last, and down the walk past the well and through the wood, where she had many times gone during the last few months to the most sweet and peaceful spot in all the world, she thought—where her mother and her little brother and sisters lay; and here, after a while, her father found her. He was not free from restlessness either, it seemed. Jean rose as he drew near.

"Where is your sister? Should you have left her?" asked he doubtfully.

Jean shook her head and laughed.

"They shut the door upon me."

"Ay! He's in earnest, yon lad. You like him, Jean? Though it's soon to ask."

"Not too soon. I liked him the first glance I got of him. He has a good, true face. Yes; I like him."

"It doesna take you long to make up your mind," said her father laughing. But he was evidently pleased. "You dinna like his errand? Well that was hardly to be expected. But if it hadna been him, it would have been another, and we should have lost her all the same. And it might have been worse."

"Yes, it might have been worse."

Jean was thinking what her father's feelings would have been had May's troth been plighted to Willie Calderwood. But her father was thinking that it would have been worse for him to-day had it been for Jean that the stranger had asked.

"It will be your turn next," said he with a sad attempt at jesting.

But Jean answered gravely,—

"No. I think not I'm content as I am."

Her father laughed, a short, uncertain laugh.

"Ay! that will do till the right man comes, and then—we'll see."

"But he may never come. He never came to Auntie Jean."

"Did he no'? Weel, it came to that in the end."

Mr Dawson looked up and met the question in Jean's eyes, but he did not answer it, and her lips were silent. She did not need an answer. Though she had heard nothing, she seemed to know how it had been with her aunt. Disappointment had come to her in her youth. Whether death had brought it, or change, or misunderstanding, or something harder to bear than these, she knew not; but however it had come, it had doubtless been a part of the discipline that had wrought toward the mingled strength and sweetness of her aunt's character, so beautiful in Jean's eyes. She forgot her father in thinking about it.

And for the same reason her father forget her. There were none like his sister in his esteem. None, of all the women he had seen grow old, had lived a life so useful, or were so beloved and respected in their old age as she. Her life—except for a year or two—had never been solitary in a painful sense, he thought. It had been, and was still, full of interest— bound up with the lives and enjoyment of others, as much as the life of any married woman of them all.

"And if she were to die to-night, there are more in Portie that would miss and mourn her than for many mothers of families, and that is not more than all would acknowledge who ken what she is and what she has done in the town."

But for his daughter? No, it was not a life like her aunt's that he desired for her. His eye came back to her as the thought passed through his mind. She was gazing straight before her, in among the trees, but it was not the brown buds nor the opening leaves that she saw, he knew well.

What could it be that brought that far-away look to her eyes. Was she looking backwards or forwards? Where were her thoughts wandering? Her look need not have vexed him. It was a little sad, but she smiled as though her thoughts were not altogether painful. He could not but be uneasy as he watched her. He loved her so dearly, she counted for so much in his life, that he longed for her confidence in all things, and he knew that there was something behind that smile which he could not see.

"Weel?" said he as she turned and met his look.

"I should go back to the house, you are thinking? Yes, I am going. But, papa—it will not be very soon? May's going away, I mean."

"That is all before us. I can say nothing now. I doubt all that will be taken out of our hands, my lassie. He is in earnest, yon lad."

"But, papa—it is surely our right to say when it is to be? And May is so young—not nineteen yet."

"Just her mother's age, when—"

He rose as if to go, but sat down again and said quietly, "A few months sooner or later will make little difference, and we could hardly expect that he would hear of making it a matter of years. Nor would I wish it."

"But it will not be—just at once?" said Jean. She had almost said "not till the 'John Seaton' comes home."

"Well, not just at once. There is time enough to decide that."

Mr Dawson looked doubtfully at his daughter. The look he had wondered at had left her face. She had grown pale and her eyes had the strained and anxious look that had more than once pained him during the winter. The question over which she had wearied herself then was up again.

"Shall I speak to him about Geordie? Shall I tell him how he went away?" But he did not know her thoughts, and fancied she was grieving about her sister.

"My dear, it is hard on you for the moment. But it is not like losing your sister altogether."

"Papa! It is not May I am thinking about. It is—Geordie. Oh, papa, papa!"

"My dear," said her father after a pause, "it will do no good to think of one who thinks so little of us. Think of him! We maun ay do that, whether we will or no'. But I whiles think he maun be dead. He could not surely have forgotten us so utterly."

His last words were almost a cry, and he turned his face away.

"Papa!" said Jean with a gasp, and in another moment she would have told him all. But before she could add a word he was gone—not back by the path to the house, but through the wood the other way, slowly and heavily with his head bowed down. Jean looked after him with a sick heart.

"It is my mother he is thinking of, as well as his son. Oh! I wish I hadna spoken?"

She sat down in a misery of doubt and longing, not sure whether she were glad or sorry that he had given her no chance to say more. How little and light her own anxieties looked in the presence of her father's sorrow! The silence and self-restraint, which day after day kept all token of suffering out of sight, made it all the more painful and pitiful to see when it would have its way! Miss Jean, his sister, had seen him more than once moved from his silent acceptance of pain and loss, but his daughter had never seen this, and she was greatly startled, and sat sick at heart with the thought that there was no help for his trouble.

For even if she were to tell him now that her brother had gone to sea in the "John Seaton," there would hardly be comfort in that; for it was more than time that the ship were in port, and though no one openly acknowledged that there was cause for anxiety, in secret many feared that all might not be well with her. No, she must not tell him. The new suspense would be more than he could bear, Jean thought; and she must wait, and bear her burden a little longer alone.

The tears that she could not keep back, did not lighten her heart as a girl's tears are supposed to do, and though she checked them, with the thought that she must not let their traces be seen in the house, they came in a flood when she found her sister's arms clasped about her neck and her face hidden on her breast. But she struggled against her emotion for her sister's sake, and kissed and congratulated her, and then comforted her as their mother might have done. And May smiled again in a little while—indeed what cause had she to cry at all, she asked herself, for surely there never was a happier girl than she.

And they both looked bright enough when they came down to dinner, and so did their father. Jean wondered and asked herself whether the sight of his moved face and the sound of his breaking voice, had not come to her in a dream.

He only came in at the last moment, and if he guessed from May's shy looks that something had happened to her, he took no notice, and every thing went on as usual, though a little effort was needed against the silence which fell on them now and then.

Of course after dinner, the girls went to the parlour and young Corbett went with them; and when, by and by, their father and Mr Manners came in to get some tea, Jean knew that May's fate was decided, as far as her father's consent to her marriage could decide it.

Pretty May blushed and dimpled and cried a little when her father came and kissed her and "clappet" her softly on her shoulder, and in rather an uncertain voice bade "God bless her."

Then Mr Manners brought her to Jean. "Will you give me your sister?" said he gravely. "Since she seems to have given herself to you, I may as well," said Jean kissing her sister and keeping back the tears that were wonderfully ready to-night.

"And remember your first word was a promise to stand my friend."

"Only I don't think you seem to stand in need of a friend just now," said Jean laughing.

"Ah! but I may need one before all is done. And you have promised."

Chapter Fifteen.

Mr Dawson's Will.

It would doubtless have been agreeable to Mr Dawson had Mr Manners been a richer man than he seemed to be, but he did not allow even to Miss Jean, that this want of money was a serious drawback to the satisfaction he felt in consenting to his daughter's marriage.

"He is a man whom I like much, and money is a secondary consideration," said he.

"That's true," said Miss Jean.

"Not that he is without means, and he has a good professional income. They will do very well. It is true I havena kenned him long, as ye say; and I dare say ye think I have been in haste with my consent. But just wait a wee. He'll ha'e your good word. For ye ken a man when ye see him."

"If they truly love one another—that is the chief thing."

Mr Dawson laughed.

"They do that."

"And what does Jean say?"

"She'll tell you herself. There has been little time to say any thing. He is to be brought over to see you to-day. I wished to send for you, but Jean said it was more becoming that he should come to you. Jean has her ain notions about most things."

"Ay, she has that."

"And ye'll come hame with them to Saughleas? There are two or three things that I would like to have a word with you about. And ye'll be sure to come."

But Miss Jean did not promise. She liked best to be at Saughleas when there were no strangers there, she said. Mr Dawson was ready to resent her calling Mr Manners a stranger, so she said nothing. The matter could be decided afterwards.

Probably Jean was only thinking of what was due to her aunt, when she insisted on taking their new friend to make her acquaintance in her own house. But it was a wise thing to do for other reasons than Miss Jean's "dignity," which her niece might very well have left to take care of itself.

The house was like herself,—quiet, simple, unpretending, but with a marked character of its own; and no one could fail to be impressed with his first glimpse of Miss Jean, sitting in her quaint parlour, with its shelves of brown old books, its great work-basket, and its window looking to the sea. She was an old woman now, and not very strong; but the inward calm which earthly trouble had no power to disturb, had kept disfiguring wrinkles from her face, and the soft wavy hair that showed under her full-bordered cap was still more brown than grey.

Some who had known Miss Jean all her life declared that she was far more beautiful at sixty than she had ever been in her youth. And naturally enough. For a life of glad service to a loving Master, a helpful, hopeful, self-forgetful doing of good as opportunity is given, for His sake, tell on the countenance as on the character; and the grave cheerfulness, the trustful peace that rested on the old woman's face were beautiful to those who had eyes to see.

It was not May, but Miss Dawson, who came with the visitor that morning.

"Auntie Jean, I have brought Mr Manners to see you," said she coming in unannounced.

Miss Jean received them kindly, but with a certain gravity.

"Yes, your father has been here. He told me who was coming," said she, and her eyes sought Jean's gravely and earnestly. Jean nodded and smiled, carrying her aunt's look to the face of Mr Manners.

"Yes, auntie, that is the way of it." Then Miss Jean gave him her hand again. "The Lord keep and guide you both. And the Lord deal with you as ye shall deal with the bairn that is willing to leave her father's house to go with you."

"Amen!" said Mr Manners, and he stooped and touched with his lips the soft wrinkled hand that had been offered him.

They had not very much to say to one another for a while. It was Jean who kept up the talk for a little, remarking upon the "bonny day," and the flowers that were coming out earlier than usual, and on the sea, which was seen at its best to-day, she said, a sparkling blue that faded to pale green and grey in the distance.

"You have a wide view of it here," said Mr Manners who was leaning against the ledge looking out.

There was nothing to be seen from Miss Jean's usual seat, but the sea and one rocky cape in the northern distance. "It is company to me," said she. "It is ay changing."

"But it is dreary whiles, aunt, very dreary, when the wind blows loud, and the winter is here." Miss Jean smiled.

"I think winter makes less difference to my outlook than it does to yours, Jean, my dear. It's ay the sea, and ay the same, yet ay changing ilka day o' the year, be it summer or winter. It is like a friend's face to me now after all that's come and gone."

It was not easy getting below the surface of things, because their thoughts were of the kind not easily spoken. Miss Jean said least, but she looked and listened and was moved by the soft flowing English speech of their new friend, in a way that filled her with amazement, "after all these years," she said to herself.

By and by May came in, leaving Hugh Corbett in the pony carriage at the door. She hesitated a moment, shy, but smiling, on the threshold, and then Mr Manners led her forward to be kissed and congratulated and made much of by her aunt.

"Ye'll try and be a good wife—as your mother was," said Miss Jean softly, and she gave a tearful, appealing glance toward him who had won the child's heart.

"I love her dearly," said he gently. "And I will care for her first always."

"I believe ye," said Miss Jean.

What with his good, true face, his kindly ways and winning-speech, he had won her good word, as easily as he had won Jean's "who liked him at the first glance," as she had told her father.

Mr Manners' visit was necessarily brief, but when he went away, he carried with him the good-will, and more than the good-will, of them all. Even young Corbett, who had at first resented the break made in the pleasant life they had been living of late by his monopolising Miss May's time and attention, agreed with the rest at last. They became mutually interested over shells and seaweeds, beetles and birds' nests, and they were very friendly before Mr Manners went away.

Before his departure Mr Manners put Jean's friendship to the test.

"If you are on my side, I shall be able to bring about that on which I have set my heart, and I must remind you of your promise."

Jean laughed.

"It seems that you are like to get that on which you have set your heart without the help of any one."

"Ah! but how would it have been if you had set yourself against me? Or if you were to do so even now?"

"It is too late for that now, and I don't think you are much afraid."

"Jean," said he gravely, "I want my May for my very own on the first day of August." Jean was not so startled as she might have been. "I did not think you would be willing to wait very long. But the first of August! That is not much more than three months. It will look like haste."

There were, it seemed, many good reasons for that which looked like haste. The chief one was this: Mr Manners looked forward to two full months of leisure after that time, which could not happen again for another year. He had set his heart on carrying his bonny May to Switzerland for the whole two months.

"Think what that would be in comparison to a winter marriage, and then straight to a dull house in a London street!"

"Will she find it dull, do you think?" asked Jean smiling. "Ah! that may be very possible, even though I know she will go willingly. Miss Dawson, I feel as if I were guilty of wrong-doing in thinking to take my darling from a home like this, to such a one as I can give her, even though I believe she loves me."

But Jean smiled still. "You need not fear."

"Thanks. I will not. But in those two months, think how we should learn to know each other, as we could not in my busy days in London! And she would learn to trust me. And it might be if you were to be on my side. As to preparations—dresses and things—"

"It is not that. All that is quite secondary. I mean I could see to all that after," said Jean to his surprise. "It is something quite different that I was thinking about."

It was the return of the "John Seaton" with her brother George on board of which she was thinking, and she was wondering whether it would be right to let her sister go, if he should not be home before that time. But she could not speak to Mr Manners of this. Indeed she could speak of nothing for the moment. For May came into the room, and her lover intimated triumphantly that her sister agreed with him as to the important matter of the time.

"And you know you were to leave the decision to her."

"I agree with you that preparations need not stand in the way. As to other things, I cannot decide. It was something quite different that I was thinking of."

But she did not say what it was, even to her sister, and from that time it was understood that the marriage was to take place on the first of August, and that, if possible, Mr Manners was to pay one more visit before that time.

In the quiet that followed his departure, the anxiety which in her interest in her sister's happiness she had for the time put aside, came back again to Jean. She strove to hide it from her father, and devoted herself to May and her preparations, with an earnestness which left her little time for painful thought. There was less to do in the way of actual preparation than might have been supposed—at least less than could be done by their own hands. The "white seam" that had employed Jean's fingers through so many summer afternoons and winter evenings, came into use now.

"I meant them for you, quite as much as for myself, and I shall have plenty of time to make a new supply before I need them," said she when May hesitated to appropriate so much of her exquisite work.

There was plenty to do, and Jean left herself no time for brooding over her fears. She kept away from the shore and the old sailors now, and from the garrulous fishwives of the town. She would not listen even to the eager reasoning of the hopeful folk who strove to prove that as yet there was no cause to fear for the ship; and she did keep all tokens of anxiety out of her face as far as her father saw; which perhaps was because he was occupied more than usual at this time with anxieties of his own. But when Mr Manners had been gone a month and more, and they were beginning to look for his return, something happened which would have made it impossible for her to hide her trouble much longer.

Mr Dawson had never yet taken any important step in business matters, or in any matter, without first talking it over with his sister. He did not always take her advice, and she never urged her advice upon him beyond a certain point; but whether her advice was accepted or rejected, there was no difference in their relations to each other because of that. He claimed her sympathy when the next call for it came, none the less readily because he had refused to be guided by her judgment, nor was she the less ready to hear and sympathise.

> "The breaks,
> Which humour interposed, too often makes,"

never came between these two, and her judgment guided him, and her conscience restrained him, oftener than either of them knew.

Long ago he had spoken to her about some change that he wished to make in his will, and some words of hers spoken at the time, hindered him from obeying his own impulse in the matter. He knew that it was not wise to delay the right settlement of his affairs, and now the arrangements necessary in regard to his daughter's marriage portion brought the matter up again, and made some decision inevitable.

That his son was dead, or worse than dead, he could not but believe, now that another year had gone bringing no word from him. In his silent broodings, he had in a sense got accustomed to the misery of the thought. He was dead, or, if he lived, he was lost to him forever. Even if he were living, his long silence proved to his father that he never meant to come home while his father lived.

He might come afterwards; and then his coming might bring trouble upon his sisters, unless all things were settled beyond the power of change. And so it must be settled. But, oh! the misery of it!

To think that his only son might come when he was dead, and stand where they had stood together at his mother's grave, and have only hard thoughts of his father! How could it ever have come to such a pass between them! The memory of those first days of their estrangement, seemed to him now like a strange and terrible dream. Had he been hard on his son? He was but a lad,—he repeated many a time,—he was but a lad, and he had loved him so dearly.

Nothing could be changed now. In the silence of the night, often amid the business of the day, his heart grew soft towards his son, and he repented of his anger and his hardness toward him. But nothing could be changed now, and the future of his daughters must be made safe against possible trouble when he should be no more.

He had nothing that was new to say to his sister, except that the year that had gone by bringing no word of him, made it less likely that they would ever hear from him again; and she could only listen sadly and acknowledge that it was even so.

But though there was not much that was new to be said, they were rarely left alone together that their talk did not turn on this matter. Mr Dawson's mind was so full of all that must be gone into and arranged in view of what he had to do, that he was sure to speak of it, and to dwell upon it, more sometimes than was wise. And so it happened that Jean, coming in from a solitary walk in the gloaming to the parlour, where there was no light, was startled by hearing her father say,—

"I think that will be a just division. I will make it up to her aster, but it is Jean who must have the land. I will not divide, and I will not burden the land."

Jean heard the words without fully taking in their meaning, till her aunt said in her grave, firm voice,—

"And if he ever should come home, you may trust to my Jean to deal kindly and justly with her brother."

"Papa," said Jean coming forward, "I heard what you were saying."

Mr Dawson did not answer for a moment, then he said, "It might have been as well if ye hadna heard. But a while sooner or later can make less difference than it would if ye werna a woman o' sense."

"Papa! Have you forgotten—Geordie?" Her father answered nothing. Her aunt put out her hand and touched hers, and Jean knew that the touch meant that silence was best. But she could not keep silence.

"Papa, you think that he is dead, but he is not. He will come home again. And how could we look him in the face if we were to wrong him when he is away! As for me, I will never take what is his by right—never. You must give the land to whom you will, but not to me." Still her father did not utter a word. "Whisht, lassie," said her aunt; "ye dinna ken what ye are saying. Dinna grieve your father, Jean."

But Jean was "beside herself," her aunt thought.

"Papa, was it not for George that you bought the land? Have you had much pleasure in it since he went away? But, papa, he will come again. He is sure to come home—soon."

Jean's voice faltered a little. That night her father had come home anxious and burdened with fears for the safety of the "John Seaton." There had been some of the sailors' wives inquiring for news, and there was no news to give them though it was more than time; and though Mr Dawson had spoken cheerfully to the women, the few words he spoke, and the grave face he wore at his own tea-table, had made it plain to Jean that his fears were stronger than his hopes.

He looked up at Jean when she said so eagerly that her brother was sure to come home, as though he expected her to say more. But how could Jean say more, knowing what she knew? It was too late now to tell that her brother had sailed in the "John Seaton." She could only look at him with pitiful, wet eyes, and repeat over and over again,—

"Papa, he will come home. He is sure to come. We must always hope. And when he comes, he must not know that you ever thought of putting—another in his place. It must not be me. Even if I could give it all back to him, it would not be the same. He could never believe you had forgiven him if you were to do as you said. And, oh! Auntie Jean, he is sure to come home. We can only wait and hope?"

"Only wait and hope and pray. He will come if it is God's will. And if he shouldna, God's will is best."

There was nothing more to be said. But did the old man sitting there with his face hidden in his hands assent to his sister's words? Had God's will been best? If he could have had his will, all should have been very differently ordered, as far as the past of his son was concerned. As for the future—did he wish for his return? Could the misery of their long estrangement ever be forgotten or outlived?

The bright-faced, happy, loving lad never could return—never. What was his son like now? What could he hope from him, or for him, after what he knew of him?

Oh, yes! he loved him, pitied him, longed for him; but if it were God's will that he should come home again, would God's will be best? God Himself could not blot out the past, and make them to each other all that they had been before this trouble came between them. He groaned aloud in his misery, and then he remembered that he was not alone. He rose up as if to go, but sat down again, putting great constraint upon himself.

"We'll say nae mair about it now, lassie," said he hoarsely.

"No, papa, only this, Wait a little while. George will surely come home—or—we shall hear that he is dead. I think he will come home—soon."

"Will our Geordie, our frank, true-hearted, noble lad ever come home to us again, think you? Could God Himself give him back to us as he was?"

"Whisht! George, man," said his sister gravely. "Think what ye're saying! All things are possible with God."

"Ay! to him that believes, but that is beyond belief—to me," said the old man with a sob.

"Papa," said Jean touching his bowed head with her hand, "He will come home—soon."

"And whether he come or no', we have just to live our lives and make the best of them," said Mr Dawson rising; and he went away with no word of good-night.

Jean lent her young strength to the weakness and weariness of her aunt as they went up the stairs together, but there were no more words spoken between them. They kissed one another in silence, and each knew that the other could not lighten the burden of care and pain that had fallen on both.

Though they had waited so long and so anxiously for the return of the "John Seaton," it took the Dawsons by surprise at last. But from the moment that the white sails broke the line of the far horizon, the ship was watched by an ever-increasing crowd gathering on the pier, and on the high rocks above the town.

Glasses were passed from hand to hand, while some looked doubtful and grave, and others joyfully declared that it was the long-expected vessel. In an anguish of hope and fear fathers and mothers, wives and sisters, waited. Some wept and prayed, and wandered up and down, others sat in still excitement counting the moments till the suspense should end.

It was Sunday afternoon and so none of the Dawsons were in the town. Even Miss Jean was at Saughleas. In the excitement of the moment none thought of sending word to the owner of the ship. Not one of all the anxious mothers and wives who were waiting but had more at stake than he.

"But when we are sure, and when I've seen our Tam, I'll be off to Saughleas to tell the twa Miss Jeans," said Robbie Saugster to his sister Maggie, who was waiting and hoping like the rest.

"Ay. They'll be glad—or sorry," said Maggie with a sob.

"The twa Miss Jeans, said he!" repeated Mrs Cairnie, who was wandering up and down, anxious and intent as all the rest, though there was no one belonging to her on the ship, or on any ship that sailed. "The twa Miss Jeans! And what is it to them? Ay, I ken fine the auld man is chief owner, and weel he likes his siller. But the twa Miss Jeans! what is it to them? Except that they may ha'e had their ain thochts for a' the puir bodies that ha'e grown feared this while," added the old woman relenting.

"They ha'e had many an anxious thought, and many a kind word and deed for them—I ken weel," said another woman whose eyes were on the ship.

"An' sae do I," said another who was sitting on a stone with her baby in her arms, because her trembling limbs would not support her. "What would I ha'e done but for auld Miss Jean since my man sailed."

"Ay; and they say auld Miss Jean has been through it all."

"And whether or no', she kens how to weep wi' those who weep."

"But she'll 'rejoice with them that do rejoice' this time, for as sure as I ha'e e'en to see, yon's the 'John Seaton'!"

"And I'se awa' to the pier head," said Robbie. "Are you coming, Maggie?"

Maggie took two steps after him, then she turned.

"Come, Mrs Barnet. It'll soon be over now. I'll carry wee Jamie." And the crowd moved with them.

It was the "John Seaton." All saw that by this time. There was but a thin kirk that night, for none could force themselves away from the shore, and some who set out for the kirk, turned aside with the rest to meet and welcome those who were coming home. But the kirk was empty and the crowd increased before the "John Seaton" touched the pier.

The first who reached the deck was Robbie Saugster, and the first man he saw was Willie Calderwood, tall and brown and strong, a hero in the boy's eyes.

"Our Tam?" said he with a gasp.

"Tam's a' richt. Tell your mother I'll be round to see her."

There was no time for more. The folk pressed forward, and all noticed that the mate's face was graver that it ought to have been. There was something wrong.

"Is Mrs Horne here? Or my mother?" asked the mate. "Is that you, Robbie Saugster? Run to my mother's house and say I bade her go to Mrs Horne's, and bide till I come there."

Robbie was off like a shot. "Is it ill news?"

"If it's ill news, the laddie should speak in and tell auld Miss Jean."

"Miss Jean is unco frail."

"Miss Jean is ower at Saughleas."

"And is it Captain Horne? And when did it happen?"

"Puir woman! Her turn has come at last!" Many voices took up the "ill news," telling it gravely till it went through the throng. Even those who had got their own safe home again, spoke their welcome gravely, thinking of her who had to hear heavy tidings.

Chapter Sixteen.

The "John Seaton."

Mrs Calderwood stood waiting outside Mrs Horne's door, when her son came there.

"Is it you, mother?"

"Is it you, Willie? Thank God?"

"Amen. Mother, I bring heavy news to this house."

"Ah! poor soul! I dared not go in till I knew the worst. Is it long since it happened?"

"Three months and more. He was long ill, and glad to go."

"And must I tell her? Oh, if Miss Jean were here!"

"I will tell her, but I wanted you here. Does she ken that the ship is in?"

"She must ken, I think. But it is no' like her to go out among the throng. She's just waiting. God help her, poor woman!"

"Ay, mother, *ye* ken."

"But, Willie—I must say one word. George Dawson? He sailed with you?"

"Yes, mother, but—"

A voice from within bade them enter, and there was time for no more. We shall not enter with them. The first tears of a childless widow suddenly bereaved, must not be looked upon by eyes indifferent. There was much to be told—much that must have made her thankful even in her bitter sorrow. But it was a painful hour to the returned sailor, and there were tears on his cheeks when at last he came out to clasp his joyful only sister at the door.

But he could not linger long. He had more to do before he returned to the ship.

"I must go to Saughleas," said he, as they paused at the corner where his sister must turn towards home.

"To Saughleas? Oh! Willie let me go with you," she cried clinging to him. "Mother will maybe bide with Mrs Horne a' nicht. Oh, Willie, let me go! I'll keep out o' sicht, and naebody will ken. If ye maun go, let me go with you."

"I maun go. I promised Geordie."

"Geordie? Have ye seen him? Did he sail in the 'John Seaton'? And has he come home?"

"Ye dinna mean that ye never heard that he sailed with us?"

"I never heard. Did Miss Dawson ken? It must have been that that made her e'en grow like my mother's when she looked out over the sea."

They were on their way to Saughleas by this time. They had much to say to one another. Or rather Marion had much to say, and her brother had much to hear. A few words were enough to tell all that he needed to tell until his mother should hear him also.

But Marion had to give him the news of a year and more,—the ups and downs, the comings and goings of all their friends and acquaintance; the sickness of one, the health of another; the births and deaths; the marriages past and in prospect. With the last the name of May Dawson was mentioned, and being herself intensely interested in the matter, Marion went into particulars.

"He is an Englishman; but they all like him. I like his lace. Yes, I saw him once, and Jean made me sing a song to him—'The bonny House o' Airlie.' And auld Miss Jean likes him, she told my mother. He is no' a rich man, and folk wonder at Mr Dawson being so well pleased. But what seems strange to me is, that May should be married before her sister. And I whiles think, that maybe if he had seen Jean first—but love goes where it is sent, they say," added Marion gravely.

"And her sister's turn will come next," said Willie.

"Oh! as to that—" said Marion, and then she was silent, adding after a little, "and *he* was an Englishman too. May is nice, ye ken, but there's no' another in all Scotland like Jean."

They were approaching Saughleas by this time. They went slowly round the drive to the open hall door. The summer gloaming was not at its darkest yet, and there were no lights visible. As they stood for a moment at the door, they heard enough to make them aware that a messenger had preceded them.

"It's Robbie Saugster, Miss Dawson. He says he has news for you—or for Mr Dawson, I canna say which. Will you come but the house and see him? or will I send him ben to you?"

But Jean did not need to answer. Robbie had followed his message.

"Miss Dawson, it's the 'John Seaton.' She's won safe hame. But there's ill news. It's the Captain. But I saw Willie Calderwood, and he said—"

It was hard on Robbie that after all his trouble, the telling of the news should fall to another. A heavy hand was laid on his shoulder, and a voice said,—

"That'll do, Robbie, lad. I'll say my ain say."

And then Jean stood face to face with Willie Calderwood. For one wonderful moment they clasped hands and gazed into each other's eyes. Not a word, not even the name, of George was spoken. And then came a joyful cry from May,—

"It is Willie Calderwood. Oh, Willie! Willie! Papa, the 'John Seaton' has come."

Then there was a minute or two of confusion in the hall, hand shaking and congratulations, and then Mr Dawson ordered lights, and they went into the parlour where auld Miss Jean was sitting, for she had not moved with the rest. She drew down the young man's handsome head and kissed him.

"Oh, your happy mother!" said she softly.

But the mate of the "John Seaton" did not sit down. He stood erect beside Miss Jean's chair, with his eyes cast down upon the floor. He must go back to the ship at once. He would report himself at Mr Dawson's office to-morrow; he had come to-night because of a promise—

"Did I hear something about ill news?" said Mr Dawson. "Jean, what was it the laddie said about Captain Horne."

"Yes," said the sailor, "it is bad news. It is three months and more since we lost him; a heavy loss. A better sailor never sailed—nor a better man."

There was silence for a minute.

"His wife! Puir body!" said Miss Jean.

"My mother is with her," said the sailor. "They were wishing for you, Miss Jean, to tell her. I almost think she kenned what was coming."

The young man seemed to forget where he was for the moment.

There were more questions asked, and more particulars given, and all the while the mate stood beside Miss Jean's chair, making his answers clear and brief, and suffering no sympathetic friendliness to soften voice or manner, except when he spoke to Miss Jean.

"And are there any more sorrowful hearts in Portie the nicht?" asked she gravely. "Did a' the lave win hame?"

"Saugster, the second mate, did not, nor two others. But nobody need grieve for Saugster. There was never less occasion. He'll be home all right, I hope soon."

And then he told how they had met in with an American fishing vessel partially disabled from encountering a heavy storm, and far out of her course. She had lost four of her men, one of them the mate, from the capsizing of a boat. The captain was down with fever, and the ship was at the mercy of the winds and waves as there was no one on board who had the knowledge or skill to sail her.

"We might have taken the rest of the men on board, but it would not have been right to abandon their ship, and as Tam Saugster and—two others were willing to go, there was nothing to be said. I dare say they are safe in Portland harbour by this time."

Mr Dawson asked some questions as to the cargo and value of the vessel taken in charge, and the mate answered them briefly, and then he said, "And now I must go. I came to-night, because of a promise I made—"

Jean had been sitting all this time in the shadow of her lather's high-backed chair, a little out of sight. She rose now and stood gazing at the mate with dilated eyes and a face on which not a trace of colour lingered. He did not look at her, but at her father, who had risen also, ready to give his hand at parting.

"It is a letter," said the sailor. "I must give it into your own hand, as I promised George."

"George!" repeated Mr Dawson suddenly falling back into his chair again, with a face as white as Jean's.

"Yes. He sailed with us. You surely must have heard of that."

"I heard nothing of it."

"Well, that is queer?"

He hesitated and remained silent, as he might not have done if he had seen the agony of the father's face. Jean had stretched out her hand and touched him. She was trying to say something, but her lips uttered no sound.

"My son! my son! Oh, dinna tell me that he didna come home?"

It was an exceeding bitter cry.

"He didna come home—"

"Oh, Willie, tell him?" cried an eager voice, and his sister sprang forward and a hand was laid on the old man's arm. "He hasna come home, but he's safe and well and he is coming home. And he is—good now. He was ay good, but now he is sorry, and he's coming home. And—Oh, sir, I beg your pardon—" added Marion, coming to herself, and she would have darted away again, but Jean held her fast.

Willie's heart softened as he met the old man's look.

"George was one of the two that went with Saugster. There is no better sailor than Tam, as ye ken; but he's open to the temptation o' strong drink. If there is any one that can keep Tam straight, it's George. I dare say they are in port by this time."

"Willie," said Miss Jean, "tell us how it happened that he sailed with you. Surely you should have told us before you let him go?"

"I did my best, Miss Jean. He came on board that last morning with some of the men who had been making a night of it on shore, but I did not know it till we were nearly ready to set sail. I did my best to persuade him to stay at home. I sent three different messages to his father, but he couldna be found; and I wrote a line to—"

Mr Dawson groaned.

"I had heard that he had been seen in the town, in company with Niel Cochrane of the How. I went there to seek him, and the ship had sailed before I came back again."

"It was to be," said the sailor. "And though I was sorry at the time, I was glad afterwards, and ye'll be glad too, sir. It has done him no ill, but good. He has gathered himself up again. He is a man now—a man among a thousand. And ye havena read your letter."

A curious change had come over the young man's manner, though there was no one calm enough to notice it but Mr Manners. He had for the greater part of the time not been looking at Mr Dawson, but over his head, or at any one else rather than the master of the house when he spoke. But now he sat down near him, his voice softening wonderfully, and his face looking like the one that was leaning on Miss Dawson's shoulder on the other side of the old man's chair.

It was a very handsome face, but for that Mr Manners would have cared little. It was a noble face, strong and true; a face to trust, "a face to love," said he to himself. He had heard of Willie Calderwood before, as he had by this time heard of the most of May's friends, and he had gathered more from the story than May had meant to tell. And now he noticed that the handsome face had hardly turned towards Jean, and that Jean had not spoken since he came into the room.

Mr Dawson opened his letter with fingers that trembled. There was only a line or two, and when he had read it, he laid it on the table, and laid his face down upon it without a word; and when he lifted it again there were tears upon it.

"Oh, Willie, man! if ye had brought him home! There is nothing of mine but ye might have had for the asking, if ye had but brought him home!"

The young man rose and walked up and down the room once or twice, and then sat down again, saying gently,—

"I had no right to prevent his going. He was in his lather's ship of his own will, and though he submitted to command through all the voyage, that was of his own will too. And I am no' sure that I would have kept him, even if I could have done it. It was to save life that he went. Danger? Well, it turned out that there was really less danger than was supposed when he offered to go. I went on board with him and we overhauled the ship and did what was needed to make all safe. As to its being his duty—he had no doubts o' that. It was to save life."

"Dinna go yet, Willie, man," said Mr Dawson, putting out his hand as the mate rose. "We are a' friends here. This is Hugh Corbett, his father was your father's friend. And this is Mr Manners who has come seeking our May. It is no secret now, my lassie."

The two shook hands heartily—each "kenning a man when he saw him." And then the sailor offered his hand to May. And if Jean had had any doubts remaining as to the nature of the mutual interest of these two they were set at rest now. May blushed, but met his look frankly, and for the first time since he came Willie smiled brightly—a smile that "minded" Jean of the days before trouble of any kind had fallen upon them.

The rest of the story might have kept till another day, as Willie said, but he yielded to entreaty and sat down again. He had nothing to tell of George's story before he found him on board ship. He had come home meaning to see his father, but had fallen into bad hands, and, discouraged and ashamed, had changed his mind, not caring whether he lived or died. If he had not been allowed to go in the "John Seaton," there were other vessels leaving Portie in which he could have sailed.

"I could only have kept him at home by using force, or by betraying him, as he called it. I thought he was better at sea with a friend than on shore with those who did him no good—for home he would not go. So I risked the captain's anger and said nothing. But I never supposed but you would hear about his sailing, as there must have been more than one who knew it."

No one made any reply to this. Captain Horne, a good and just, but stern man, was sorely displeased when he found that his owner's son had sailed secretly with them; and he showed his displeasure by ignoring his presence on board after the very first, and leaving him to suffer all the hardships of the lot he had chosen. George accepted the situation, asked no favours, and shirked no duty, but lived in the forecastle, and fared as the rest fared there.

After a time he grew strong and cheerful and did his part for the general entertainment, chatting and chaffing—singing songs and spinning yarns, and winning the good-will of every man and boy on board. Nor did he lose his time altogether, as far as self-improvement was concerned. He read every book on board, and at leisure times gave himself to the reading of mathematics and the study of navigation with his friend, and had done it to some purpose, his friend declared.

They reached the Arctic seas in good time, and had there met with more than the usual success, so that they had good hope of getting home to Portie before the year was over. But after that heavy storms had overtaken them, and they had driven before the wind many days and nights without a glimpse of sun or star, and so had drifted far out of their course. They had taken shelter at last in an unknown bay and had lain ice bound for many months.

Here sore sickness fell on Captain Horne, against which—being a man strong and brave and patient—he struggled long, only to yield at last, and take to his berth helpless, and for a time, hopeless. A good man, a true Christian—("ane o' your kind, Miss Jean," said the sailor),—he had yet fallen into utter despondency, out of which, strangely enough, the foolish lad who had wandered so far from home, and from the right way, had helped him.

When he came to this part of the story, the mate rose and took two or three turns up and down the room again; then he came and stood beside Miss Jean's chair, saying softly,—

"Sometime, Miss Jean, when Geordie comes home, ye must ask him about it. I could never tell you all he was to the sick man in those days. No son ever served a father more faithfully. No mother ever nursed, cared for, and comforted a sick child with more entire forgetfulness of self. Whiles he read to him out of the Bible, and out of other books, and whiles he talked to him and told him things that he had heard—from his mother, I dare say, and from you, Miss Jean, and whiles—once at least in my hearing—he prayed with him, because in the darkness that had fallen on him the old man couldna pray for himself I mind that night well."

There was a long pause after this, and then he went on; "Geordie will tell you all about it better than I could do. A good while before the end, light came back to the captain—and, oh! the brightness of it! and the peace that fell on him! The good book says 'It is more blessed to give than to receive,' and that was the way with Geordie. For as much good as came to our captain through him, there came more to himself; and it came to him first.

"You are one of those, Miss Jean, who believe in a change of nature,—coming from darkness to light—from 'the power of Satan onto God.' Well, I would have said that Geordie needed that change less than most folk, but it was like that with him. Even I, who saw few faults in him before, could see the difference afterward. But it canna be spoken about, and it is more than time that I were away."

However he sat down again for a moment on the other side of the table where he had been sitting before, and went on to tell, how after a few bright days, the captain died, and they buried him in the sea.

At last they got away from the ice, and were beginning to count the days, before they might hope to see the harbour of Portie, when they fell in with the ship in distress, and this ended in Tam Saugster being sent to take her to her port, and in George going also, to help Tam to withstand his foe. For the "John Seaton" was a temperance ship, and Tam had tasted nothing stronger than tea or coffee since he lost sight of Portie harbour.

"He had sailed with us, just to give himself another chance, he said, and, poor lad, he had gone far the wrong gait—and he was another man; a fine fellow truly, when he was out of the way of temptation. And whiles I have thought it was for Tam's sake, more even than for the sake of the Yankee ship and its crew, that George was so fain to go. It cost him much no' to come home with us, for he had come to a clearer sight of—two or three things,—he told me. But I think he made a sort of thank-offering of himself for the time, and even if I could have hindered him, I could hardly have found it in my heart to do it. And he is sure to come soon."

"He is in safe keeping," said Miss Jean.

"Yes, he is that, and we may hear from him any day." There was not much more said. Mr Manners had some questions, and so had Miss Jean, and May asked if her brother had changed much as to looks; and Mr Dawson looked from one to the other as each spoke, but he did not say another word, nor did Jean till Willie rose to go. "Now, Marion, it is late and we must make haste." Then Jean said softly—it was the first word she had uttered since he came into the house—

"No, Marion. It is too late to go. Willie will tell your mother that you are going to bide with me to-night."

Of course that was the wisest thing for the girl to do, as Mrs Calderwood might remain all night with poor Mrs Horne, and it was necessary that her brother should go back to the ship. And so the mate went away alone.

Chapter Seventeen.

Home Coming.

That night Mr Dawson and Miss Jean sat long together, when the others had gone away, and for the most part they sat in silence. Mr Dawson had some thoughts which he would not have liked to tell his sister,—thoughts which he knew she would call wrong and thankless—which he would gladly have put away.

The good things of this life, the glad surprises, the unhoped for reprieves from sorrow, rarely come without some drawback of regret or pain. That he should have got tidings of his son; that he should be coming home, and glad to come; that he should be well and worthy, a man to honour and to trust,—how utterly beyond his hopes had this been yesterday!

His son was coming home; but, alas! he could never have his light-hearted, bonny laddie back again. George was a man now, "knowing good and evil." It could never be again between them as it had been before their trouble came.

"Ane o' your kind, Miss Jean," the mate had said; "a changed man."

Mr Dawson's thoughts went back to the time of his sister's trouble, when she had become "a changed woman." All the anger and vexation, that had then seemed natural and right, because of her new ways, had passed out of his heart, a score of years and more. It was as though it had never been. He glanced up at her placid face, and said to himself, as he had said before many times, "A woman among a thousand." But he remembered the old pain, though it was gone, and he shrank from the thought that he might have to suffer again through his son.

"He is a man now, and must go his ain way," he said to himself, moving uneasily on his chair and sighing. "We canna begin again where we left off. Ungrateful? Yes, I dare say it would be so called; but, oh! Geordie, my lad! I doubt your way and mine must lie asunder now."

Miss Jean too had some thoughts which she would not have cared to tell, but they were not about George; for him she was altogether joyful. If Willie Calderwood's words about him were true, and he were indeed "a changed man," nothing else mattered much in Miss Jean's esteem. The "good," for which he had God's promise as security would be wrought out in him whether by health or sickness, by joy or sorrow, by possession or loss, and through him might be brought help and healing, higher hopes, and better lives to many. The Master who had chosen him would use him for His own work, and that implied all that was to be desired for any one to Miss Jean.

But in the midst of her joy for him, she could not forget Jean's silence, and Willie Calderwood's averted eyes. And though she told herself that possible pain and disappointment could work good to her niece as well as to her nephew, she could not but shrink beforehand from the suffering that might be before her. But it was not a trouble to be spoken about.

Neither had spoken for a long time, when the door opened and Jean came in. She was wrapped in her dressing-gown, over which her long hair hung, and her face looked pale and troubled.

"Are you here still, Auntie Jean? No, don't go, papa," said she as he rose. "I have something to tell you."

"It maun be late. I thought you had been in your bed this hour and more," said her father.

"Yes, papa, I was in bed, but I couldna sleep."

"For joy, I suppose?" said he smiling.

"Yes, for joy and—because—papa, I knew that my brother had sailed in the John Seaton."

"You knew! And never spoke?"

"Would it have been better if I had spoken? Would you have suffered less? But I did not know it till after the ship had sailed, and I thought it would break your heart to know that he could have been here and gone away again, without a word. I tried to tell you afterwards, and you, Auntie Jean, as well. I longed to tell you. I could hardly bear the doubt and fear of the last few weeks. But I thought if it was so terrible to me, what would it be to you!"

Mr Dawson did not answer for a moment. He was thinking of the stormy nights of last winter, and the dread in her eyes as they looked out over the angry sea.

"No wonder that you were anxious often, and afraid."

"Ought I to have told you? But you are not angry now, papa?"

"There is no good being angry—and you did it for the best."

And then Jean told them about the note that Robbie Saugster had brought too late to let her see her brother before the ship sailed. Miss Jean said it had doubtless been wisely and kindly ordered, that the lad would come home and be a better son, and a better man for the discipline of the time. And then when they went upstairs together, she added a few joyful words to Jean, about the change that had come to her brother, and about the peace that would henceforth be between his father and him. But she would not let her linger beside her for any more talk.

"Ye need your rest, my dear, and we'll baith ha'e quieter hearts, and be better able to measure the greatness of the mercy that has come to us. And other things will take a mair natural look as well."

Though Mr Manners had only one more day at Saughleas at this time, he accepted Mr Dawson's invitation to walk with him to Portie in the morning. Mr Dawson wished to show him the "John Seaton," and Mr Manners wished to see again the fine young fellow, who might, if he chose, henceforth have the command of the ship. Mr Dawson had something to say to him on the way.

"You will get a scanter portion with your wife than you would have gotten if—we had heard no news."

"Oh! My wife! My bonny May," said Mr Manners with smiling eyes. "But then I shall have a brother—I who never had one—and I shall have a right to my share of the family joy."

Mr Dawson did not speak for a moment.

"There will be something at once," and he named a sum, "and there will be something more at my death."

Then he went on to mention certain arrangements that were to be made, and Mr Manners, of course, seemed to listen with interest; but when he ceased speaking, he said gravely,—

"I have only one fear, lest the joyful expectation of having her brother home again, may make May wish to delay her marriage."

"As to that—if he come at once he will be here long before the first. And if he should delay—no, I do not think that that ought to be allowed to interfere with your plans."

"Thank you," said Mr Manners. "Oh, he will be sure to be here in time."

"Wha kens?" said Mr Dawson. "It seems beyond belief that I should ever have my son back again. I never can in one sense. He is a man now, and changed. I wouldna seem unthankful; but, oh, man! if ye had ever seen my George, ye would ken what I mean."

He was greatly moved. If he had tried to say more, daylight as it was, and on the open road, his voice must have failed him. They walked on in silence for a while—for what could Mr Manners say?—and before they reached the High-street, he was himself again.

There were many eyes upon him as they went down the street, for by this time it was known through all the town that George had sailed in the "John Seaton." But "the old man took it quietly enough," some said, and others, who saw him in the way of business through the day, said the same. The sailors in the "John Seaton," when later he and Mr Manners went down to the pier, saw nothing unusual in his rough, but kindly, greetings. There was not one of them but would have liked to say a kindly and admiring word of "Geordie"; for "Geordie" he had been to them all, through the long year; and doubtless it would have pleased the father to hear it. But he heard nothing of it there.

It did not surprise these men to see that he took it quietly. Their own fathers and mothers took quietly the comings and goings of their sons. But it would have surprised them to know that the old man kept silence because he was not sure whether his voice would serve him if he should try to speak. He turned back again for a minute when Mr Manners and the mate came on deck, when all had been said that was necessary on that occasion, and it would have surprised them to know that it was to shut himself into the little cabin where George had so long served and comforted the dying captain, and that he there knelt down and thanked God for His goodness to his son.

He seemed to take it quietly as far as people generally saw during the next ten days; but Jean put away all remorseful thoughts as to the silence she had kept during the last long year.

"He never could have borne the long suspense," she said to herself, as she watched him through the days and heard his restless movements through nights of sleepless waiting. He never spoke of his son, or his anxiety with regard to him; but Jean took pains to speak of her brother to others in his hearing; and sometimes she spoke to himself, and he listened, but he never made reply.

"He will grow morbid and ill if this continues long," she said one day to her aunt.

"It will not continue long," said Miss Jean.

"No, he will come soon, if he is coming."

"Oh, he is coming! ye needna doubt that. He is no seeking his ain way now. He'll come back to his father's house."

And so he did, and he found his father watching for him. He did not go all the way to Portie, but stopped, as his father knew he would, at a little station two or three miles on the other side of Saughleas, and walked home. It was late and all was quiet in the house. Summer rain was softly falling, but Mr Dawson stood at the gate as he had stood for many nights; and George heard his voice before he saw him.

It might have been said—if there had been any one there to see—that Mr Dawson "took it quietly" even then. There were not many words spoken between them, and they were simple words, spoken quietly enough. How it happened neither of them could have told,—whether the father followed the son, or the son the father,—but instead of turning to the terrace, where the drawing-room window stood open to let them in, they turned down the walk, past the well into the wood; and whatever was said of confession or forgiveness was said by the grave of the lad's mother, in the stillness of the summer midnight, in the hearing of God alone.

No one but Jean knew that night that George had come home, and Jean did not go to her brother till she had heard her father shut himself into his room. Mr Dawson himself brought food to his son, and wine, and watched him as he partook of it. But when he would have poured out the wine, he staid his hand.

"I promised Tam Saugster—we promised one another—not to touch or taste before he comes home to Portie."

"It is for his sake then?"

"And for my own," said George gravely.

His father was silent. Strangely mingled feelings moved him.

"Is he so weak that he cannot refrain? Is he so strong that he can resist?"

Even in the midst of his joy in having his son back again, "clothed and in his right mind," he was more inclined to resent the implied weakness, than to rejoice in the assured strength. But he uttered no word of his thoughts then or ever, though George did not release himself from his vow even when Tam Saugster came home to Portie "a changed man" also.

When the house was quiet again, and the lights were out, Jean stole softly to her brother's room, for one embrace, one kiss, a single word of welcome. But she would not linger.

"We couldna stop, if we were once to begin, Geordie; and you are tired, and my father would be ill-pleased. I only wanted to be sure that you were really home again. And I'm no' sure yet," she added laughing and touching with caressing fingers the soft brown beard, that she could just see, for a faint gleam of dawn was breaking over the sea. They looked at each other with shy pleasure, these two. Jean blushed and smiled under her brother's admiring eyes, but she would not linger.

"My father will hear us, and he will not be pleased," said she going softly away.

But was it not a joyful morning?

"May, are you ready? Come down quickly. I have something that I want you to see."

"May, I think it is I who have something to see," said George, as his younger sister came in. One might search the countryside and find no other such brother and sisters as these three. The father looked at them with proud but sorrowful eyes, for their mother was not there to see them.

George was changed, even more than his sisters. He had gone away a lad, and he had come back a man. There was more than the soft brown beard to show that. He had grown taller even, his father thought, he had certainly grown broader and stronger. The colour that used to be as clear red and white as his sisters' was gone. His face was brown and his eye was bright and steady, and his smile—when it came—was the same sunny smile that his father had so longed for during the sorrowful days of his absence. But it did not come so often as it used to come, and at other times, his face was touched with a gravity new to them all.

But there was no gloom on it, and no trace of any thing that those who loved him would have grieved to see. It was a stronger face now than it had been in the old days, but it was none less a pleasant face, and in a little while they forgot that it had changed. It was George's face. That was enough.

"It is a *man's* face. And he'll show himself a man yet, and do a man's share in the work of the world," said the proud and happy father. And in his heart he acknowledged his son's right to take his own way and live his own life, even though the way might lie apart from his, and though the life he chose might not be just the life that his father would have chosen for him.

"Your aunt should have been here, Jean. You should have sent for her," said Mr Dawson in a little.

"I will go and see her," said George. "I will walk in with you to the town, by and by."

"But we must have her here, all the same, for a day or two. Ye'll send for her afterward, Jean."

But they did not go in the morning as they meant to do. They lingered long over the breakfast-table, and then in the garden and in the wood, and the father and son went down the burn and through the green parks beyond, never thinking how the time was passing, till Jean came to tell them that dinner was waiting.

After dinner they went to the town. But they did not go down the High-street. They were both shy at the thought of all the eyes that would be upon them there.

"And it should be your aunt first," said Mr Dawson.

So they went down a lane that led straight to the sea and then turned to Miss Jean's house.

"You'll go in by yourself and I'll step on and come back in a while," said his father.

He had not stepped far before a hand touched his arm, and a pair of shining eyes met his.

"Oh, Mr Dawson! Is it George come home? And isna your heart like to break for joy?"

There were tears as well as smiles on the beautiful face that looked up into his with joyful sympathy and with entire confidence that sympathy would be welcome. For an instant Mr Dawson met her look with strangely contending emotions. Then a strange thing happened. He took the bonny moved face between his two hands, and stooping down, kissed it "cheek and chin" without a word.

He would not have believed the thing possible a minute before, he could hardly believe if a minute afterwards, as he turned back again towards his sister's house. Mrs Cairnie coming slowly down the street saw it—and then she doubted, telling herself, that "her e'en were surely nae marrows," or that the last "drappie" she had taken at "The Kail Stock" had been ower muckle for her, and the first person to whom she told the story thought the same.

Bonny Marion's mother and brother saw it from the window of their own house: he with amazement, she with dismay.

"It maun be that Geordie has come home, and that the joy of it has softened his heart," said Willie.

"Ay. He has gotten his son back again?" said Mrs Calderwood. And Willie knew that his mother was thinking of her child who would never return.

Marion came dancing in with the glad news. She told it soberly after a glance at her mother's face. And then they all sat waiting, knowing that George and his father would pass that way.

But George did not pass. Both men stood still before their door, and George's hand was laid for an instant on his father's shoulder. They knew what he was saying though they did not hear him speak, and then Mr Dawson went on "looking grave, but no' angry," Marion whispered, and George came into the house.

Mrs Calderwood received him as she had received her son, kissing him and thanking God for his safe home coming at last. Their meeting could not be all gladness, remembering how they had parted. George was very white and silent. Even Marion's bright face and joyful welcome could not win a smile. Willie and he had much to say to each other, but all that must wait till another time. George could stay but a moment, for his father was waiting for him at the pier.

That night Mrs Calderwood and her son sat together in the gathering gloaming, and after a long silence Willie said, "Would it break your heart altogether, mother, to think of leaving Portie?"

"Hearts are no' so easily broken as I used to think. I could leave it, if it were the wisest thing to do. I could leave even Scotland itself, for that matter."

"Yes, it would end in leaving Scotland—if any change were to be made. But as far as you are concerned, you needna be in haste for a time."

"A while sooner or later would make little difference," said his mother.

Nothing more was said; but from that night, Mrs Calderwood knew that it might come to leaving Portie with them, and she set herself calmly to look the possibility in the face.

George came home about the middle of July, and the preparations for May's marriage were nearly completed by that time. Jean had determined that it was to be a very pretty wedding, and so it was; and having said this, little more need be said about it. It was like all other pretty weddings— that is to say like pretty weddings in the north. The guests were many, and merrier than wedding guests usually are in other regions.

Mr and Mrs Seldon came from London to be there, and other friends came from other places. George was "best man," and there were many bridesmaids. Marion Calderwood was one of them, and Willie was an invited guest. But at the last moment Willie failed them, and the only reason given, was the unsatisfactory one of "business before pleasure." On the very morning of the marriage he left home "for London, or Liverpool, or somewhere,—before I was up," said Marion, who came early to put on her pretty bridesmaid's dress in Jean's room; and George, when

May questioned him, said with absolute truth, that not a word had passed between him and Willie as to the reason of his going away.

Mr Manners might have cast some light on the matter, though he also could have said that no word had been spoken with regard to it. Intent on making the acquaintance of George, they had set out the night before the wedding for a long walk along the shore, and meeting young Calderwood, he turned at their invitation and went with them.

Probably Mr Manners learned more about both of them in listening to their conversation with each other than he would have had he had one of them to himself. As it was he enjoyed it much. They went far and before they returned the gloaming had fallen.

Standing for a moment at the point where the High-street of Portie turns off from the road which leads in one direction along the shore, and in the other out towards Saughleas, they heard a voice, familiar enough to George and Willie, coming through an open cottage window.

"Weel, weel! I maun be gaen. Ilka ane kens her ain trouble. And them that ha'e nane, whiles think they ha'e, and that's as ill to thole till real trouble comes, and then they ken the difference. But I maun awa' hame."

Mrs Cairnie lingered, however, at the open door.

"Eh, woman! wha's yon comin' up the High-street? Wha would ha'e thought it? The Dawsons are on the top o' the wave enow! Do ye no' see, woman? Yon's young Miss Jean's Englishman."

Mr Manners had not followed all the speech, but he understood the last part of it, and never doubted that it referred to himself, "though she has mistaken the lady's name," said he, turning laughing eyes on young Calderwood.

But Willie did not meet his look. He was looking down the High-street, and George was looking at Willie whose face had grown white through all its healthy brown. Mr Dawson was coming slowly up the street, and by his side there walked a young man large, and fair, and handsome; a gentleman evidently whom neither of them had ever seen before. A groom driving a dog-cart followed slowly after.

"It must be Captain Harefield. May has spoken of him," said Mr Manners.

It was Captain Harefield. Mr Dawson introduced him as they came up, and from his father's manner George knew that he was pleased at the meeting.

"I have been trying to persuade Captain Harefield to come to the marriage to-morrow," said he. "It is short notice, I know, but not too short, if you will come out to Saughleas to-night and see the bride."

Captain Harefield murmured something about an engagement, but he looked as though he would willingly be persuaded to break it. Mr Manners first, and then George added a word, and he yielded, and he and Mr Dawson drove off in the dog-cart at once.

"Ye'll come with us, Willie?" said George laying his hand on his shoulder, in boyish fashion. The friends looked at one another, and both changed colour a little.

"No' the nicht, I think, Geordie."

Then they shook hands and the mate went rapidly down the street, and the others were more than half way to Saughleas before George uttered a word.

That night Willie Calderwood startled his mother by saying suddenly after a long time of silence,—

"I am off to-morrow morning for Liverpool, mother. I have a letter that I meant to show to George, but I couldna, and you must tell him. I have a chance to be second officer on one of the great ocean steamships. What do you think of that, mother? I think I'll take it."

"Then you've given up all thoughts of the 'John Seaton'?"

"Yes. This is a far better post—as you must see, mother, with a chance of promotion. I mean to command one of these fine ships yet."

"But must you go so soon? You are expected to go to the marriage to-morrow."

"Yes. And I would have liked to see the last o' May Dawson. But 'business before pleasure,' ye ken, mother; and nobody will miss me, I dare say. And Marion will say all that is needful to the bride."

Willie spoke cheerily—too cheerily, his mother thought, to be quite natural. "No thought of Jean Dawson shall ever come between my mother and me," Willie was thinking. "Even if she cared for me, it could never be; and I must get away from the sight of her, or I shall do something foolish, and give my mother all the old pain over again." Then after a long time of silence, he said, "If you were to live in Liverpool, or near it, mother, I could see you oftener than if I had to come to Portie."

"Yes, I have been thinking of that."

"Marion wouldna like it?"

"No, I dare say not. But it might be well for her to have a change."

"Well, then, that is settled. But there need be no haste, mother."

"A month or two sooner or later would make little difference."

And then they were silent again. Mrs Calderwood was thinking, "I am sorrier for her than I am for him. He is a man, with a man's work to do, and he will forget her. But as for Jean—she's no' the kind of woman to forget."

So Willie kissed his sister in her morning sleep, and was away long before she opened her eyes on May's marriage day. If any one but his sister missed him amid the gay doings of the day, no one said so. The eyes and thoughts of all were on the bride and her attendant maidens, and it was a sight worth seeing.

May behaved as a bride should, who of her own free will is leaving her father's house to go to the house of her husband. Jean stood by her and her quietness kept the bride quiet also. But even Jean's colour changed many times as they stood with all the kindly admiring eyes upon them.

And when the ceremony was over, and the breakfast, and the speech-making, and the few painful moments of lingering that followed, and the happy bridegroom had at last gone away with his bonny bride, then nobody saw Jean till a long hour and more was over.

Chapter Eighteen.

Another Proposal.

Captain Harefield was at the wedding an honoured guest, as all could see, and for a very good reason, it was said. Through the Blackford groom, it had come to be known in Portie that a change had fallen on the fortunes of Captain Harefield.

Through the sad and sudden death of a distant cousin, he had become heir to a large estate in one of the southern English counties, and though he might have a while to wait for the full enjoyment of his inheritance, and for the tide that was to come with it, there was in the mean time a happy change in his circumstances as far as money was concerned. He had not come to Blackford House this time, to escape duns. And his sister had not come to take care of him.

The chances were that he had an object in view in coming, and on the wedding day more than one of those who saw the looks he cast at the bride and her maidens, had felt satisfied as to what that object might be. Mr Dawson was one of these.

There were several guests still in the house, when a week had passed. Mr Dawson and his sister were sitting one afternoon on the terrace, when Captain Harefield rode up, and in a little he had joined Miss Dawson in the garden. The father watched them as they came and went among the trees.

"Jean has the ba' at her foot this time, I'm thinking," said he. "Weel, weel! It it pleases her, it will please me."

"She'll never please ye in that way. Dinna think it."

"I'm no' so sure that it would please me—no' so sure as I was this time last year. But I think she might be satisfied."

"She'll need a stronger hand to guide her."

"She has strength and sense to guide *him*, and that might do as well."

"It wouldna be for her happiness were she to be persuaded to such a marriage," said Miss Jean gravely.

"Persuaded! No, that is not likely. But, Jean, I like the lad, though he is no' a Solomon, I confess, and he has a high place in the world—or he will ha'e ane—and Jean would do him credit."

"High place or no', he is no' her equal in any important sense. If she cared for him, she might guide him and put up with him, as many another woman has to do. As to persuading her—no one could do that; but if she thought your heart was set on it, she might persuade herself to her ain unhappiness."

"I'se never persuade her. And I would ha'e ill sparin' her. But it would be a fine position, and she would keep it we'll."

"Ay, if she could take it with a good conscience. But that she canna do," said Miss Jean.

When the bustle attending the wedding was over and all the guests were gone, a new life began at Saughleas. As far as George was concerned, it was not just the life his father would have chosen for him. But George was a man now, and every day that passed proved to his father that he was a man that might safely be trusted to guide himself. It would have pleased his father that he should at once have taken his place as the young laird of Saughleas. There were many signs among the other proprietors of the neighbourhood, that he would have been welcomed to the houses of people who had held hitherto only business intercourse with his father.

There was no need for George to return to the counting-house again. Mr Dawson acknowledged himself to be a richer man than was generally supposed, and George, as the heir of Saughleas, might "take a long tether," as far as the spending of money was concerned.

And he need not lead an idle life. All the congenial occupations of a country gentleman were open to him, to say nothing of the amusements which only men of comparative leisure could enjoy. Or he might farm his own land. Whether he could make such farming profitable to himself might be doubtful, but he might do good in the countryside, and he would thus have an opportunity of bringing himself into contact with people whose acquaintance was to be desired,—the lairds and gentlemen farmers of the north.

It was to his sister oftener than to his son that all this was said; and listening to him, Miss Jean could not but wonder what had become of the sense and judgment that had guided him through all his life till now.

"When you are dead and gone, and George has a son of his ain, he'll get willingly in the countryside what you are so anxious for him to take now. It would bring neither the honour nor the pleasure that you are dreaming about for him, if he were to turn his back upon—the shop—for that was the foundation o' your fortune, though you are a banker and a ship-owner now. Let George win his ain way, as his father did before him; it will be mair to his credit, and mair to his happiness, than any such change as ye would fain see in his way of life. And he'll be far safer."

"A body would think to hear ye, Jean, that I was like to be ashamed o' the shop, and the makin' o' my ain way in the world; I'm so far from that, that I seek no other credit or honour in the countryside than what I have won as a man of business. But it might be different with my son."

"Weel, honour and consideration seldom come the sooner for the seeking. They'll come to George in good time, if he shall deserve them. It's little honour he would be like to get from men o' sense if he were content to sit down with what you ha'e won for him, putting himself in the place that ye ha'e honestly and honourably won for yourself. That would be for the honour o' neither you nor him, though ye may think it."

"It was for him I won it. There would be neither pleasure nor profit for me, at my time o' life, in seekin' any change. But I acknowledge it would be a pleasure to me to see my son taking his right place in the countryside. It is no' as if he werena fit for it. Just look at him! Who is there to compare with him? And he has as good blood in his veins as the most o' them, when a' is said."

"He'll get his right place in time, never fear. And he'll get it all the readier that he's no' in haste about it."

In the mean time George was in his father's office, setting himself to the mastering of all details and succeeding therein, in a way that astonished his father. It was that part of the business that had to do with shipping interests which he liked best, and which chiefly claimed his attention at this time. His father acknowledged that he had a clear head, and a power of application that would stand him in stead either as merchant or landed proprietor. And the pleasure he had in his son's companionship, and in his sympathy with his work, went far to keep him silent as to any change in his present course.

As for George, he was for the most part silent also, because he was unwilling by opposition to his father's wishes to put in jeopardy the new and pleasant relations existing between them. But to his sister and his aunt he spoke plainly enough.

If any of them were to have special consideration from their neighbours, it must be because of his father's life, and what he had accomplished in it. As for his assuming the position of the young laird of Saughleas while his father continued the laborious life of a man of business, that would be only contemptible. If he were to take his own way in life, he must win the right to do so, and he made no secret of the possibility that, as the years went on, his way of life might in some respects be different from his father's.

He pleased his father in one way. He took great interest in all that concerned the management of the estate. He was fond of the place as his home. They agreed in most things which concerned its prosperity and prospects, and if George was less eager than his father in his desire to add to its extent, he did not vex him by showing this too plainly. They differed in opinion about this, and about other things often. But Mr Dawson put great restraint upon himself at such times, striving to remember that George had a right as a man to hold his own opinions and to act upon them though they differed from his. George, on his part, felt no temptation to fail in the perfect respect he owed to his father, in his words and in his ways. And so, in course of time, things bade fair to adjust themselves to the satisfaction of both.

As was to be supposed, Jean and her aunt looked on with deep interest, while the father and son were thus happily though warily renewing their acquaintance, but they said little about it, even to each other. During the first month after May went away there was much going on at Saughleas. Emily Corbett, who had come for the wedding, stayed a while, and Hugh stayed also, though he was strong and well and able for any thing now. There were young people coming to the house for their sakes,—Marion Calderwood, who was Emily's chief friend, and the young Petries, and others; and there were expeditions here and there, and garden parties at various houses; and Jean's time and thoughts were much occupied.

Captain Harefield made one of such parties now and then, but not so frequently as had been the case last summer. He was a person of more importance at Blackford House now than he had been then, and though his sister was not there to take care of him, there were others there ready and willing to do the work in which it must be confessed she had failed. He was so good-natured, and so unaccustomed to exert his own will against any one who assumed the right to guide him, that he was easily taken possession of. It was agreeable also to be made much of, to be consulted and included in all arrangements for business or pleasure, so that he did not find his stay at Blackford House "a bore," as he had done last summer, and he was less inclined to stray away into other parts to look for pleasure.

The less frequently that he came to Saughleas, the more kindly and frankly he was received by Jean, who liked him very well since he seemed to have put foolish thoughts out of his head. But he came often enough to put foolish thoughts into the heads of other people. The young people who came to the house, watched with interest the Captain's shy devotion, and Jean's friendly indifference, not quite sure the last was altogether real. Mrs Seldon, during the weeks of her stay, never doubted as to his object in coming, and sensible of the importance attached to having a place in county society and a title in prospect, she doubted as little as to the result of his devotion, and Mr Dawson, with a mingling of feelings which he could not easily have analysed, repeated to himself that "Jean had the ball at her foot, whatever way it might end." But Miss Jean held fast to her first opinion, that Jean was safe from any temptation to yield to him, and so was another who had not had Miss Jean's experience.

"Oh! Miss Jean, I am the most unfortunate little creature in all Portie, I think. I'm ay doing or saying something that I shouldna."

"My dear, ye are worse than unfortunate if that be true. What have ye been at now?"

"It was quite true, what I said, only I wish Mr Dawson hadna heard us. We were speaking about—about Miss Dawson—"

Marion hesitated. She was not quite sure how Miss Jean herself would like to hear that the young folk had been discussing her niece and her affairs so freely.

"It was only that he heard us. I'm ay vexing Mr Dawson, I think."

"Are you?" said Miss Jean, smiling.

"Ay, am I. Don't you mind the apple-tree that was broken, and don't you mind?" several other circumstances that it vexed the girl to remember. But Jean herself coming in, the vexation of the moment could not be discussed and Marion was not sorry.

It had happened thus. She had come early to Saughleas with the young Petries intending to set out at once on an expedition that had been planned to the Castle, but something had delayed several of their party, and the younger folk were whiling away the time of waiting, chatting and laughing as they sat on the grass. By and by the well-known dog-cart passed.

"Haloo! There is your Englishman, Marion," said Hugh Corbett. "I wonder he didn't come in. He'll be back again to go with us, unless we make haste to get away."

"Well, and why should not he come with us? The more the merrier," said his sister.

"And he's no' *my* Englishman," said Marion with dignity; "and for that matter ye are only an Englishman yoursel'."

"Only an Englishman! Just hear her!" said Hugh.

"And ye're not even an Englishman. You are neither one thing nor the other," said Grace Petrie laughing. "If ye were to bide a while in Portie, ye might maybe pass for a Scotchman, however."

"Oh, indeed! Might I? That's encouraging."

This was a favourite subject of discussion between these young people, and much banter passed with regard to the nationality of the Corbetts.

"But he is no' Marion's Englishman anyway," said Jack Petrie in a little. "He only falls back on Marion when Miss Dawson's company is no' to be had."

"And it's only because Marion saves him the trouble of saying a word. She is such a chatterbox," said Hugh. "And he'll have to fall back on her altogether soon, I'm thinking."

"I'm sure that's no' what our Milly thinks," said Jack. "She says that Miss Dawson—"

"Your Milly! She judges other folk by hersel'! Miss Dawson wouldna look at him," said Marion Calderwood.

"But she does look at him, whiles," said Grace.

"But that's because she's no' ay thinkin' about—about the like o' that Him indeed! He might as well go and ask for one of the young princesses at once."

They all laughed and exclaimed.

"Well, she would be no more above him in one way than Miss Dawson is in another. A baronet? What o' that? Any body might be a baronet, I suppose," said Marion.

"But nothing short of a lord will do for Jean Dawson, ye think. I doubt she'll bide a whilie," said Jack scornfully.

"And she can afford to bide a whilie. Miss Dawson is sufficient for herself," said Marion loftily. "But I don't expect you to understand me, Jack; and I don't think it is nice for us to be speaking that way about Miss Dawson."

"I agree with you," said Emily.

"So do I," said Hugh. "But I have one question to ask, and only one. Who of all the gentlemen you have ever seen would you think good enough or great enough for Miss Dawson."

"Oh! as to good enough, that is not what Marion means," said Grace.

"No. Nor great enough," said Emily. "Well—just suitable—worthy of her, in every way? In mind, body, and estate. Come, let us hear."

"Yes, come, let us hear."

"In mind, body, and estate," repeated Emily laughing. "I think enough has been said already," and Marion rose to go away. "But if ye will have it—I never saw any body in every respect worthy of Miss Dawson—except, perhaps—But yet—" Marion hesitated, and then added,—

"I dinna believe there is another in all Scotland like Miss Dawson."

"I agree—nor in England either," said Hugh. "But I rise to ask a question—"

He had risen, but it was evidently with the design of intercepting Marion, who was moving over the grass intent on getting away.

"I leave it to the company if we have not a right to hear what is to be said; and, what is more, you are not going away till you tell us."

He did not touch her, but he looked quite ready to do it.

"Nonsense, Hugh! You are not to vex Marion," said his sister; but she drew near with the rest to listen.

"'Not one in all Scotland,' she said," repeated Grace laughing.

"Let us stick to the point," said Hugh.

Marion reddened and fidgeted, and measured the distance with her eye with the evident intention of running away, and all this Hugh noted—nodding and smiling.

"Ye canna gar Marion speak, if she's no willin'. I've seen her tried," said another Petrie.

"Why shouldna I speak?" said Marion, realising the impossibility of getting away. "Except that—it's no' a thing to speak about—here. What I mean is this. But yet if she were to give her whole heart to any one—he would be the right one—even if—but she would never care for one who was not worthy. Now let me go."

"Yes—certainly. Well?"

Marion had made up her mind to say no more. But when Grace Petrie, tossing her head and laughing, said that she could guess who the exception might be, she changed her mind again.

"Well!" said Hugh, drawing still near as she receded. "'Except, perhaps,' whom?"

"I except no one that ever I saw, for there is no one that ever I saw who, in all things—in mind, body, and estate, as you say—I would think fit for Miss Dawson. But what I was going to say was—except, perhaps—George—only he is her brother, ye ken."

"George!" echoed, many voices.

"And what's George more than another?" asked Jack scornfully. "She'll be saying next, that there's naebody like *him* in all Scotland."

And then Marion, glancing up at the window beneath which they had been sitting, met the wondering look of Mr Dawson.

"He must have heard every word," said Grace in a whisper.

Marion turned and fled to seek comfort with Miss Jean.

They went away to the Castle, and Miss Dawson went with them; Captain Harefield came to the house soon after they set out, but he did not follow them, though Mr Dawson suggested that he might easily overtake them before they reached the place. It was Mr Dawson himself he had come to see; and when they all came back, and the young folk had had their tea and were gone home together in the moonlight, her father had something to say to Jean.

"It's a comfort that you can just leave it to Jean herself," said his sister, when he told his news to her. Of what her own opinion might be she said nothing, nor was she curious to hear what Mr Dawson might think now about the chance that his daughter had of becoming the wife of Captain Harefield. "It is a thing that she must decide for herself; and indeed she will let no one else decide it."

There was a measure of comfort in that view of the matter. For though Mr Dawson was ambitious for his daughter, Captain Harefield as a man with expectations was by no means so interesting to him personally as he had been last year when he had none. He knew by Jean's face at the first word spoken, that her aunt was right.

"I gave him his answer last year," said she.

"But it's no' an unheard of thing that a woman should change her mind," said her father dryly.

"I have had no reason to change my mind, but many reasons against it. Fancy my leaving you and George and the happy life we are just beginning, to go away with a stranger to folk that would look down on me, and think he had thrown himself away?"

"I could make it worth their while to think otherwise." But Jean shook her head. "Last year you might, when he had nothing."

"As for his friends—ye need ha'e little to do with them. I dare say none o' them can ha'e a higher sense o' their ain importance than his sister, Mrs Eastwood, and I think ye could hold your own with her."

"If it were worth my while. But, papa—he is nothing in the world to me."

"He is not a clever man, I ken that. But I like him. He is sweet tempered, and he is a gentleman, and he cares for you. And I think, with you to stand by him, he might be a good man and a useful."

"But, papa—the weariness of it, even if I cared for him."

"But that might come in time."

"No, papa. I am not—going with him. He will find some one who will care for him, and who will fill the high position that he can give her better than I could do."

In his heart the father did not believe that, but he only said,—

"Very likely. You must please yourself I only wish you to ken your ain mind, and understand what you are refusing. He will be Sir Percy Harefield, and there may come a time when you will regret your refusal."

"I don't think it, papa."

"As for not wishing to leave your brother and me—George will marry sometime, and then you will be but second with him, though he may be first with you."

"Of course he will marry, papa. And I will be 'Auntie Jean' to his bairns. And I'll ay have you, papa."

"But, Jean, I want you to understand. When George marries it is my intention to give up Saughleas to him. His wife will be mistress here then."

He watched her face as he said this. She was not looking at him, but out at the window, standing in the full light. She turned to him with a smile like sunshine on her face.

"Then I could live with Auntie Jean when you didna need me any more. 'The twa Miss Jean Dawsons!' Wouldna ye like that, Auntie Jean? But, papa," she added gravely, "it wouldna please George to hear you speak of giving up Saughleas to him."

"He need not hear it till the right time comes. There need be no haste. His choice will be the wiser the longer he waits, let us hope."

"And you are not vexed with me, papa?"

"So that you are sure o' yourself. That is the main thing. You might take longer time to think about it."

"No, no. A longer time would make no difference. It would not be fair to Captain Harefield—and I am quite sure of myself."

Miss Jean, as her manner was, had kept silence during the whole interview.

"Her time will come, I dare say, but she is fancy-free at present," said her father as Jean left the room.

"She has done wisely this time," said her aunt. "And it is well that she should wait till her time come."

"That is well over," said Jean to herself. "And I can wait—yes, though it be all my life—if so it must be."

For Jean had found herself out long before this time—before the "John Seaton" had come home even. She knew that she "cared for" Willie Calderwood as she could care for no other man. And since that night when they had clasped hands and looked into each other's eyes she had not been ashamed of her love. For there had been more than the gladness of home coming in Willie's eyes, his hand-clasp had told of more than friendship.

True he had guarded eyes and hands and voice since then, and he might keep silence still for years—there was cause enough, Jean acknowledged, remembering "bonny Elsie." But he "cared for her," and she could wait. "Patiently? Yes, hopefully, joyfully," she had told herself often, and now she said it again as she sang softly to herself as she went about the house.

But that night her brother came home with a sadder face than usual, for he had heard sad news, he said. Willie Calderwood had declined the command of the "John Seaton." He was about to sail as second officer in one of the great ocean steamships. Indeed he had already sailed, for his note to George was written at the last moment, he said; and he must cross the wide Atlantic twice before she should see him again.

"It is not so bad as a year's voyage to the north," she told herself. "Portie is his home while his mother is here and Marion."

But he had spoken no word to her before he went, as he might have done, if he had been going away to the dangers of the Arctic seas. That was the pain to her. But she comforted herself. Though she knew his pride was strong, she thought that his love would prove stronger still, and he would speak when the right time came.

But when Willie had crossed the sea twice, and twice again, still he did not come to Portie. He went instead to London, and there he fell in with an aunt of his father's who, in years long past, had been the wife of a London merchant, but who was a childless widow now. She had been left with a large house and a small income more than thirty years ago, when she was young and courageous, and she had put aside all the traditions of the class into which marriage had brought her, and had fallen back on the belief in which she had been brought up in her home in the north, that honest work honourably followed was a blessing to be thankful for, rather than a burden to be borne.

So her head and her hands and her house were all put to use, and she had lived a busy and a happy life since then. But she was growing old now, and her heart longed for her own land and kindred, so when she saw Willie, and heard of his mother who was a widow, and his young sister Marion, she begged them to come to her for a while.

It is doubtful whether Mrs Calderwood would have had the courage to accept the invitation, if the thought of leaving Portie had not been already familiar to her; and it is equally doubtful whether she would have had the courage to go away, if this invitation had not come. It was for a visit that they were going, she said, but her house was given up, the few things which she valued and could not take with her, were safely put away in an empty room in Miss Jean's house. And no one knew when she might be expected in Portie again.

Jean had not often seen Mrs Calderwood since the day she had gone to ask Marion to visit her at the time her sister May was in London, but she saw her now in her aunt's house, where the last few days of the mother and daughter were passed, and though they both strove against it, there was a shadow of embarrassment between them.

"We'll maybe see May in London, and we'll be sure to see you when you come to visit her there," Marion said, including both George and Jean in her words.

"London is a large place, and Mrs Manners has her own friends," said Mrs Calderwood.

"We shall find you out, never fear, and we winna forget you even if you should live in London all your life."

Marion laughed and then looked grave.

"But that can never happen," said she.

If Jean was grave and silent for a while at this time, no one noticed it but her aunt, and she did not remark upon it. Indeed she was grave and a little sad herself for she greatly missed both mother and daughter, who had been her dear friends and daily visitors for many a year, and she confessed to a strange feeling of loneliness in her house by the sea.

Jean came often to see her and so did George, but she seldom spoke about the Calderwoods to either of them. Now and then a letter came from Marion to Jean or to her aunt, but after the very first these letters said nothing about coming home to Portie again.

And Jean waited. Not unhappily. Far from that, for her life was a busy one. She had much to do and much to enjoy in her father's house and beyond it. She strove to forget herself, and to remember others, and made no one anxious or curious because of her grave looks and her sadness.

She just waited, telling herself that if so it must be, she would do as her aunt had done, and wait on till the end.

Chapter Nineteen.

George.

They had three years and more without a break of the happy life to which Jean had looked forward when her brother came home. The days seemed all alike in the quiet routine into which they fell; but no one wished for a change.

If Mr Dawson had misgivings as to how his son, after his long wanderings round the world, would settle down into the man of business, intent chiefly on the work which the day brought to his hand, they were all put aside after a time. George fell into his place with an ease which indicated a natural aptitude for the kind of work expected from him; and during a slight but tedious illness, which kept his father a few weeks at home, George filled his place in the counting-house with a success which proved that in all but experience, he was fitted, and might be trusted to hold it to as good purpose as ever his father had done. He had the same clear head, and the same directness of purpose in his dealings with other men; and he had, what his father even in his youngest days had never had, the natural kindliness of heart and temper that won good-will without an effort.

Mr Dawson had always been respected as an honest man,—a man of his word; but when their fellow townsmen discussed the father and son in their new relations, as they were not slow to do, it was said of George, that he was "a true gentleman"; and by this it was meant, that the temptations which his father, as a man of business had all his life successfully resisted, the son would never see as temptations at all. While those who came into business relations with him saw that he would probably be as successful in the making of money as his father had been; they also saw that he cared far less for it; and with better opportunities for knowing, they would also have seen that he spent a good deal of it in a manner, which, according to his father's judgment, would bring but poor returns. The poor folk of Portie, the sailors' widows and orphans, and the "puir auld wivies" of the town, knew about it, though even they oftener saw Miss Jean's hand in the help that came from him, than his own.

"Ane o' Miss Jean's folk," they called him, and so he was, in that he served the same Master, and loved the service. But he did not offend nor grieve his father by openly casting in his lot with these people as his aunt had done. There was not the same need. Miss Jean had found in communion with the despised little flock in Stott's Lane, the help and comfort which she had failed to find in the kirk of her fathers. But times had changed since then. In the kirk of their fathers in Portie as well as elsewhere there was found in George's day the personal consecration, the fervour of love, the earnestness of service, which in the old days had made the folk of Stott's Lane "a peculiar people." George was content to remain with them, and his aunt had no desire that he should do otherwise.

And then he went quietly on his way, unconscious that the eyes of all Portie were upon him; not just watching for his halting, yet with a certain movement of expectation to see him fall into his old light-hearted, careless ways again. He did not begin his new life among them with any definite plan of work. He had no such faith in his own strength or wisdom as to make him hopeful as to what he might do for any one. But this work came to him, as in one way or another work will come to all who wish to serve.

It came to him out of the every-day work of his life, which brought him into contact with ships and sailors, either setting sail, or coming home after a voyage. He sent away those who were going with a friendly "God speed," and met those who returned with a kindly greeting, and was frank and sympathetic with all, because it was his nature to be so; and the men liked him as every body who came near him had liked him all his life. And his sympathy and their liking opened the way for the help which he could give, and which some of these poor fellows needed badly enough.

By and by he found himself in the midst of work which had come to his hands he scarcely could have told how;—certainly not from any impelling sense of the duty which he owed to this class of his townsmen, and not consciously from any thought of the service that he owed them for his Master's sake. One needed his help, and another, and he gave it gladly, taking pleasure in it, and before he knew it, his hands and his heart were full. It was in one way humble work enough that he did—speaking a word of caution to one, laying a restraining hand on another, guiding another past an evident danger, helping another firmly to withstand the temptation of strong drink, too often the sailor's strongest and wiliest foe.

All this led him at times into dark places, and queer companionships, where was needed a strong arm as well as a cool head and a persuasive tongue. For "poor Jack," just off a long voyage with money in his pockets, was considered fair game in Portie as in other places; and even in Portie, where dark deeds could not be easily hidden, dark deeds were sometimes done. Though the influence of the respectable part of the community could be brought to bear more readily and directly on the doers of such deeds, than could be the case in larger places, yet direct interference, either to prevent or to punish, was not always effectual. "Poor Jack" himself was often as eager as his enemy to resent and resist such interference, and those who ventured upon it, sometimes fared ill between them.

To these poor fellows George gave both time and interest, and not in vain. In all his dealings with them they were made to feel that it was not a sense of duty merely, that brought him near them. He understood them, and liked them and their ways, and was their friend. They believed in him, and did, to please him, what they would hardly have been brought to do from higher motives. After a time they trusted him entirely, as well they might. He loved them. There was nothing that he would not do to help them— few things that he did not do for some of them. In the many ways which genuine personal interest can devise, he befriended them and theirs. In sickness he helped them by helping those to whom they belonged—which was well, and he put his own hands on them, which was better,—putting his strength to gentle uses: soothing, restraining, comforting them, as he never could have done if he had not loved them, and if they had not had confidence in his love.

And because he loved them, they were not unwilling to listen to him when he told them of a "greater love," the love of One who grudged not to give His life for their sakes. He never told it in many words, and he did not for a good while try to tell it to any but the sick and the suffering, as he got a chance for a word with them one by one. But later, when there were occasions, now and then, for sharp though kindly words of rebuke where numbers had gathered, words of gentleness were sure to follow about the love that could keep them in all straits from yielding unworthily to wrong-doing. And if such occasions grew more frequent as time went on, it was because of no plan or intention of his.

Little of all this was known in Portie, except among the men themselves and their families, and among the ill-doing folk who would fain have made gain of their folly; but the result was visible enough in the better lives of some and added comfort of many a home in the place. But to no one did George's work do more good than to himself. It gave him an interest in life which business, engaged in conscientiously for the sake of pleasing his father and making up to him for the disappointment which the last few years of his life had caused, could never have supplied. It did more to establish him permanently in Portie, and to make him content there, than did the partnership into which during the second year he entered with his father.

He grew more like his old self, his father said to Miss Jean, giving the new partnership, and the increased interest and responsibility which it implied the credit for it. In Miss Jean's eyes, he was as little like the wilful lad who had given cause for many anxious thoughts in the old days, as could well be, except that he had the same sunny temper and the same winning ways, and was well-beloved as he had been in his most foolish days. Now he was a man to be trusted as well as loved. He was a graver man than he might ever have become without the discipline of sorrow through which he had passed, and the remorseful memory of the worse than wasted years that followed; but his "trouble," as the suffering and sinning of those years were vaguely called, had not harmed him. At least good had come out of it all. He was grave, but he was not gloomy; and though he availed himself less than pleased his father of the opportunities given for mingling in such society as Portie and its neighbourhood afforded, he made home a different place to them all.

These were happy days to Jean. Between her and her brother, as to all that filled his life and made the future hopeful, there was perfect confidence and sympathy. She helped him in his work among the sailors and their wives and families, and among the fishers of the neighbourhood, by doing many things that only a woman's tact and skill and will could do, and she helped him even more by the eager sympathy with which she listened and advised when she could not put her own hand to the work.

They were true friends as well as loving brother and sister, and as time went on, their father began to fear that they might grow too well content with each other and the life they were living, and so fail of the higher happiness which he coveted for them, and which was the right of such as they.

"There is time enough," said Miss Jean comforting him.

"Yes. He is young, and he will surely forget," said his father. "And as for Jean, she is fancy-free."

To this Miss Jean made no reply. She was not sure of either the one thing or the other. But she saw that the brother and sister seemed content, and that they were doing willingly and effectively the work that fell to their hands, and in her esteem life had nothing better to give than this.

"All that you wish for them may come in the natural course of things, but ye must have patience and no' try to force it," said Miss Jean. "And in the mean time, ye ha'e ay one o' May's bonny boys to fall back upon for Saughleas, if that is what is in your mind."

For they had lately heard of the birth of Mrs Manners' second son, and much rejoicing had it caused.

"I wonder ye're no' thinkin' o' going south to see your new grandson. The change would do you good, and it would be a great pleasure to May."

"There is nothing to hinder, if Jean will go with me."

But there was much to hinder Jean it seemed. May had better nursing than she could give her, and she would much rather make her visit when her sister should be well and strong and able to go about with her. And then George had been promising to take her to Paris and perhaps farther, later in the summer, and they could visit May at the same time. Besides—she told her father privately she would not go away and leave her aunt so long alone just at present, for she was never strong in the spring; and her father could urge her no longer.

Jean had another reason, of which she could speak to no one, why she did not wish to leave Portie at this time. She had heard from one of the young Petries of the hope they had of a visit from Marion Calderwood and her brother, and Jean would not leave home and lose the chance of seeing them.

Willie Calderwood had never been in Portie again, and Jean had never seen him, since he left it on the morning of her sister's marriage day, and that was a long time now. She had waited patiently, but she longed for the time of waiting to be over. She knew now how well she loved him, and in her heart she believed that he loved her as well. He had never spoken, he might never speak; but whether he spoke or not, she had a longing unspeakable, just to see his face and touch his hand again. She had been quite happy during these two years, she told herself; but her heart sprang gladly up at the thought that her time of waiting might be nearly over. She had never spoken his name even to her brother, and he had been as silent to her, but she sometimes thought that George knew how they cared for one another, and that he kept silence because he knew it would not be well to speak. But all the same, Jean would not lose the chance of seeing Willie again. So, after some consideration, Mr Dawson set off alone. He reached London late at night and did not go to his daughter's house until the morning. She lived in a pleasant part of a pleasant suburb, in a little house which stood in the midst of a tiny garden, which was enclosed within high walls. They had removed to it recently, and Mr Dawson had never seen it before. It was a very pretty place, he thought as he entered—a little confined perhaps, for the high walls were not very far apart—a little like a prison, he could not but fancy, as the gate was locked behind him.

Mr Manners had already gone out for the day, the neat little maid told him, and Mrs Manners was not down yet, but she would be down presently. She was well and so was baby.

But he was not left alone long, and then he had another greeting. He thought for a moment that it was May who came toward him with outstretched hand. It was not May. It was a tall, slender, dark-eyed girl with a blooming face in which there was something familiar. He knew who it was as soon as he heard her voice.

"Didna Jean come with you?" A shadow fell on the bright face at his answer. But it passed in a minute.

"It is good to see a 'kenned face' again. Mrs Manners is very well, and so is baby—such a darling! Mrs Manners is coming down-stairs to-day for the first time. She will be down soon," added the girl more sedately, as if she had got a little check. She was thinking of the time when she stood before Mr Dawson with the broken branch of the apple-tree in her hand, and oddly enough, so was he. But the sight of Marion Calderwood stirred no angry feelings now. That was all past. The ill that had come to his son through Elsie Calderwood had been changed to good. The sudden glad remembrance of the son he had left at home—a man strong, earnest, good—softened his heart and his voice as he looked on the girl's wistful face, and he smiled kindly as he said,—

"England seems to agree with you, my lassie."

Marion shook her head.

"But it is no' home," said she. "I like Portie best." Then she took courage to ask him about the place, and about the folk in it, and the changes that had taken place since she left. Trifling questions some of them were, but they were asked so eagerly, and the answers were listened to with such interest, that he could not but take pleasure in it. Nobody was forgotten. From Miss Jean herself to poor old Mrs Cairnie, every body in Portie seemed to be a friend of hers, and all that concerned them of the deepest interest to her. Mr Dawson had difficulty in recalling some of the folk she asked about.

"Ye should come back and renew acquaintance with them all."

"Oh! wouldna I like it! And maybe I may—some day. We thought Miss Dawson was coming with you," said Marion with a little change of face and voice!

"Jean? yes, I thought that too; but she had some good reasons of her own for staying at home. Her aunt is not just so strong as she might be, and she didna like to leave her. She'll come soon, however. She is a friend of yours, it seems."

"She was ay good to me," said Marion softly, and there was nothing more said for a while.

"But what have I been thinking about all this time?" said Marion suddenly.

She left the room and returned almost immediately with a child in her arms—May's eldest, a beautiful but rather delicate looking boy of a little more than a year old.

"This is George Dawson—the precious darling. He is just a little shy at first, but he is not going to be shy with his own grandpapa, is he, my pet, my darling, my bonny boy?" And she fell into a soft babble of fond words, which would have had no meaning to an indifferent listener, but the grandfather listened, well pleased. The "bonny boy" showed his shyness by clinging to his nurse, but he looked at his grandfather bravely enough, and did not resent the cautious advances made to him. He was persuaded to show all his pretty tricks of action and speech, and smiled, and cooed, and murmured his baby words; and it would not have been easy to say whether his nurse or his grandfather was most delighted at the success of the introduction.

"And now," said Marion, "I think we may tell grandpapa our secret. And it will not be long a secret now, will it, my bonny boy? For mamma is coming down to-day, and all the world must know."

Then setting the child safely in a corner, she moved a step or two away, and held out her arms. Then there were more sweet foolish words, and then the venture was made, and two or three uncertain steps taken, and the little hero was safe again in her arms.

Again and again, with a skill and courage that increased as the distance was lengthened, the journey was made in triumph. Then Marion knelt down, and steadying the child before her, said softly and firmly,—

"Now go to grandpapa." And forgetting his shyness in the glory of success, away he went with eager, faltering steps, and sprang joyfully into the old man's arms. The door had opened softly and the young mother, pale but smiling, stood on the threshold seeing it all. As the child turned she stooped and held out her arms, and again he crossed the space between them with quick, uncertain steps; and May kissed her father with her child in her arms.

Then, after a whispered word, Marion went out and returned in a little carrying a tiny bundle with trailing white robes, and presented to Mr Dawson another grandson. If she had been at all afraid of him at first, her fear had not outlasted the play with the child, and Mrs Manners saw with mingled surprise and amusement the good understanding between them, and the interest her father allowed to appear in the pretty ways and pleasant words of the girl whom in the old days they had found it best to keep a little out of his sight.

He listened to their lamentations about Jean's not coming patiently, and answered with a good grace, more questions in ten minutes than ever she had ventured to put to him in as many days.

"She has wonderfully improved since she left Portie," said he, when Marion had carried away the baby again.

"She was ay a bonny lassie," said May.

She was not going to put him on his guard against the fascinations of her friend by praising her too earnestly.

"I like her to be here with me when I cannot go out. She is very nice with Georgie."

That was all she said to him, but she told her husband that night, that Marion, with the help of the "bonny boy," had made a conquest of her father.

Chapter Twenty.

Marion.

That was but the beginning. Mr Dawson might have had a dull time for the next few days, since Mr Manners was more than usually engaged, and Mrs Manners was not permitted to come down-stairs very early. But he did not. There was the boy, and there was Marion, ready to show one another off to the best advantage for his admiration and amusement. And when the boy was carried away by his nurse, Marion still considered herself responsible for the entertainment of the old gentleman of whom, since he had showed himself inclined to unbend, she had ceased to be afraid.

She read to him, she sang to him, she talked to him about many things—about the leaders in the *Times*, the fishing interests, the prospects of a good harvest. And when other subjects failed there was always Portie to fall back upon. Her interest in all that pertained to her old home and its inhabitants was inexhaustible.

"Oh! we are never at a loss," she told Mrs Manners, when she asked her how they had got through the day.

It might have come to that, however, if Mrs Manners had not judiciously suggested a change. When one morning Mr Dawson said he must go into the city, his daughter suggested that business and pleasure might be united for once, and he might take Marion. His business took him to the Bank of England, and there Marion found her pleasure. For he took her through all that wonderful place and showed her what was to be seen, to her great delight.

Then they threaded their way through the crowds of Cheapside, and came to the great cathedral which hitherto Marion had only seen in the distance. It was almost too much in one day, she thought, the Bank of England and Saint Paul's. But did she not enjoy it? They only meant to go in to rest for a minute, but hours passed before they came out again.

Then Mr Dawson took her to lunch at a curious little place near Ludgate Hill, and then they moved through crowds again along Fleet Street till they came to Temple Bar and turned into the Temple.

Oh! the peace and quiet of the place, after the jostling and noise and confusion of the great thoroughfare! Marion fancied herself walking in a dream, as they wandered through the silent courts, and listened to the soft "plash, plash" of the fountain, and then sat down to rest under the trees of the garden.

A score of names famous in history and fiction rose to her lips. They had not said much to one another all the morning. Marion had said only a word now and then in her delight at the wonderful things she saw, but as they sat a while to rest and catch the cool air blowing from the river before they set out for home, her lips were opened, and she talked a good deal more than she would have been likely to do to Mr Dawson, or any one else, in other circumstances.

Foolish talk some of it was, about unreal folk who will still live forever because of the genius that called them into being. Unknown names most of them were to her listener; and in another mood and place, he might have called it all folly or worse. But he listened now with the pleased interest that one gives to the fancies of a child. And all she said was not foolish, he acknowledged as she went on. There were little words now and then, clear and keen and wise, which pleased him well.

But nothing that was seen or said that day pleased him so much as this.

"You have made a day of it together," said Mrs Manners laughing, as she met them at the door. "You must be tired enough by this time."

"Yes, I am tired. And no wonder. I think I never had so much pleasure in one day in all my life before."

She did not say it to him. He only heard it by chance as she passed up the stairs. But he said to himself that there should be more such days for one so easily pleased before he left London.

And so there were. They saw together pictures and people, parks and gardens. They went to Richmond and Kew and Hampton Court, and to more places besides. Mrs Manners went with them sometimes, but their energy and interest were too much for her, and usually she let them go without her. And Mr Dawson was fain to acknowledge to himself that he had a share in the pleasure which he meant to give "the blithe and bonny lassie" at such times.

She was "blithe and bonny" at all times, but when he saw her, as often happened, moving about among the guests that sometimes filled his daughter's pretty rooms, none more admired and none more worthy of admiration than she, he owned that she was more than that.

They were not just well-dressed, well-mannered nobodies that Mrs Manners entertained. Many of them were men and women who had been heard of in the world for their worth or their wisdom, or for good work of one kind or another done by them. And this blithe and bonny lassie, who enjoyed her play with the child and her sight-seeing with the old man, was not out of place among them. She was young and a little shy of folk that seemed great folk to her, and she was very quiet and silent among them. But many eyes followed her with delight as she moved up and down among them in her pretty evening dress; and she had words of wisdom spoken to her now and then as well as the rest, and she could answer them too, on occasion, as he did not fail to see.

She sang too, not only the old songs that delighted him, but grand, grave music, to which they listened who were far wiser about such things than he. She was a wonder to him at such times, but in the morning she was just as usual, "bonny and blithe" and easily pleased.

"Ye mind me whiles of our Jean," said he to her one day, and he could not but wonder at the sudden brightness that flashed over her face at the words. Mrs Manners laughed.

"That is the very utmost that can be said, papa. You cannot go beyond that. There is no one like Jean in. Marion's eyes."

"Am I like her? Maybe I may grow like her, sometime," said the girl softly.

All this time May had been keeping a wise silence with regard to her friend. She believed that he would see all that was good and pleasant in her all the more readily that they were not pointed out to him; and so it proved.

The days passed quickly and happily and came to an end too soon. All this time Mrs Calderwood had been at the seaside with her old friend, who had needed the change, and when they returned Marion was called home. She was glad to go home, but at the same time she acknowledged herself sorry to leave.

"For I think I never had so much pleasure all my life before. Only I am afraid my mother will think I cannot have been much comfort to you."

"She will be quite mistaken then," said Mrs Manners laughing and kissing her. "You have been a great comfort to me."

A great surprise awaited Marion when she reached home. She found her mother pondering gravely over a letter which she held in her hand, and the shadow of care did not—as it ought to have done—pass from her face as her daughter came in. It deepened rather; and in her pre-occupation she almost forgot to return the girl's greeting.

"Is any thing wrong, mother? Is it Willie?"

"No, no. It is a letter I have gotten from Miss Jean." She spoke with hesitation. Marion looked wistfully at the familiar handwriting of her old friend.

"Miss Jean asks you to visit her in Portie. It seems her nephew and niece are thinking of a journey, but Miss Dawson doubts about leaving her aunt, who is not strong. Miss Jean thinks she would go if you would promise to go and stay with her a while."

"Oh! mother! I should so like it." Marion held out her hand for the letter, but her mother did not offer it to her; she read bits of it here and there instead.

"'I have said nothing about it to Jean, and shall not till I hear from you. They would likely set off at once if you would promise to let Marion come to me, and that would please you, though—'

"'If you decide to let her come, she might travel here with young Mr Petrie, who, I hear, is soon to be in London. Though I think myself it might be better for her to come at once, in the company of my brother, who will not likely stay much longer.'"

"Oh, mother! I should so like to go. And is that all that Miss Jean says?"

"All she says about your visit."

"You don't wish me to go. Why, mother? It is nae surely that you canna trust me so far away? I am not more foolish than other girls, am I?"

Mrs Calderwood looked at her a moment as though she did not understand what she was saying. Then she laughed and kissed her.

"Nonsense! dear. You are a sensible lassie and discreet. I would be sorry to disappoint Miss Jean, though she has friends enough in Portie one would think. But it is the first favour she has ever asked of me, and many a one she has done me."

"But, mother, I think this is a favour to us—to me at least. Oh! it seems too good to be true."

"Well, we will think about it."

"And, mother, if I should go, I would like—wouldn't you? rather to go with Mr Dawson than with James Petrie."

Her mother's face clouded again.

"What ails you at young Mr Petrie?"

Marion shrugged her shoulders.

"Oh! nothing. Only I like Mr Dawson better—better than I could have believed possible. He has been very good to me. I haven't told you yet. Mother, I think he must have grown a better man since George came home."

Her mother said nothing. She did not think well of Mr Dawson. She did not wish to think well of him. When she had heard from Marion that he had come to his daughter's house, her first impulse was to recall her at once. The impossibility of leaving her old friend, or of permitting Marion to travel alone, prevented her from acting on her first impulse, and when she had time to consider the matter, she saw that it would be better for her to remain. It was not likely that Mr Dawson would see much of her, and whatever he might feel, he would not do otherwise than treat politely his daughter's guest.

That he should "begood to her," that he should put himself about, as she knew he must have done, to give her pleasure surprised her, but it did not please her. She had forgiven him, she told herself. At least she bore him no ill-will for the share he and his had had in the trouble of her life, but she wished to have nothing at all to do with him, either as friend or foe.

But Miss Jean's friendship was quite apart from all this. It had been a refuge to her in times of trouble long before she lost her Elsie, and this invitation was but another proof of her friendship, and she would let her daughter go.

As for her escort—Mrs Calderwood was as averse to accepting James Petrie as such, as her daughter was, though from a different reason. But she was equally averse to any appearance of presuming on the kindness of Mr Dawson. Fortunately the matter was taken out of her hands.

Mrs Manners came the next day empowered to plead that Miss Jean's invitation should be accepted, and when she found that this was not necessary, she found courage to propose that instead of waiting for any one, Marion should hasten her preparations and go on at once with her father.

Trouble! What possible trouble could it be for her father to sit in the same railway carriage with the child? As for Jamie Petrie—it was easy seen what he was after. But it would be quite too great a grace to grant him at this early stage of—of his plans and projects. Oh! yes. Of course it was all nonsense, but then—

But the nonsense helped to bring Mrs Calderwood to consent that Marion should go at once. And so it was arranged.

It would have pleased Mr Dawson to take Marion with him to Saughleas, but this she modestly but firmly declined, because her mother expected her to go at once to Miss Jean's house by the sea, and there she was kindly welcomed.

It was like getting home again, she said. The sound of the sea soothed her to sleep, and it woke her in the morning with a voice as familiar as if she had never been away. She was out, and away over the sands to the Tangle Stanes, and had renewed acquaintance with half the bairns in Portie, before Miss Jean was ready for her breakfast.

The bairns had all grown big, and the streets and lanes, the houses and shops, had all grown narrow and small, she thought. But the sea had not changed, nor the sands, nor the far-away hills, nor the sky—which was, oh! so different from the sky in London. Marion had not changed much, her friends thought. Some of them said she was bigger and bonnier, but she was blithe and friendly and "a'e fauld" still—and London hadna spoiled her as it might very easily have done. At any rate she meant to enjoy every hour of her stay, and that was the way she began.

She did not miss Jean either, for George had been called away on business for a few days and when he returned they were to set out on their travels. During these few days Marion saw much of her friend. Jean was graver than she used to be, Marion thought; but she was kind and friendly, and could be merry too, on occasion. They had much to say to one another, and they spent hours together in the old familiar places, in the wood and on the rocks by the sea, and heard one another's "secrets," which were only secrets in the sense that neither of them would have been likely to tell them to any one else.

Marion told her friend all that she had been seeing and doing and reading, and some things that she had been hoping, since she went away, and Jean did little more. She told what her brother was doing and the help she tried to give him, and she told of the life that seemed to be opening before them.

Not such a life as they used to plan and dream about for themselves, when they were young; a quiet, uneventful, busy-life, just like the lives of other people. Judging from the look on Jean's face it did not seem a very joyful life to look forward to. Marion regarded her friend with wistful eyes.

"No. It will never be that, I am sure—just like the lives of other people, I mean."

"And why not? Well, perhaps not altogether. It will be an easier life than the lives of most people, I suppose. It will not just be a struggle for bread, as it is for so many. And we can do something for others who need help, and we need not be tied to one place every day of the year, as most folk are. And by and by we will be 'looked up to,' and our advice will be asked, and folk will say of us, as they say of my father, that 'they are much respeckit in the countryside.' And by that time I shall be 'auld Miss Jean,' and near done with it all. But it is a long look till then."

"But it may be all quite different from that. Many a thing may happen to change it all."

"Oh! many things will happen, as you say. May and her bairns will be coming and going, and the bairns will fit into the places that the years will leave empty, and George will need a staff like my father, and I will grow 'frail' like Auntie Jean, and sit waiting and looking at the sea. And ye needna sit lookin' at me with such pitiful e'en, for who is waiting so happily as she? And yet who will be so glad to go when her time shall come?"

Marion said nothing, but turned her eyes seaward with a grave face. Jean went on.

"Yes, many things will happen, but it will be just the same thing over again. The ships will sail away, and there will be long waiting, and some of them will come home, and some will never come, and the pain will be as hard to bear as if it had never come to many a sore heart before. And some folk will be glad, and some will be at least content, and some will make mistakes and spoil their lives and then just wait on to the end. Marion, what are you thinking about?"

"I'm wondering if it is really you who are saying all that. And I am thinking that is not the way Miss Jean would speak."

"Oh! Miss Jean! No, she has won safely past all that. But once, long ago, before she had learned the secret of peaceful and patient waiting, she might have been afraid of the days. Come, it is growing cold. Let us go on."

They rose from the Tangle Stanes where they had been sitting and moved away, and Jean said,—

"And as for you—Are you sure it is to be the grand school after all? Well, you will come back when the heat and burden of the day is over to take your rest in Portie. And you will be a stately old lady, a little worn and sharp perhaps, as is the fate of schoolmistresses; but with fine manners, and wisdom enough for us all. And the new generation of Petries will admire you and make much of you—not quite as the Petries of the present day would like to do," said Jean laughing. "And behold! there is Master Jamie coming on at a great pace. Shall we let him overtake us? Or shall we go in and see poor old Tibbie and let him pass by?"

They were on their way to Saughleas, where Marion was to pay her first visit. Miss Jean had gone on already in the pony carriage, but the girls were walking round by the shore. There was no reason why Marion should wish to avoid Mr James Petrie, except that she wished no one's company when she had Jean's, but she was quite willing to go into Mrs Cairnie's house where she had been several times already. It was a different looking place from the house to which Miss Jean had taken Mrs Eastwood long ago. Mrs Cairnie's daughter Annie had returned and was going to remain, and the place was "weel redd up," and indeed as pleasant a dwelling, of its kind, as one would wish to see. Poor old Tibbie had lately met with a sad mishap, which threatened to put an end to her wanderings, and keep her a prisoner at home for some time to come. Annie had come home to care for her, with the design of earning the bread of both, by making gowns and bonnets for such of the sailors' wives and fisher folk, as were not equal to the making their Sunday best for themselves.

But a different lot awaited her. She had gone away with the English lady "to better herself," it was said; but that was only half the reason of her going. She went because she feared to be beguiled into marrying a man whom she loved, but whom she could not respect, because of his enslavement to one besetting sin.

The love of strong drink had brought misery to her home, since ever she could remember. It had driven her brothers away from it and had caused her father's death and her mother's widowhood, and she shrank with terror from the thought of living such a life as her mother had lived. When her lover entreated her, saying, that being his wife she might save him from his sin, she did not believe it; but she knew that in her love and her weakness she might yield her will to his, and lose herself without saving him. So she went away with a sore heart, and when her mother's accident had made it necessary for her to come home again, she hardly could tell whether she was glad or sorry to come.

And the first "kenned face" she saw as she drew near home was the face of her lover. He did not see her. He had stepped from another carriage of the train, into the little station a few miles from Portie. Young George Dawson's hand rested on his shoulder, for the single minute that he stood there, a very different looking person from the wild lad she had left years ago.

"Yon's young Saughleas," she heard one fellow-traveller say to another. "And yon's Tam Saugster. He's hame again, it seems."

"I ha'e heard that he has gathered himsel' up wonderfu' this while back. He is a fine sailor-like lad."

"Ay. He's his ain man now. And he'll be skipper o' the 'John Seaton' before she sails again if young George Dawson gets his way, and they say he gets it in most things with his father."

Then Annie saw the sailor spring back into the carriage again as the signal was given, and she got a glimpse of George Dawson's kindly face as they passed, and then she saw nothing for a while for the rush of tears which she had much ado to hide.

"The skipper o' the 'John Seaton'! Ah! weel, he has forgotten me lang syne, but that is little matter since he has found himsel'."

But Tam had not forgotten her, and whatever he might have done at the time, he did not now resent her refusal to take as her master one who could not master himself. That very night as she sat in the gloaming listening to her mother's fretful complaints, and taking counsel with herself as to how they were to live in the coming days, a familiar step came to the door, and Tam lifted the latch and came in without waiting to be bidden.

All the rest was natural enough and easy. The next time Tam sailed he was to sail as master of the "John Seaton," and he was to sail a married man, he said firmly, and what could Annie do but yield and begin her preparations forthwith. The cottage in which Mrs Cairnie had hitherto had but a room, was taken, and Tam set himself to making it worthy to be the home of the woman he loved.

And a neat and pleasant place it looked when Jean and Marion went in that day. Into the pretty parlour the bride that was to be looked shyly, scarcely venturing to follow them.

It was Marion who displayed to Jean the various pretty and useful things already gathered.

On the mantel-piece was a handsome clock, and over it the picture of a ship with all her canvas spread, sailing over smooth seas, in the full light of the sun of an Arctic summer day. There was a low rocky shore in sight, and the gleam of icy peaks in the distance; but the ship with the sunshine on the spreading sails was the point of interest in the picture—and a pleasant picture it was for the eyes of a sailor's wife to rest upon. They were both Mr George Dawson's gift to the bride, Marion told Jean. Jean nodded and smiled.

"Yes, I know," said she.

"Miss Dawson," said Annie taking one step over the threshold where she had been standing all the time. "It is all your brother's work, and you must let me say to you what I canna say to him. Though he had done no more good in the world, it was worth his while to live, to help in the saving such a lad as Tam Saugster."

"They helped one another," said Jean softly.

"Ay. That I can easily believe. There are few men like Tam when ance ye ken him."

"And Jean thinks there are few like George," said Marion smiling, as they came away.

"And isna that what you think of your brother?" said Jean.

"Oh! yes; and with good reason," Marion said; and the rest of their talk was of their brothers, till they came to the gate of Saughleas.

Chapter Twenty One.

A Meeting.

Mr Dawson and Miss Jean were sitting on the terrace by the parlour window as they went in. Jean knew by many signs that her father and Marion had come to be very good friends, and she was prepared to see him give her a warm and kindly welcome. But she was a little surprised at the ease and pleasure with which Marion met him. She did not turn away after a shy brief greeting, as the young people who came there were rather apt to do, but smiled brightly and answered merrily when he asked her whether she had enjoyed all that she had expected to enjoy when she came to Portie. And then she sat down on the grass at Miss Jean's feet, and looked round with a sigh of satisfaction at "the bonny place."

"What kept you on the way?" asked Miss Jean. "Oh! we came round by the shore," said her niece, "and we sat a while at the Tangle Stanes, and then we went in to see Mrs Cairnie—and by the by—we didna see her after all."

"She was sleeping," said Marion.

"And we were admiring the fine things that Captain Saugster has been gathering for his bride," said Jean.

"That would hardly have kept you long," said Mr Dawson. "A few chairs and a table, and a bed and blankets, and some dishes."

"But we saw more than that; didna we, Marion?"

"Yes. Even Annie herself wasna thinking of chairs and tables and dishes. It was of the new home that is to be there, we were thinking, and it never might have been, if—Jean, tell them what Annie said."

"Tell it yourself," said Jean.

"I canna just mind all," said Marion with hesitation. "But it was to Mr George Dawson that they owed it all—their happiness, I mean—and that it was a grand thing to have a hand in saving such a lad as Tam."

"She thinks muckle o' Tam, it seems," said Mr Dawson laughing. "And he is a good sailor, if he can only keep hold o' himsel' where the drink is concerned."

"His Master will keep hold of him, I trust," said Miss Jean.

"And is he to sail the 'John Seaton,' papa?" asked Jean.

"That is what George says. There is a risk, but we'll take it, and Tam will be none the less safe for the responsibility, let us hope."

"Annie is proud and glad, and so are all the Saugsters," said Marion.

"But the proudest and gladdest of all must be—George."

"Ay, even the angels are glad over a sinner repenting," said Miss Jean.

Mr Dawson looked from one to the other.

"Saved, is he! And George did it? But Tam has hardly been tried yet."

"Oh! yes. He is surely to be trusted now. Three whole years since he has touched a glass. Yes, nearly three years Annie told me once—and I think she wouldna be vexed at my telling you, because—George belongs to you," said Marion, turning a soft bright glance on Mr Dawson. She rose in her eagerness, and stood before them, and with softened voice and changing colour told the story of one dark night on board the "John Seaton," when some kind word of George's had touched a sore spot in poor Tam Saugster's remorseful heart, and had opened his lips to utter all his shame and sorrow over a life worse than wasted. The very first thought of hope that had come to Tam since Annie forsook him, came when George laughed at him for saying that his life was nearly over. He was but a lad yet, and his life was before him, and the way was to let the past be past, and begin again with better help than he had asked for yet. And Tam was not ashamed to say that his tears had fallen fast into the sea as he listened, and if he had been his own brother, George could not have been more patient with him, or have done more for him than he had done. "And I think," added Marion, turning her shining eyes on the old man, "that George must be even happier than his friend."

She paused suddenly, turning a startled look to Miss Jean, who had gently touched her hand. Jean was looking at her father with a smile upon her lips, but he was looking away to the sea.

"Shouldna I have said it? Was it wrong? Tell me what you are thinking about, Miss Jean," said Marion in dismay.

"I'm thinking the wind has been making free with your hair, my lassie, and it is near tea-time."

Jean kissed her laughing.

"Come with me and put your hair in order, as auntie says. No, never mind. There is nothing to look grave about. It was only that my aunt was surprised to hear any body say so many words to my father, and about George too. Oh! yes, he liked it, you may be sure. I'm glad that he heard it anyway."

"But I'm afraid that Miss Jean must have thought me—forward," said Marion, hesitating over the hateful word.

"Nonsense, you are not a child any longer. And she was as well pleased as I am that my father should hear it all."

It was Mr Dawson who broke the silence that fell on them when the girls went away.

"She is an outspoken lassie yon."

"Ye canna judge her as ye might any o' the common sort," said Miss Jean shortly.

"I'm no' seeking to judge her. She seems a nice lassie enough. I like her frank, free way."

"She's but a bairn—though she is the height of our Jean, and coming on to womanhood," said Miss Jean with a sigh.

"Ay. She is a weel grown lassie," said Mr Dawson, rising, and then he went away and moved up and down the walks, pausing at shrub or tree, or flower bed, as his manner was when he was at leisure, and he only returned in time to give Miss Jean his arm when they were called into the house.

That evening they were so fortunate as to have the company of James Petrie and his sisters, and several other young people, among whom was Mr Charles Scott, to whom the eldest Miss Petrie was engaged. The young people enjoyed themselves, but Marion was not able to forget the touch of Miss Jean's fingers upon her arm, and she was rather grave and silent, the others thought. They had music, in which she took her part, singing a song or two, and then Miss Petrie played her masterpiece, a very grand piece indeed, in the midst of which Mr Dawson went out to the little gate to wait for his son.

He had gone there many times since that first night of his son's coming home. He did not always wait till he came in sight. He moved away sometimes, as his footsteps drew near, slow to acknowledge to himself, or to let his son see how much his home coming meant to him. But to-night he waited.

"There are young folk at the house to-night," said he, as though giving a reason for being in the garden at that hour.

"The Petries are there, and young Scott, who seems to be one of them. And your aunt is over and her visitor. Will you go and see them?"

"Oh! yes, surely; only I would need to go upstairs first. Jamie Petrie! What brings him here? I thought that was over," said George with a laugh.

"Is it Jean you mean?" said Mr Dawson gravely. "But it's no' Jean the nicht."

Very evidently it was not Jean, Mr Dawson thought when he went in again. Young Mr Petrie had eyes for only one, and that was Marion, who, sitting at Miss Jean's side, seemed busy with a piece of worsted work. Mr Petrie was talking eagerly and confidentially, as though he had a right as well as a pleasure in doing so.

"He has put Jean out of his head soon enough," said Mr Dawson to himself, by way of accounting for the uncomfortable feeling of which he was conscious at the sight.

"Are we to have no more music? Will you not give us another song, Miss Petrie?" said he.

Certainly Miss Petrie would give him more than one, but Marion Calderwood must come with her—not to sing, but to turn her music for her, a task to which Mr Scott was not quite equal. And so it happened that Marion was standing gravely at her side, in the full light of the lamp, when George came to the door of the room. He stood for a moment, with his eyes, full of wonder and pain, on the fair thoughtful face of the girl, and his father saw him grow white as he gazed.

"He hasna forgotten," thought he with a sudden, sharp pang of regret and anger.

Would the memory of the dead girl ever stand between him and his son? He had not thought Marion like her sister; but as he saw her now, standing so still with a face of unwonted gravity, there came a vivid remembrance of the young girl who in his hearing had said so quietly and firmly to her mother,—

"He will never forget me, and I will never give him up."

"She should never have been brought here. What could Jean have been thinking about? What could I have been thinking about myself?"

When he looked again George was gone. When, however, he came into the dining-room, where they were all assembled later, he appeared just as usual, and greeted the young people merrily enough. But Mr Dawson forgot to notice him particularly, so startled was he by the sudden brightness of Marion's face at the sight of him. George did not see her at first—at least he did not seem to see her, and she stood beside Miss Jean's chair, her smile growing a little wistful as she waited for his coming. Miss Jean looked grave as she watched her.

"George," said his sister, laying her hand on Marion's and drawing her forward, "George, who is this? Have you forgotten our wee Maysie?"

No, that was not likely, he said; but he could scarcely have been more ceremoniously polite in his greeting had she been a strange young lady from London, and not the Marion whom he had petted and played with as a child. He lingered a moment beside her, asking about her mother, and if there had been any news from her brother, and then he went to his place at the table, and made himself busy with his duty there.

Something was said about the anticipated trip to the continent, and the time of setting out George had intended to leave at once if his sister were ready, but he found he must stay in Portie a few days longer.

"But next week, Jean, we must go, or give it up altogether."

"The sooner you go now, the better, or the best season will be over," said Mr Petrie.

"Oh! as to that, any season is good for what we mean to do."

"Still, the sooner the better. Could not I do what would be necessary to let you go at once?" said his father.

George laughed and shook his head.

"I am afraid not. It seems I stand pledged to be best man at Captain Saugster's marriage, and he has no idea of putting off the happy day for a month or more—since his time may be short. So he is to hasten it on instead, and I must wait and see him through it."

"That will hardly be fair on Annie," said Miss Jean.

"Oh! she is ready, I dare say; and she can finish her preparations afterwards," said Miss Petrie.

"And it is to be very quiet. Indeed, hardly a wedding at all in the usual sense," said George.

"But that is rather mean of Tam, I think," said Mr Petrie. "He ought to give a dance on board the 'John Seaton,' if he is to have the command of her."

His sisters were charmed with the idea. And would not Mr George put the thought into Tam's head?

"The 'John Seaton' is not in yet. He would hardly consent to wait for that," said Mr Scott.

"Don't you call it a risk, giving a man like Tam Saugster the command of a vessel like the 'John Seaton'?"

Mr Petrie asked the question not at George, but at his father.

"There is ay a risk of one kind or another about all seafaring matters," said Mr Dawson quietly.

"But there ought to be a fine wedding. Tam is quite a credit to the town now. We could all go to the dance," said Miss Annie Petrie.

"But I am afraid Tam would not long be a credit to the town if the whiskey were to flow as freely as it usually does at sailors' weddings. That could hardly be dispensed with, the whiskey, I mean. It would test Tam's principles at any rate, in which I cannot say I have very great faith," said James with a little sneer.

"I think keeping out of the way of temptation might be a better proof of his wisdom," said Mr Dawson coldly. "I doubt, Jean, your aunt is getting wearied. She should be allowed to go."

But Jean had long ago sent word to Nannie that her mistress was to stay at Saughleas for the night. The young people did not linger much longer. George went out with them to the gate, and did not return till the rest had gone upstairs. Nor did they see him in the morning. He had taken an early breakfast and gone away long before any one was down.

On each of the three days that passed before Jean and her brother went away, George went to his aunt's house as was his daily custom; but he scarcely saw Marion. The first day she had gone out, the next his father was with him, and the third time there were several of Marion's young companions with her, so that no word passed between them till the day of Tam Saugster's marriage.

"If marriage it could be called," said some of Tam's indignant friends, "going off on the sly as gin he were ashamed o' himsel'."

They were by no means ashamed of themselves. Tam and Annie went quietly to the manse with Tam's father and mother, where Miss Dawson and her brother and Marion Calderwood and Maggie and Robbie Saugster were waiting for them, and they "got it putten ower quaietly," as Tam's father rather discontentedly said. His judgment doubtless approved of "a teetotal" marriage in Tam's case, but neither his taste nor his sense of the fitness of things was satisfied. Who had a better right to feast their friends and "fill them fou" on such an occasion than the Saugsters? And to go back to Tam's house just to tea and jelly and fushionless sweet cakes!—It might be prudent, but it wasna pleasant, and any thing but creditable, in his father's opinion.

And while he grumbled secretly the bride's mother, poor Mrs Cairnie, openly resented and railed at the manner of the marriage as mean, and as a confession of most shameful weakness on Tam's part. Even shrewd and sensible Mrs Saugster, though joyful over her returned prodigal and thankful to escape the risks attending a marriage as usually ordered in their rank of life, even she did not think it wrong to connive at the brewing of a steaming bowl of "toddy" for the comforting of the old folks when Tam and his wife had set out on their week of pleasure, and all the rest of the young folk were gone away.

It was a "bonny nicht," Jean said, as they lingered in their walk down the street. Over the soft glow of sunset fading in the west hung the pale new moon, and a star showed here and there among the grey wreaths and flakes of cloud that floated far beneath the blue. The tide was out, and over the sands came the soft "lap, lap" of tiny waves, with a sound more restful than silence. They stood still a minute at the point where they were to turn into the High-street.

"We may as well go home the long way. It is not late yet," said Jean.

"Going home the long way," meant turning back, and going over the sands, the mile that lay between the town and the Tangle Stanes, and they turned with one accord.

"It is our last night for a while," said Jean, and scarcely another word was spoken till they found themselves climbing the broken path that led to the High Rocks. The night air blew cool from the sea, and Jean led the way to the sheltered seat a little further down. The two girls sat down together, and George stood above them with folded arms, looking out upon the sea.

They spoke about "the happy couple," who had gone away to begin their new life together, about Tam's long voyage and Annie's hopeful waiting, and the chances they had of happiness, because they loved one another. And then they went on to other things, some of them glad, and some of them sad, and "do you mind that time?" and "have you forgotten this?" they said, and sometimes they sighed, and sometimes they smiled, and at last they fell into silence. By and by Jean rose and moving upward, paced up and down the narrow ledge, as she had done so many a time before in so many a mood. The two who remained were silent still, busy with their own thoughts, till George, stooping down and speaking softly, said.

"Marion, do you mind one day coming here with—Elsie and me?"

"Ay, George, I mind it well."

Marion turned, and took in both hers the hand that he held out to her.

"Poor George!" said she, drooping her head till her cheek just touched it. Then she rose and stood beside him still holding his hand. George stood with his face turned away, and neither spoke or moved for a good while.

"George, do I mind you of her? Does it grieve you to see me?"

George turned and met the look in her sweet wistful eyes.

"You mind me of her, but it does not grieve me to see you—my dear little sister."

And then George did an unwise thing. He clasped and kissed her, and held her to him, "as I might have clasped and kissed my own sister," he said to himself afterward, trying to still the voice that said it was not wise.

And Marion went home smiling in the darkness, and saying to herself,—

"Now I have two brothers, and which of them I love best; I'm sure I canna say."

So George and Jean set out on their travels next day, and Miss Jean and her visitor were left to entertain one another, and they did not find it a difficult thing to do. Miss Jean had lived too much alone, to care even for pleasant company continually, and Marion had friends and engagements enough to call her away, so as to leave her to her solitude for a while each day. And whether she was out with her friends, or at home with Miss Jean, she was happy as the day was long.

They had many quiet hours together, when the wisdom which had come to the elder woman out of her sore troubles and solitary days which God had blessed, and out of willing service given to the needy and the suffering for His sake, was spoken for the good of the girl who had all her troubles and her solitary days before her. These were the hours that afterwards Marion liked best to remember.

It seemed a very happy world to her in those days. Nothing evil or sad seemed possible to her in her young strength and hopefulness. And even trouble itself, sickness or pain or disappointment, if it brought to her what had come through all these to Miss Jean—a heart at peace, a heavenly hope, surely even of these things she need not be afraid. When she said something like this to Miss Jean, her old friend smiled and answered,—

"Surely not. Even when you feel the pain you needna fear the evil. And when the pain hurts most—is worst to bear, I mean—it doesna really harm. Why should I fear for you?"

"And do you fear for me more than for the rest?" said Marion gravely.

"I ought to fear less for you than for some, because I hope ye're one who winna lose the good which is meant to come out of all trouble. But ye're young and bonny and winsome, and whiles troubles come to such that pass others by; and a heart both strong and tender, such troubles hurt sore.

But the sorer the pain the deeper and sweeter the peace, if it sends you to the feet of the Master," added Miss Jean cheerfully.

There was silence for a little while, and Miss Jean looked up with surprise at Marion's first words.

"Am I bonny, Miss Jean? As bonny as our Elsie was?"

Miss Jean looked at her a moment without speaking. Elsie Calderwood had indeed been a bonny lassie, but looking at her sister, Miss Jean could not but acknowledge that she was far more than that. She was like her sister. She had the same sweet eyes and lovely colour, the same wealth of shining hair. But in the face before her Miss Jean's discerning eye saw a beauty beyond that of mere form and colouring. It might have come to Elsie too, with cultivation, and a higher intelligence, and the wisdom that experience brings. But Miss Jean, remembering well the girl who was dead, saw in her living sister's face a beauty that had never been in Elsie's.

"Does your mother think ye're like your sister?" said she, evading the question.

"My mother hardly ever speaks about my sister. But once—some one said—that I minded him of her."

As she spoke, a feint, sweet colour overspread her face. Her eyes did not fall before the grave eyes of her old friend, but there came into them a soft, bright gleam, "like a glint o' sunshine on the sea," Miss Jean told herself as she gazed.

"Ay, ye're like her. I think them that mind her weel would say that ye're like her."

Marion's head drooped and rested on her hand.

"Whiles I wonder how it would have seemed if Elsie hadna died."

"It was a mysterious Providence indeed, her early death. The living should lay it to heart," said Miss Jean; and then she took up the book that lay at her hand—a sign that no more was to be said at that time.

Chapter Twenty Two.

Young Mr Petrie.

That night Mr Dawson came to invite them to pass a few days at Saughleas. He "wearied" there alone in the mornings and the long evenings, and there was no good reason why he should be alone, when they could come to visit him without leaving any one but Nannie to miss them. Nannie putting in her word, said she would not object to being left since the change would be good for them both.

"And as Mrs Petrie asked you for a few days, Marion, my dear, if you like you can go there instead."

"Oh! Miss Jean! If you please?"

Marion's face fell so decidedly that Mr Dawson laughed and insisted that Marion must come also, and Miss Jean had nothing to urge against it since both were pleased.

"Mrs Petrie is very kind, but she canna really care very much; and I see some of them every day," said Marion, fearing to appear ungrateful.

"Miss Jean will be all the better o' her company when ye're in the toon," said Nannie privately to Mr Dawson. "And as to thae Petrie's—we ha'e eneuch o' some o' them at a' conscience;" which was Marion's opinion also.

The days passed happily at Saughleas. Marion enjoyed the garden and the woods and fields, and every growing thing in them, as only they who have been long shut up in a dull house in a dull city street can do, and her delight in all that Saughleas had to offer was pleasant to see. Mr Dawson went to the town every day, but some days he did not stay there long, and Marion and he grew as friendly among the flowers and fields, as they had been among the wonderful sights of London during the first days of their acquaintance. The shyness which old associations had brought back since she came to Portie, passed quite away, and the frankness which had been her chief charm to the old man returned, and they took pleasure in each other's company.

"I'm going over to the brae to see a fine new plough that Mr Maclean has got. Have ye a mind for a walk, my lassie?" said Mr Dawson as they met one afternoon in the kitchen garden behind the house.

Marion had been longing for a walk and was delighted to go. There was a cold wind blowing from the sea, and she went to the house for a shawl, but came back in a minute with a clouded face.

"The Petrie's—at least young Mr Petrie is at the gate," said she.

"And ye would rather bide at home? Weel—"

"Oh! no! But if I go in for the shawl he will see me; and it is not so very cold."

"I doubt ye may find it some cold on the hill, but run ye away through the wood, and I'll ask Phemie for a wrap of some kind."

"And it winna be rude?—to Miss Jean, I mean—I'm no' caring for Jamie Petrie."

Mr Dawson laughed.

"He'll think the mair o' your company when ye come back," said he.

It was a successful afternoon on the whole. They walked quickly at first through the fields, but when they got over the hill, they took it leisurely. Then Mr Dawson said a word about young Mr Petrie's disappointment, and Marion looked grave.

"He is very kind—they are all very kind, and I am afraid you will think me ungrateful. Oh! yes, I like him well enough, but it was only the other night that he was at Miss Jean's—"

"And I dare say he will come back again."

"Oh! yes, I dare say he will. Oh! I like him well enough, but I get tired of him whiles."

"Well, never think about it."

"I'm no' caring for *him*. But I hope Miss Jean winna be ill-pleased."

"She needna ken that ye saw him," said Mr Dawson much amused.

Marion shook her head.

"I doubt I'll need to tell her."

"Nonsense! It was my fault. Ye would ha'e stayed if I had bidden you."

"Yes, that is true. And Miss Jean must see that I would far rather please you than Jamie Petrie."

"That's as may be, but for once in a way you may be excused."

Though they were away for a long time, they found Mr Petrie sitting with Miss Jean when they returned.

"Come awa'," said Miss Jean. "Where have ye been? and what can have keepit ye sae lang? Mr James and I have been wearyin' for our tea."

"Oh! well, ye'll enjoy it all the mair for that, and so will we," said Mr Dawson.

Marion went away to arrange her hair which the wind had blown about, and when she returned Mr Dawson was asking Mr James what news the afternoon's post had brought. But Mr James had left before the post came in.

"Then you must have been here a good while. It is a pity that ye hadna been in time to go with us. We went over to the brae to see the new plough that the farmer has gotten. Miss Marion explained the philosophy of the thing to us."

"Miss Marion is in some danger of becoming a learned woman, I hear," said Mr James, with an uncomfortable smile on his lips.

"In danger? Oh! weel, I dare say ye're right. I'm no' sure but there is danger in it. I canna say that I think very learned women are best fitted for the kind o' work that most commonly falls to a woman's hand."

"But for the work of a schoolmistress," said Marion eagerly. "I am going to be a schoolmistress,—not a governess, not a teacher in a school merely, but the mistress of a school."

"You mean if you cannot do better," said Mr Petrie. "Better? But that is what I have been thinking about all my life. My plans are all laid—only—"

"But then you could just let them all drop, if any thing *better* should present itself, as James says. But what are your plans? if it be fair to ask," said Mr Dawson. Marion did not laugh, but answered gravely, "First I must make 'a learned woman' of myself, and that will take a good while. I used to think I would have a young ladies' school, but I have changed my mind. Young ladies are troublesome, and I think I would prefer to teach boys."

Mr James whistled. Mr Dawson said, "Well, and what would you teach them?"

"Whatever they needed to learn. I can hardly tell yet about it. But Mrs Manners has promised me her boys."

"She is to lose no time it seems," said Miss Jean smiling.

"Oh! but you forget, I have to educate myself first. I am afraid I should have to be a great deal older before people would trust their boys to me. But that is what I mean to do." Marion spoke gravely.

"And ye'll do it too, if you set yourself to do it," said Mr Dawson.

"And she could hardly set herself to a better work," said Miss Jean.

But Mr Petrie by no means agreed with them, and expressed himself to that effect with sufficient decision. He ridiculed the idea, and being very much in earnest, he was not so guarded as he might have been, and allowed a tone of contempt to mingle with the banter which he meant to be playful, and at the same time severe. Marion answered lightly enough, and was in no danger of being angry as Miss Jean feared, and as, after a time, Mr James hoped she might be. The necessity of making his peace with her would have pleased the young man better, than her laughing indifference to his opinions, or to his manner of expressing them. But she was so friendly in her manner, and so willing to oblige him by singing his favourite songs when Miss Jean sent her to the piano, that he had no excuse for returning to the subject again.

His errand, he told them when he rose to go, was to ask Miss Marion to join his sisters and some of their friends in walking to the Castle the next day, and after an inquiring glance at Miss Jean the invitation was accepted with sufficient readiness.

"And if the day should not be fine, it is understood that you will spend it with my sisters, and the Castle can wait till fair weather."

To this also Marion assented with a good grace, and the young man went away assuring himself that he ought to be content. He might have been less so, had he seen the shrug of her pretty shoulders, and heard her voice as she said to Miss Jean,—

"What should the like of James Petrie ken?"

When she was gone for the night, Mr Dawson, laughing, told Miss Jean of the manner of their departure for the brae that afternoon. Miss Jean looked grave.

"Ye dinna mean to say that ye think the lassie did any thing out of the way?" said Mr Dawson. "She said she doubted she would need to tell you, though I'm sure I canna see why."

"I wasna thinking about that I was wondering whether after all, I had done a wise thing in bringing her down here."

"I have wondered at that myself, whiles, though I acknowledge I had a part in bringing her. But it depends on what ye brought her for."

Miss Jean said nothing.

"If it were to do young Petrie a pleasure, I think ye ha'e nothing to regret."

But Miss Jean shook her head.

"I'm no' so sure o' that," said she.

"As to how his father may be pleased, that is another matter."

To this Miss Jean made no answer.

"And if I mind right, ye once thought Jamie Petrie would ha'e little temptation to look that way, and little chance of success if he did."

"That is just what I thought, but I was wrong it seems as to the temptation. As to the success—I canna say, but—"

"But why should you be downcast about it?"

"It is for the lad I am sorry, because I doubt he has disappointment before him. He should have been content to bide awhile. She is but a lassie, with no such thoughts in her mind."

"She looks like a woman."

"Ay, she does that. But she is but a bairn in some things. She is no' thinkin' o' him. She doesna even amuse herself with him. He is just Jamie Petrie to her, and that is all. I'm wae for the lad."

"His father and mother will be all the better pleased."

"That may be, but I dinna think it."

Then Miss Jean told in few words a story to which Mr Dawson listened with varying feelings,—the story of James Petrie's love and what was like to come of it.

He had seen her in London about six months since, Miss Jean said, and had made his admiration very evident to the mother whose surprise was great; for like the rest of the world she had given him credit for a degree of worldly wisdom greater than a serious attachment to a penniless girl would seem to imply. He made no formal declaration of his suit, to which indeed Mrs Calderwood would not have listened, as Marion was in her eyes little more than a child. In her heart she believed and hoped that his fancy would pass away, or be put by prudent thoughts out of his head, without a word spoken.

For she did not want him for her daughter. He was a rich man's son, and would be a rich man himself one day. By years of steady attention to business, and by exemplary conduct generally, he had proved himself worthy of a certain confidence and respect. But whatever other people might think of him, he was not in the opinion of Mrs Calderwood worthy to have as his wife her beautiful and intelligent Marion, and she determined that he should not speak if she could prevent him.

Marion was pleased when he came, and liked him as she liked all the rest of the folk of Portie, who had been kind to her all her life, liking them all the more that she had left them, and saw little of them. Her mother feared that, flattered by his admiration, she might fancy it was more than liking that she felt for him, and that should he ask her to become his wife, she might accept him, and repent it all her life as many another woman has done. She must hear nothing of this till she was old enough to know her own mind about it, and wise enough to make no such terrible mistake.

But by and by, when there came friendly advances from the father and mother, showing that they were aware of their son's feelings and intentions, and at least did not disapprove of them, Mrs Calderwood was much moved. Marion might at feast hope for a kindly welcome among the Petries. She was not sure that she was right in wishing that nothing might come of it.

There was another view to be taken of the matter. Her own health was by no means firm, and she had no expectation of living many years. Her son in his profession could hardly hope to give a home to his sister for years to come, nor could he give her personal care and guardianship should she be left alone. It was well enough for Marion to talk about making herself independent by keeping a school. Her mother had given her every chance to prepare herself for it, if such was to be the work of her life. But the girl was too young and too pretty to be fit for any such position for years to come, and the mother's heart shrank from the thought of the struggle and the weariness that even in the most favourable circumstances such a life must bring to her child.

Was it right for her to hesitate when a home among her own people was opened to her? Might she not live a quiet and happy life, beloved and safe from the manifold difficulties and dangers that beset even the most successful women, making their own way in the world? A word of encouragement from her would make the young man speak, but whether to give it or withhold it she could not decide.

In the discomfort of her indecision she sought counsel of Miss Jean. But what could Miss Jean say but just what she had said to herself, that it must depend on Marion's own feeling whether such a word should be spoken.

Out of this had come Miss Jean's desire to bring Marion to Portie for a little while. The girl would learn to know the young man with so many pleasant chances of intercourse, as she never could do in his brief and infrequent visits to London, and she would also come to a better understanding of her own feelings with regard to him. It is likely that Mrs Calderwood understood her motive and intention, though no word passed between them with regard to it. All this Miss Jean told in as few words as might be to her brother. "I doubt it hasna answered," added she. "Such plans seldom answer. But why should you take it to heart. They maun please themselves," said Mr Dawson impatiently. "I acknowledge I am surprised that old Petrie should pitch on a penniless lass for his son. It is nae what I should ha'e expected of him, and I ken him weel."

"He didna pitch on her, I doubt it is but making the best of a bad matter, with him. Mrs Petrie was ay fond o' Marion, and she is a peacemaker. And James is as determined as his father and not altogether dependent on him. And the old man has the sense to see that his son must judge for himself. And any thing is better than dispeace in a family. And now that he has seen her again, the father likes Marion."

"And are ye satisfied that such a marriage would be the wisest thing for her? James Petrie is a good business man, capable and honest. But when ye ha'e said that, it's a' there is to say. As for her—ye ken best about her."

"There are few like her, and there are plenty like him. But if they loved one another, that would make them equal in a sense, and they might live happily enough. But she's no' thinkin' about him."

"But why should you vex yoursel' about it."

"I doubt I was wrong to bring her. And I'm sorry for the young man."

"Oh! as to that, he'll win over it, as he has done before. There is no fear."

But Miss Jean still looked grave and troubled. "That was different. Our Jean was the most beautiful woman and the best match in the town, and no doubt he believed that he was in love with her, but this is different; and it will do him harm, I fear."

"Well, I canna see that you are needing to make yourself responsible for Jamie Petrie's well-being, if that is all."

But that was not all. Miss Jean had anxious thoughts about others besides James Petrie. Her anxiety she could not share with her brother however, and she said no more.

Nor was Mr Dawson more inclined to carry on the conversation. The pain of past years was sharply stirring within him, though even his sister did not guess it from his words or his manner. Indeed he hardly knew it himself, till they fell into silence; but that night his head pressed a wakeful pillow, and the ghosts of old troubles came back upon him.

How vividly it came back to him, all that he had suffered in those nights long ago when he could not sleep for the pain and the anger and the utter disappointment in his hopes for his son! In those nights he had sometimes had a doubt whether he had wrought wisely toward the desired end, but he had never doubted as to the wisdom of that end—till to-night.

Was John Petrie, whose judgment when exercised beyond the even routine of business, he had never highly valued—was John Petrie showing himself wiser in yielding to the wishes of his son, than he had been in resisting the wishes of his?

What an influence for good in a man's life must be the love of such a girl as Marion Calderwood. Had bonny Elsie been one like her? Remembering the sweet, calm eyes of the girl so long dead and gone, the gentle strength, the patient firmness by which she withstood not him alone, but her own mother whom she loved, rather than break her promise to the lad who loved her, he could not but doubt whether he had judged wisely then, and whether he had afterward dealt wisely with his son.

Ah, well! That was all past now, and good had come out of it to George. But would he ever forget? Would there ever come to his son's home in future years one who would be to him all that Mary Keith had been to him. "He has not forgotten her," he said to himself, remembering his pale looks when first his eyes fell on Elsie's sister. But he was young yet, scarce five and twenty, and his life was before him, and all might be well. At any rate nothing could be changed now.

He had a troubled, restless night, and the first sight he saw when he looked out in the early morning was Marion walking up and down among the flowers. She was walking slowly, with a graver and more thoughtful face than she was used to wear in his presence. She saw the beautiful things around her, for she stooped now and then over a flower as she passed, and touched tenderly the shining leaves as she bent her head beneath the overhanging branches. But she was evidently thinking of other things, and paused now and then looking out upon the sea.

"A strong, fair woman," he said. "She will make a man of James Petrie, if there's stuff enough in him to work on—which I doubt. If they love one another—that is the chief thing, as Jean says, and the folk that ken them both will mostly think that she has done well."

Miss Jean went in to Portie that day, having her own special work to attend to there, and it was understood that for this time the visit at Saughleas was over.

Marion went to the Castle with the rest, but she did not go with them to Mr Petrie's house to pass the evening. She came straight to Miss Jean's, having Mr James Petrie as her escort, and it so happened that Mr Dawson met them both on their way thither.

"Something has come to her since morning," he thought as he watched her approaching.

She was walking rapidly and steadily, carrying her head high and looking straight before her, with the air of being occupied with her own thoughts, rather than with Mr Petrie's eager, smiling talk.

"I'll hear about it from Jean," said Mr Dawson to himself, with a feeling of discomfort which he did not care to analyse.

But he heard nothing from Miss Jean. If she had any thing to tell, it could not be that which he had at first expected to hear. For young Mr Petrie, whom he saw as he saw him every day, did not carry himself like a triumphant lover, neither did he look downcast, as though he had met with a rebuff. He was just as usual, seemingly content with himself and with the world generally.

"I dare say it was but my own imagination," said the old man, wondering a little that he thought about it at all.

He did not see Marion the next day when he called at Miss Jean's house, nor the next, nor for several days, and friendly though they had become, he still felt a certain disinclination to ask Miss Jean about her. He caught a glimpse of her on the third morning as he was coming down the High-street, but she turned toward the shore before he came near. She had not seen him, he thought.

When he did see her at last, sitting sedately, her eyes and her hands occupied with her work in Miss Jean's parlour, the same thought came into his mind.

"Something has happened to her. Some one has been saying something to vex her, whatever it may be. But young lasses are whiles easily vexed."

The next time that Miss Jean was asked to spend a day at Saughleas, it rained heavily, and she could not go, and when she was asked again, Marion was engaged to go somewhere else, and Miss Jean went alone.

"Oh! ay, she is quite right to please hersel'," said Mr Dawson coldly, when Miss Jean explained that it was necessary that she should go and visit Miss Spence that day, because the visit had been put off more than once before.

"Miss Spence was a friend of her mother lang syne," said Miss Jean.

Mr Dawson did not ask, as he had meant to do, what had happened to vex the girl, though he guessed from Miss Jean's manner, that whatever happened, it was known to her.

Chapter Twenty Three.

Danger and Reconciliation.

It had been arranged that Mrs Manners and her children should return with George and Jean for a visit, but when the time came it was decided that it was too late in the season for the northern journey, and in order to make amends to the sisters for their disappointment, it was proposed that George should go home alone, and that the sisters should spend a few weeks together at the seaside.

Jean hesitated long, before yielding to her sister's entreaties, though she acknowledged she had no reason for refusing the pleasure, since it had been proposed by her father, and since her aunt was well, and nothing had happened to make it necessary to go home. She yielded at last, however, and George went home without her.

He did not go alone. He had spent many words in trying to persuade Willie Calderwood, who had just come to London for a day or two, to go with him; and at the last moment Willie decided that it was possible for him to go for a single day, to bring his sister home. It might be long before he would see her again, for his next voyage was to be a long one.

In a week he was to sail for Australia, not as commander of the vessel this time, but if all went well, he had the hope of making his second voyage as commander of a fine new ship that was to be ready for him by the time his present engagement came to an end. He had been fortunate, during one of his Atlantic voyages, in coming under the notice of a great merchant and ship-owner, who was capable of appreciating his high qualities as a sailor and as a man. The offer of a ship was made by him and accepted by Willie, and now he could with certainty look forward to a successful career in the profession he had chosen.

They reached Portie only just in time, they were told, for the "John Seaton" was to sail that very day, and it would have been hard indeed if Captain Saugster should have missed the sight of his friends. They were hardly in time for speech. The ship was to sail at noon, and the new skipper was busy with a thousand things, and had only time for a word, and a grip of the hand when they went on board.

They walked about, and lingered here and there, and had something to say to most of the ship's company as well as to the skipper, and Mr Dawson grew soft-hearted as he watched the friendly looks that met his son wherever he turned. George had a word for most of them, a promise to one, a caution to another, a joke with a third, a kind word to all.

"Ye're no' to vex yourself about your mother and the bairns, Sandy. Miss Dawson will see that they are cared for if the sickness should come again. Donald, man, be thankful that ye're leaving your temptation behind ye, and that ye're to sail under the temperance flag this time. Gather strength to withstand your foe, by the time ye come home again. I suppose we must call ye a man now, Jack. Dinna forget the mother and grannie. They winna forget you."

Mr Dawson kept near his son when he could do so without too evidently appearing to be listening to him, and he heard all with mingled feelings. George's way had never been his, and it was only a qualified approval that he had been brought to give to his son's method of dealing with the men, but he could not but be pleased and proud at the many tokens of respect and affection with which he was regarded by them all. Even the strangers among them turned pleased looks to the young man, as he moved up and down among them.

"It is a pity but you had come sooner, that you might have had a longer time on board," said Mr Dawson, as he took his way to Miss Jean's house in company with the two young men. "Ye might almost take an hour or two's sail with them and land at F— or C— and be home to-night, or early in the morning."

Before twenty-four hours were over he would have given much that he had not uttered the words. But George and his friend caught at the idea, and before they went into the house all arrangements for going with Captain Saugster for a few hours' sail were made. Miss Jean looked grave when the plan was spoken of, but she said nothing in the hearing of her brother.

"Ye winna bide awa' long, and make us anxious," said she.

They must not stay long, for Willie had but a single day, or at most two to see all the folk he wanted to see in Portie, and they would be certainly home early in the morning. There was no time to discuss or even to consider the matter. Willie had only a word or two with his sister, but he followed every movement of hers with glad, proud eyes; and when she went for a moment out of the room, he said softly to Miss Jean, "She has grown a woman now, our wee Maysie."

And Miss Jean said as softly and a little sadly, "Ay, has she!"

Did George's eyes follow her too? His father could not but think so.

"For the sake of the girl who is dead," he said to himself with a pang.

Marion's eyes were only for her brother, but she had few words even for him. They had little time for words. They bade Miss Jean and Marion "good-bye" in the house. By and by, Mr Dawson saw Marion standing a little apart from the group of women gathered on the pier, but when he looked again she was no longer to be seen. He was a little disappointed. He thought if they had walked up to his sister's house together, he might have said a word to dispel the cloud of shyness or vexation that had somehow come between them since the day she had gone with the Petries to the Castle.

He would not make much of it, by speaking about it openly, nor could he bring himself to ask his sister about it. Miss Jean was not easy to approach on the subject of the Calderwoods. She had never said one word to anger him at the time when she had thought him hard and unreasonable with regard to them, and neither had she noticed by word or look the interest with which he had come to regard her young visitor; and her silence made it all the more difficult for him to speak. But when he went in on his way home, as it drew towards gloaming, and found her sitting alone in her darkening parlour, he asked her why she did not have lights brought in, and where was her visitor.

"Marion went over to the Tangle Stanes with the skipper's wife and Maggie, and I dare say she has gone hame with her. Her troubles are begun, puir body—Annie Saugster's—I mean."

"What should ail her? She has just the troubles that ay maun fa' on sailors' wives."

"Ay, just that," said Miss Jean.

"And she kenned them a' beforehand. And what gude could a lassie like that do her? She has had small experience o' trouble anyway."

"She has a tender heart—and she shows her sympathy without many words. And folk like her," said Miss Jean. There was a moment's silence, and then Mr Dawson said hesitating,—

"What ails her this while? Is it only as her brother says, that she is growing a woman, that she is so quiet? Or has any thing happened to vex her? I have hardly got a word from her since she left Saughleas. Is it James Petrie that's to blame?" added he with a laugh.

Miss Jean regarded him gravely for a minute.

"Yes, I think it was something he said. I ken it was, for she told me."

"And did she give him his answer?"

Miss Jean shook her head.

"It's no' what ye're thinkin'. That question hasna been asked yet," said she. "And I doubt he'll need to put it off, for a while. He didna help his ain cause by what he said, though he meant it for that. He was telling her about—about George and her sister Elsie."

Mr Dawson said nothing in the pause which followed.

"Of course she had heard something,—that they cared for one another,—and that George's heart was nearly broken when Elsie died. But she had never heard of your displeasure, nor of some other things. Though how he thought it would help him to tell all this to her, I canna tell—unless he may be afraid that—But she is to go hame with her brother, it seems, and I hope that no ill may come o' my bringing her here."

"Nonsense, Jean! What ill should come of it? And why should you take the blame of it? It was her mother's doing, sending her here. And if it should end in her agreeing with James Petrie, ye may be sure she will be well pleased."

"I'm no' sure. Though, puir body! she maybe was thinking o' that too."

"It is to be supposed that she kens her ain mind about it. James Petrie will be a rich man some day. Doubtless she thinks of that."

"Less than ye would suppose. But she is not a strong woman, and if any thing were to happen to her, the lassie would be left alone almost. She would be safe here among douce, well-doing folk, like the Petries, and in time she might be content enough."

"But how should he think to help his cause by—by telling that tale? And what kens he about it?"

"He kens just what other folk ken, and guesses something, I dare say. He thought to help his wishes by letting her ken, that when George looked kindly at her it was for her sister's sake."

"George!" repeated Mr Dawson in dismay. Miss Jean had not been betrayed into saying this, though that was her brother's first thought.

"Yes. She is like her sister—and he hasna forgotten *her*. But I think it was chiefly your anger and vexation that he held up to her—as against his own father's kindness."

"But George?" repeated Mr Dawson. "Yes. But it is not George I am thinking about, but Marion. And her mother too. Do ye ken that though he has ay gone to see Mrs Calderwood whenever he has been in London, George had never seen her daughter after the time of May's marriage till he saw her the ither night at Saughleas? That was her mother's will. What with one thing and another,—his love for her sister, and his friendship for her brother, and his being lost from hame so long—the lassie was ay inclined to make a hero of George. And minding on Elsie, and all she had suffered, the mother grew to have a fear that was unreasonable, lest Marion should come to care for him beyond what should be wise. So she kept her out of his sight, and she would never have let her come north but that she knew George was going away. She may have had her ain thoughts of young Mr Petrie—as I had myself, since he showed that he had the sense to see her value."

It was some time before another word was spoken, then Mr Dawson said,—

"I did but what I thought my duty. I did but what her mother was as keen to do as I was. I tried to prevent my son from doing a foolish thing. And I dare say she thinks that I killed her sister."

"No, it is not that. But ye ha'e ay been kind to her, and she thinks the sight of her must give you pain, and she is not at her ease. And so she is unhappy, for she has a grateful nature. Well, she will soon be away now, and whether she'll come back again with young Mr Petrie—I canna say. He'll hardly have the courage to ask her this time."

"I wouldna promise. There are few things that seem to him to be beyond his deserts—though I canna say I'm of his opinion."

Miss Jean knew that her brother was angry and that he was trying to restrain himself as he rose to go.

"A thoughtless word does great ill whiles, but I doubt this has done most ill to his ain cause, if he but kenned it. And it is a pity—" added Miss Jean.

"He'll get through it. It winna be the first time," said Mr Dawson angrily.

"Are ye awa'? I think we need hardly expect those lads till morning. They'll be enjoying the sail this bonny nicht," said Miss Jean.

"It depends on several things—the light and the tide and the wind. It was rather a foolish thing to undertake, though it was myself who first spoke of it. But we needna expect them till we see them."

And then he went away. He paused a little when he was outside the door, looking up into the sky, and over the sea, thinking whether he might not as well wait a while, rather than go home alone. It was not so fine a night as Miss Jean had supposed, nor as it had promised to be earlier. There were heavy banks of clouds on the horizon in two directions, and the moon which showed faintly through a dull haze, had a heavy ring around her and not very far away—sure token that a storm was near.

"They ken the signs better than I do. They'll lose no time."

He lingered still, going as far as the pier head which was not yet quite deserted; but he turned his face homeward at last.

"It will be a long night, I doubt!"

And so it was. Many a look he cast to the sky, which before midnight grew like lead, showing neither moon nor star. A long and heavy night it was. Sleeping or waking, it was the same; dark with fears, vague and unreasonable, which he could not put away—with painful dreams, and startled wakenings, and longings for the day which came at last—a dismal day, with a dull grey mist lying low on land and sea, darkening all things.

It brightened a little as the morning advanced, but he did not hasten early to the town. There was no real cause for anxiety he assured himself, the fog would account for their delay. They would be home soon. He was not anxious, but he shrank from the thought of the pier head and all the folk looking out for them and wondering where they were and when they would be home. And so it was noon before he called at his sister's door to assure her that there was really no cause for alarm. The fog would account for the long delay. There might have been danger to folk not so well acquainted with every nook and headland and current along the shore, but there could hardly be danger to these two.

What a long day it was! And when the gloaming began to fall, there was still no word of them. He went on to Miss Jean's house, and at the door Marion met him. He got a good look of her face this time. Whatever had grieved or angered her, was not in her thoughts now. Her eyes asked eagerly for tidings.

"No word o' them yet, but they canna be long now," said Mr Dawson cheerfully. "I have come to ask you for a cup of tea, though I dare say ye have had yours lang syne. Ye maunna be anxious, my dear. There is really no cause to fear for them as yet."

He had been saying this to himself all day, but his heart was growing sick with anxiety all the same, and though he could hide it from Marion, he knew that he could not hide it from his sister.

"We maun just ha'e patience," was all that Miss Jean said.

Marion prepared the tea herself, and went out and in and did what was to be done. She made his tea and served him as though she liked to do it, and his eyes followed her with an interest which for the moment half beguiled him from the remembrance of his fears. But there was not much said between them, and by and by he said he would step down to the pier head and take a look at the weather before it was quite dark. Marion looked as if she would like to go too, and all the old anxiety was in her eyes, as she turned them to Miss Jean.

"My dear lassie," said her old friend, "they are safe in God's hands."

"Yes, they would be safe there, even if we were never to see them again. But O, Miss Jean!—"

"Ay, lassie! Try ye and measure the blessedness o' that knowledge. It is no' in the power o' evil to harm them, whatever may befall. And, my dear, we have no reason to doubt that we shall see them again. They may be in at any moment, as my brother says."

"I might licht the lamp, mem," said Nannie at the door.

"There is no haste," said Miss Jean.

"Only its e'erie like sitting in the dark when folk ha'e anxious thoughts for company. Though there's no occasion as yet. What's a day and a nicht! Many a boat has come hame safe eneuch after many days and nichts. They may be in at any minute, and I maun keep the kettle boiling, for they'll be baith cauld and hungry."

Then Nannie retreated to her kitchen, doubtful as to the comfort she could give since her own fears were so strong.

Mr Dawson went to the pier head, but he did not linger long, he turned and wandered up and down the sands in the gathering darkness. The fears which he had refused to acknowledge during the day, he could no longer put away from him. The sickness of the heart with which he had slept and waked so many a night and morning in past years, came back again, strange yet familiar. Was it never to leave him more? Was the time coming when the happiness of the last two years would seem to him like a dream?

How many fathers had wandered up and down Portie sands, waiting for sons who had never returned! Who was he that he should escape what so many a better man had endured?

But it had not come to that with him yet. Surely God would be merciful to him, and spare so good a man as George to do His own work in the world. He was afraid to be angry, afraid to utter the rebellious words that rose to his lips, lest God should judge him for them.

"I am losing myself, I think," said he, making a strong effort to restrain his thoughts. "I may as well go back to Jean, or to the pier head."

No, he could not go to the pier head, to listen to words made hopeful for his hearing,—to see cheerful looks that would grow pitiful as soon as his face was turned away. And as for Jean—

Well, she was doubtless praying for the lad whom she loved scarcely less than he. But he was not ready for Jean yet Jean had a way of thinking her prayers answered whatever befell. If George never were to come home, it would not come into Jean's mind that God had turned a deaf ear to her cry. She would say that her prayers had doubtless been answered in a better way than she could see. That had ay been her way all her life.

"But as for me—when a time like this comes, I canna be sure. It's like putting out my hands in the darkness, never knowing that there is aught to meet their helplessness."

That had been the way when he saw death drawing near to his dear children and their dearer mother. No voice had answered, no help had come. They had gone down to the darkness of the grave, and he had been left in deeper darkness, never knowing whether the merciful God in whom Jean trusted had given a thought to him through it all.

He had gone far by this time, and he turned to avoid meeting some of the townspeople who were out on the sands waiting for tidings as well as he. The clouds were lifting, and as he turned he felt the west wind in his face, and heard a voice say,—

"If it has been the fog that has keepit them, they'll soon be in now, for it will be a clear nicht, and Willie Calderwood kens ilka neuk and ilka rock on the coast for miles. They'll soon be in now, if the fog is all that has keepit them."

"What could ha'e keepit them but the fog?" said a woman's voice. "Ye speak as if ye werena expectin' them."

"I'm no' sayin'. Only if it's the fog, they'll soon be in now."

Mr Dawson moved on lest he should hear more. Of course they would be home now, since the fog was lifting. What should hinder them? But he had a bad half hour and more as he moved up and down keeping out of the way of the groups, whose voices came to him through the darkness.

As he waited there came to him a sudden clear remembrance of Willie Calderwood's face when he came that night with tidings of his son. Oh! the joy of it! Had he not been grateful to God for His goodness then. Was there any thing which he possessed that he would have grudged as a thank-offering that night! God did seem near to him then.

"I had an inkling that night of what Jean may mean when she speaks o' the blessedness o' them that rest themselves on God."

But as to grudging! He was not so sure. Even before he saw his son, had he not been afraid lest, being "a changed man," as his friend had called him, George might have other aims and other plans of life than he had for him, and disappoint him after all? True he had hated himself for the thought, but it had been there that first night. And afterwards he had looked on with something like anger, as day by day he had seen him giving ten thoughts to the helping of others in their cares and their troubles, where he did not give one to the winning the place and the honour that his father coveted for him among men.

That had all passed away long ago; not, however, because he had ceased to grudge, but because, as the father put it, "it had answered well." George stood higher to-night in the respect and esteem of those who knew him, than he would have done had his aims and plans and expectations been those of his father, who saw all things too clearly not to acknowledge it.

George was a man among a thousand, he said to himself with a little movement of exultation, half forgetting his fears, till the wind, as he turned again, dashed the heavy drops of another shower in his face, and he saw that the clouds had gathered close again over all the sky. Unless they had already landed, the fog and the darkness which had kept them last night might keep them still. How could he bear another night of such suspense?

Another night! It might be days and nights, for all that he could tell. He turned with a sinking heart towards the town again.

"O! Geordie! Oh! my son!"

He did not know that he spoke the words aloud, but they were heard, and a hand was laid on his in the darkness.

"Miss Jean thinks you should come into the house, for you must be cold and wet," said Marion Calderwood. "Winna ye come with me, Mr Dawson? And, dear sir, there has been word of a boat that landed in the gloaming at C— Only John Fife, who brought the word, hadna heard that there were any fears for any one, and he came away without asking any questions. But it is sure to be them. And, Mr Dawson, winna ye come with me to Miss Jean?"

He had eaten little all day, and he was weary with his long wanderings up and down the sands. He scarcely caught the meaning of her words, but he knew that she was saying something hopeful, and he frankly grasped the hand she had laid on his.

"Ay. We'll gang in to Jean," said he.

He leaned on her strong young arm more heavily than he knew as they drew near the house. There was light streaming from the windows and from the open door, but before they reached it a voice said cheerily,—

"All's weel, Mr Dawson. They're coming hame safe enough."

"Glad tidings of great joy." That was what came into Marion's mind when she heard the words.

They had come already. At Miss Jean's door Marion was clasped in the arms of her brother, and George wrung his father's hand and brought him in to the light.

"The Lord is ay kind, George," said Miss Jean.

But Mr Dawson said nothing. He was too deeply moved for words for a little while, and indeed so were they all.

Nannie, notwithstanding her fears, had made great preparations for the entertainment of the wanderers, and though it might have been wiser for George and Mr Dawson to go home at once, there was no time to decide the matter before the supper was on the table, and they all sat down together. Afterwards they were glad of this, for Mr Dawson did not see either Marion or her brother again before they went away, and George only saw them for a moment, just as they were setting out.

They lingered a good while at the table, though even Willie owned himself tired enough to wish to rest. They had been in no special danger. The misfortune was that the small compass, to which they were to trust should the night be foggy and the stars invisible, had been left in the ship in the pocket of George's coat, and so they had had no means of directing their course during the night, and indeed as little during the day. They had been farther out at sea than they supposed, and when, as day began to decline, they got a glimpse of the sun they had to row hard to get sight of land before the darkness fell.

"And I canna say that I am proud o' mysel' on this occasion," said Willie laughing.

"But except for the fright that we have given you all, I canna say that I shall ever regret the day and the night we have been on the deep," he added after a moment. George said nothing, but his eyes and his smile assented to the words of his friend.

The brother and sister had many people to see and many things to do during the day that remained, so it happened that neither George nor Mr Dawson saw them when they called next day at Miss Jean's, and George only saw them a moment at the station as they were going away. There were a good many other people there to see them off as well as he. James Petrie was there, looking a little anxious and uncertain, and not so ready with just the right word to say, as he generally supposed himself to be. His sisters were there also, and some other of Marion's friends, and she was monopolised by them during the two or three minutes that remained after George came.

And it was Willie that George came to see, they thought. For he stood with his hand on his friend's shoulder, and the face of each was grave enough as they said their last words to one another.

But George got the last touch of Marion's hand, and the last glance of her sweet eyes, and the last words which Marion heard, George spoke, and they were words that she had heard him say before—

"My dear little sister."

Mr Dawson had to wait a good while for the return of his son that night, and he watched him rather anxiously from the window when at last he came in sight George moved slowly, with a graver face than usual, and though his eyes were wandering over the pleasant green of the lawn and gardens, his father knew that his thoughts were not with his eyes.

"How little I am in his life besides what he is in mine!" thought the old man with a sigh. "But so it ay maun be between father and son, and he is a good son to me—a good son. And it's no' for what I have to give him," added he with a sudden movement of both pleasure and pain at his heart. "Though bonny Saughleas were in other hands, and all my gold and gear were swept into the sea, he would be sorry doubtless, but he would be a good son still. And he would not be unhappy, for his portion—that which he has chosen for himself in life would still remain to him."

The old man's heart grew soft and a little sad, but he spoke just as usual when George came in. "Ye're late the nicht."

"Yes. I went round by the station to see the Calderwoods off. And I think I have taken longer time than usual for the walk home. I must be tired, I suppose."

"And no wonder. And so they are gone. And was nothing said about their coming back to Portie again?"

"No. There was time for few words, and there were other people there to see them off—the Petries, and Maggie Saugster, and some others."

"Was James Petrie there? Then his answer has been to his mind, or maybe he hasna asked the question. I dare say he was as wise."

To this George made no reply whether he understood or not, and in a little he left the room. But his father's first words went back to the same subject.

"It is no' so unwise a thing in James Petrie as it looks, because—"

"His wisdom has to be proved," said George gravely. And then he held out a letter to his father.

"I don't believe in bringing business to Saughleas, as a rule, but I thought it as well to let you see this to-night."

His father took it and read it. It was a business letter—important, but still it might have waited till morning.

"It is because he doesna wish to hear about James Petrie and his hopes. It is of her sister dead and gone that he is thinking," said his father with a sigh. "His is a true and tender heart, and oh! I wish that I could do him a pleasure." Suddenly there returned to him the thought that had been with him during his long wanderings over the wet sands that weary time of waiting.

"There is nothing which I possessed, that I would not have given for a thank-offering that night. And there is nothing that I would not give now."

And when George came into the room after a long hour or two, his father was pondering the same matter still.

In a few days Mr Dawson declared that it was quite time that Jean were coming home, and to the surprise of his sister and his son he announced his intention of going to fetch her.

For in the opinion of both, and certainly in her own opinion, Jean was quite able to take care of herself, whether in the house or by the way, and there was no need of his going for her sake. But he went, and stayed a few days, and they came home together. Jean had no light to throw on his motive for the journey, for he had never intimated that he thought she needed his escort home.

But in a few days there came a letter from Mrs Manners to her aunt which said,—

"The strangest thing happened when my father was in London. He went to see Mrs Calderwood, with whom he had not exchanged words for years. Marion was with me, so it was not she that he went to see. And her mother never told her what he had to say. He only left a small parcel which her mother was to give her when she came home. It turned out to be an exquisite little gold watch. Mrs Calderwood would have refused so valuable a gift for her daughter, if she had known it, which would have been very absurd, as I told Marion. For what is a few pounds more or less to my father. But I would give my own watch and chain too, to know just what was said between them.

"I have written all this to you, auntie, because my father whiles reads Jean's letters, and he might not be pleased that I have told it. But if you think it wise, you may tell George; I am sure he will be glad to hear it. And as for Marion—I do not wonder that she has stolen my father's heart in spite of him."

Mrs Manners would have paid dear for a knowledge of all that passed. In one way it was very little.

Mr Dawson sent in his name and waited in the drawing-room, and Mrs Calderwood came in a little with a smile on her lips, expecting to see George.

"I have come to say, 'let by-ganes be by-ganes' between us. If you can forgive all that is past, give me your hand."

He spoke almost harshly as his manner was when moved, but he spoke sincerely and even eagerly, and Mrs Calderwood could hardly have refused her hand, even if she had not long ago forgiven him, as she herself hoped to be forgiven.

"I have never borne ill-will, Mr Dawson," said she.

"No. And now I see it might have been different if I had been wiser. But—I was hardly myself in those days. He was my only son—and—I had lost his mother—"

He suddenly turned his back upon her and strode to the window, and stood long looking out into the darkening street. His face was quiet enough when he turned toward her again.

"The least said the soonest mended," said he; "if you will let by-ganes be by-ganes, as I said before. I have had many thoughts since I—well this while—and the other night when they were in danger together—your son and mine—I got a glimpse of what should be. They are true friends, these two; and surely there is no reason why we should be other than friends also."

Mrs Calderwood was a woman not easily moved. If he had given her time to think about it, if he had written to her, as he at first thought of doing, she would not have refused to meet his advances, but she might have met them less cordially. But when this man, whom she had long thought of as a hard man, turned a moved face towards her, and speaking with a softened voice held out his hand again, what could she do but put hers within it with some gently spoken word of kindness.

And that was all. Mr Dawson did not even sit down. He did not name Marion till he put the little packet in her mother's hand, and he did not return to see her again, though when he went away he meant to do so; and no one ever knew from him that he had been there.

But even before their sister's letter came, both George and Jean knew that in some way, not easy to name, a change had come over their father. When one day they were together in their aunt's house and she gave them their sister's letter to read, they understood that something which had burdened his conscience and embittered his temper had been cast off forever; but they never spoke of it to each other after they left their aunt's presence, and she never spoke of it to them.

But she saw, as other folk did, that in their father's company a new gentleness of word and manner made itself visible in them both, and she also saw what others could not see, that with this new gentleness George's face grew brighter, but on the face of Jean a shade of sadness fell.

Chapter Twenty Four.

Another Home.

"Weel! weel! If the marriage is wi' auld Mr Dawson's free consent, then the Ethiopian can change his skin, and that would be makin' the Bible out nae true. It's little ye ken! He's nae a man to change like that."

It was Mrs Cairnie who spoke, sitting at her daughter's door, with her crutch at her side. Young Mrs Saugster was sitting inside with her baby on her lap, and her mother-in-law and Maggie, busy with her seam, were with her.

"But Mr Dawson went to the marriage himself, and he wouldna ha'e gone but o' his ain free will," said Maggie as no one else answered.

"There's nae sayin'. Young George has the tow in his ain hand. It's as he says now, I doubt, about maist things."

"But he could hardly have wished the auld man to go against his will. And indeed Mr Dawson gets the credit o' makin' the marriage himsel', though that's likely going beyond the truth," said old Mrs Saugster. "But what I wonder at is Mrs Calderwood. She is a quait woman, but she is as stiff in her way, and as proud as ever Mr Dawson was; and though she said little at the time, she carried a sair heart and angry, for many a day after she lost her Elsie."

"Folk change," said her daughter-in-law. "Ay. And it's wonderfu' what folk can outlive."

"Mrs Calderwood!" repeated Mrs Cairnie. "What about her! It's a grand marriage for the like o' her dochter, no' to say that she has gotten her triumph ower auld George at last. It's weel to be her."

"It is all like a tale in a book. Somebody should make a ballad about it," said Maggie. "It's no' often that we see a thing comin' to the right end, as this ha'e done."

"The end hasna come yet," said Mrs Cairnie. "And it's no' that richt for some folk. Look at young Miss Jean. She has her ain thoughts, and they are no' o' the pleasantest, or her lace doesna tell the truth. And why didna she go to the marriage wi' the lave?"

"Oh! it wasna as if it had been a fine wedding. It was to be very quiet. And Miss Dawson has Mrs Manners' boys at Saughleas. She couldna weel leave them, nor her aunt."

"Weel, maybe no'. But it canna please her to think o' leaving Saughleas, and letting Marion Calderwood reign in her stead. It'll come to that, though it seems the young folk are goin' to the High-street in the mean time."

"Weel, Miss Dawson may be in a home o' her ain by that time," said old Mrs Saugster. "And whether or no', she's no' the first sister in the countryside who has had to give way before a brother's wife."

"Mother! Mrs Cairnie! to say such like things about Miss Dawson! Ye ken little about her, if ye think she would grudge to do what is right."

Maggie, red and angry, looked from one to the other as if she would have liked to say more. Her mother laughed. She knew Maggie's admiration for young Miss Jean of old, but Mrs Cairnie said sourly,—

"It's weel seen that ye belong to the rising generation. In my day lassies werena in the way o' takin' the words out o' their mother's mouth, to say naething o' folk four times their age. As for young Miss Jean, she's liker ither folk than ye think."

"Whisht, mother. See yonder is Miss Dawson coming down the street."

"Ay, she'll be on her way to the house in the High-street, though why I should be bidden whisht at the sight o' her, I dinna ken. And there's one thing sure. Naebody has seen auld George on his way to the house yet. That doesna look as gin he were weel pleased."

"Eh, woman! Ha'e ye forgotten? It was there he took Mary Keith a bride. Let him be ever so weel pleased, it will give him a sair heart to go there again."

There was a slight pause in preparation for Miss Dawson's greeting, but before she came near them, she was joined by her father and both passed on with only a word.

"He's hame again. And I canna say I think he looks ower weel pleased," said Mrs Cairnie.

"It is of Mary Keith he is thinking," said her friend. "He has a feelin' heart for a' sae down as he looks. I doubt he has an ill half hour before him."

In the mean time Jean and her father had reached the gate which opened into the garden of the High-street house. It was a large and well-built house, higher and with wider windows than most of the houses in Portie, and on the whole it was a suitable place of abode for a young man of George's means and station. There was only a strip of green between it and the street, but behind it was a large walled garden into which Mr Dawson had never been since he left it for Saughleas long ago. Indeed he had hardly seen the house since the death of his wife. He never came to the town over the fields as the young people were in the way of doing, and he always turned into the High-street from the turnpike road at a lower point than this.

"Papa," said Jean, arresting her hand which held the old-fashioned knocker of the door, "well go home to-night and come over in the morning. You are tired."

"No, no. We'll get it ower to-night," said her father in a voice which he made gruff in trying to make it steady.

Jean followed the servant into the kitchen and lingered there a while, and Mr Dawson went alone into the once familiar rooms, and not a word of sorrow or sympathy was spoken between them, though the daughter's heart ached for the pain which she knew was throbbing at the heart of her father. He was looking from the window over the garden to the sea, and he did not turn as Jean came in, so she did not speak, but went here and there giving a touch to the things over the arrangement of which she had spent time and taken pleasure during the last few weeks.

"You must have made yourself busy this while, Jean," said her father coming forward at last. "And I must say you have done well. It is all that can be desired, I would think. There are some things coming from London, however."

"Does it not look nice? George had his say about it all. I only helped. I think Marion will be pleased."

"But they should have been guided by me, and come straight to Saughleas. That would have been the best way."

"I'm no' so sure. I think it was natural and right that George should wish to be the head of his own house. No, papa. You are master at Saughleas and ought to be, and I am mistress. Oh! yes, we would both have given up willingly enough, but then neither George nor Marion would have willingly taken our places. But never mind, papa. It will all come in time, and sooner than you think. And I like to think of George bringing his bride to the very house where you brought mamma."

It was a rare thing for Jean to speak her mother's name to her father. It came now with a smile, but with a rush of tears also, which surprised herself quite as much as they surprised her father, and she turned away to hide them. It was her father's loss she was thinking of rather than her own.

"Ay, my lassie! May they be as blessed here as we were," said her father.

And so the first look of his once happy home was gotten over with no more tender words between them, and they went slowly home together, through the fields this time.

Many things had wrought toward the change which Mrs Cairnie and other folk as well saw in Mr Dawson about this time. The new life which George was making honourable among his fellow townsmen, the firm stand he took on the side of right in all matters where his influence could be brought to bear, the light hold that wealth, or the winning of it for its own sake, had ever had upon him, had all by slow degrees told on the old man's opinions and feelings. But as to his wish for his son's marriage with Marion Calderwood, it was Marion herself who had brought that about.

He had noticed her, and had liked her frank, fearless ways before she left Portie, and the sight-seeing together in London, and more still, the few quiet days which she had spent with Miss Jean at Saughleas, won him quite. It was going beyond the truth, as Mrs Saugster had said, to declare that the old man had made the marriage, though it is doubtful whether it would have come about so soon, or whether it would have come about at all, if it had not been for a question or two that he had put to his sister as he sat once in the gloaming in her house.

Then there was a softly spoken word or two between Miss Jean and her nephew, and then George went straight to his father.

"Father, I am going to ask Marion Calderwood to be my wife, if you will give your consent."

It would not have been like Mr Dawson if he had shown at the first word the pleasure with which he heard it.

"You are of age now, George, and your ain man. I have no right to hinder you."

"Father," said George, after a moment's silence, "I shall think you have not forgiven the past, if you say the like of that."

The old man's hand was raised to shade his eyes; he could not quite trust his face to hide his feelings now, but he said in a voice which he tried to make indifferent,—

"I suppose it is to be her or nobody. Is that what you would say to me?"

George made no answer to this.

"I shall never ask her without your full and free consent."

Mr Dawson's hand fell and he turned sharply upon him. "And what about her feelings, if that is to be the way?"

"I have never given her a word or a look that a brother might not give to a sister. But I cannot but hope—" added George with a sudden light in his eye, and a rush of boyish colour to his face. "And I thought you liked Marion, father?"

"Like her?" said his father rising. "George, man, go in God's name and bring her home. She shall be to me like my own daughter. And the sooner the better."

So George went to London and won his bride—"too easily," her mother said. Indeed George had more trouble to win the mother than the daughter. It was to the mother he went first.

As for her, unless she could blot out altogether the remembrance of the sorrow and the hard thoughts of all the past, how could she consent to give her child to him?

"And would it not be well to blot them out?" said George.

"Ay, if it could be done. But as for me—I canna forget my Elsie—"

"And do I forget Elsie? when Marion looks at me with Elsie's eyes and speaks to me with her voice, and—"

"And will that content my Marion, think ye? George, Marion is not just what her sister was. She is of a deeper nature, and is a stronger woman in every way. She is worthy of being loved for her own sake, and nothing less would content her, though she might think it for a while. And oh! George, I cannot bear the thought of having her free heart and her happy life disturbed. To think that she must go through all that!" said the widow with a sigh.

"Dear mother," said George—it was not the first time he had called her so—and he took her unwilling hand between his own as he spoke, "she shall not be disturbed, unless you give me leave to speak; I will go away again without a word. I will not even see her for a while. I cannot promise to give up the thought of her altogether, but I will go away now."

But Mrs Calderwood said,—

"No, George. You must see her since you are here, though you must not speak to her of this. She is no longer a child, and I fear I did an unwise thing in trying to keep you out of her sight so long. It kept you in her mind all the more—not you, but a lad of her own fancy with your name. Miss Jean ay said it would be far better to let things take their course, and so it might have been."

"And do you mean that you kept us from meeting of your own will?"

"Dinna look at me in that way, George. What could I do? You were both young, and she ay made a hero of you. And there was your father. And I wouldna have my bairn's heart troubled. Not that I mean that she cares for you, as she ought not—"

"Dear mother, let me ask her."

Mrs Calderwood made a sudden impatient movement. She loved the young man dearly. And her own son, who to her proud thought was "a man among men," was scarcely dearer. He was a son in all but the name. She loved him, and she believed in him; and even to herself, as she looked at his face, it seemed a foolish and a wrong thing to send him away.

But then it had always been in her thought that these two must never come together in this way, because of her dead Elsie, and because of the hard old man's angry scorn, which, though she had forgiven him, she could not forget. She could not change easily. It was not her nature. And she could not bear that her Marion's heart should be disturbed from its maiden peace. She moved about the room uncertain what she ought to say or do, and utterly impatient of her own hesitation. When she sat down again George came and stood before her.

"Mrs Calderwood, my father gave me God speed, and bade me bring her home."

"Oh! your father," cried Mrs Calderwood with sudden anger. "Your father has ay gotten his ain will for good or for ill, all his life long. And now to think—"

"His last words were—'She shall be to me as my own daughter.'"

Mrs Calderwood turned her face away.

"He loves her dearly," said George softly.

Still she did not speak.

"And, mother,—turn your face to me,—I love her dearly."

She turned then, and at the sight of his moved face her eyes overflowed with tears.

"Oh! George! you are very dear to me, but my Marion is all I have—"

What more she might have said, he never knew, for the door opened, and Marion came softly in with a letter in her hand. Her mother rose, but she did not move away from George, as was her first impulse, nor did she try to hide her tears. It would have been no use, for they were falling like rain over her face. Marion stood still at the door, looking at them with wonder and a little fear.

George went to her, and taking her hand led her to her mother. He was very pale and his lips trembled as he said,—

"Mother, will you let me speak to her now?"

What she might have answered she could not tell. She dropped into her seat with a little cry, and in a moment Marion was kneeling before her, and then so was George; and, of course, there was only one way in which it could end.

Mrs Calderwood said afterwards that Marion had let herself be too easily won. Marion laughed when she said this.

"I think, mother, I was won long before that day," said she.

But at the moment the mother could only give her consent. In a little, when George had taken his wife, that was to be, to the other end of the room, Mrs Calderwood picked up the letter which Marion had let fall, and opened it mechanically, letting her eye fall on the written words while her thoughts were elsewhere. But before she had read many words she uttered an exclamation and hastily went out of the room.

Her pride was to be spared at any rate. Nobody had supposed that *she* would be too easily won. The letter was from Mr Dawson; and by rights she ought to have had it before George came, for it was to bespeak her good word for him that he had written.

It was just, "Let by-ganes be by-ganes. Give your daughter to my son, and she shall be welcomed among us with all the love and honour of which she is worthy—and more cannot be said than that."

Mrs Calderwood read it and read it again, and her wonder grew. Changed! Surely if ever a man was changed, George Dawson must be to write to her such a letter as that. But when she showed it to her daughter, Marion was only surprised at her amazement. All these kind words did not seem strange to her. She had never heard any but kind words from him.

"I began to think he liked me when I was staying with Mrs Manners, and I was sure of it at Saughleas—only afterwards—and even then—" said Marion not very coherently. But she did not explain her meaning more clearly.

"The sooner the better," Mr Dawson had said, and George said the same, and so did Jean in a few sweet words that came in a day or two, and so did her aunt. Mrs Manners reminded her husband that she had told him of Marion's conquest of her father on that first day of her visit to them last year, and also that she had foreseen this happy ending. So with all belonging to George so ready to welcome her child among them, and

George himself so dear, what could Mrs Calderwood do but be glad also, and give her up with a good grace?

It was not so difficult a matter after all, she found when she had thus determined. And by and by she forgave her daughter for having been too easily won. And the visionary jealousy which had risen within her at the memory of her lost child vanished, though in her heart she doubted whether her poor dead Elsie had ever won such love as George had now to give her sister.

So the marriage day was set. It was not very soon, George thought, but the time was not unreasonably long, and it was hastened a little at the last. Captain Calderwood came home from his second voyage in his own ship sooner than was expected, and his stay was to be shorter than usual. The wedding was to be a very quiet one, and it could be hastened without interfering seriously with preparations. Marion had set her heart on her brother's being with her, and it was so arranged, and all things went well.

All things but one. At the very last there came from Jean a letter with many good reasons why she could not come with her father and brother, and with many sweet words of love to the girl "whom she would have chosen from all the world to be her sister." But Mr Dawson was there, intent on doing honour to the occasion, and Mr and Mrs Manners and Captain Saugster of the "John Seaton," and of all people in the world, Sir Percy Harefield! who did not, it is to be supposed, come without an invitation, but who possibly suggested to Mr Dawson that he would like to receive one.

And all went well. There was no large party and no regular speech-making. The bridegroom said nothing, Captain Calderwood said only, "If he could have chosen a brother out of all the world, he would have chosen no other;" and Mr Dawson remembered the words of Jean's letter to Marion, which she had shown him before she sent it away. Mr Dawson said a few words, but he was not so happy, because he could not help again expressing a wish that "by-ganes might be by-ganes," which Mrs Calderwood thought he might have omitted on that day at least.

It came to an end, and the bride and bridegroom went away, and Mr Dawson and Sir Percy Harefield went with Captain Calderwood to see his ship, and they were all very friendly together; so friendly that Sir Percy had thoughts of turning his back on London and the prospective delights of the moors, and taking the voyage with Captain Calderwood to see what the other side of the world was like.

"And what thought ye o' Willie himself?" asked Miss Jean, when Mr Dawson was telling her all this, after he had been at home a day or two. "Is he likely to be such a man as his father was?"

"There's mair o' him than ever there would ha'e been o' his father, if he had been spared, poor man. He is much thought of by his employers. I thought him stiff at first. But he thawed out and was cordial and kindly after a little. He would have made the Englishman very welcome to go with him, if he had keepit in the same mind till he sailed. But I doubt, as Jean once said o' him, he would have found him a heavy handfu' ere a' was done. I ken no greater misfortune that can befall a man than to have nothing to do in the world."

"He has his soldiering?"

"No, he hasna even that now, and he is unfortunate in caring little for the occupations that seem to pass the time for folk o' his class. He is coming north again, he says, and I dare say we'll get a sight o' him."

"He was ay an idle man, even when he was a poor man."

"Yes. But I ay think he might have been made something of, if the right woman would have taken him in hand."

Miss Jean could not agree with him.

"And whether or no', he needna come north to find her," said she.

"No, I suppose not, but it is a pity."

"George, man! I canna but wonder to hear you," said his sister gravely.

"Weel, he has a kind heart, and I canna but be sorry for him. And he is a perfect gentleman."

"Being sorry for him is one thing, and being willing to give him our best is another," said Miss Jean, with a sharpness that made her brother smile. "But I'm no' feared—"

Miss Jean paused. She was not quite sure that she had nothing to fear. To her it seemed that the Englishman had been wonderfully constant—"for the like o' him"—and she was not quite so sure of Jean as she used to be.

One day while her father was away, they had been speaking of Mr Dawson's wish that George should take his bride to Saughleas. Jean had said the best way to settle it would be for her to go away to a house of her own and then George could not refuse to take Marion to Saughleas.

"Weel," said her aunt, "I dare say that might be brought about, if you could bring your mind to it."

"I'll bide a wee," said Jean laughing, but her face grew grave enough in a minute or two.

"I have ay thought myself of some use to my father and George, but now George is away, and even my father would be content with Marion in my place."

"That is scarcely the most cheerful way to look at it, or the wisest. And it's no' like you, Jean, my dear."

"Are you thinking that I am jealous of Marion, Aunt Jean? No, it is not that I love her dearly, and I am glad for George, and for my father, since he is pleased. But are you sure that it gave *you* no pang to give up your brother to Mary Keith?"

Miss Jean smiled, and shook her head.

"I was growing an old woman even at that time. No, though she was almost a stranger to me, I was only glad for George. They loved one another."

"And besides you were an independent woman, with a life and work of your own, and content."

"Jean, my dear," said her aunt, laying down her work and folding her hands on her lap, as was her way when she had something serious to say, "unless ye are keeping something in your heart that ye have never told to me, and there be a reason for it, I would hardly say that you are looking at things with your usual sense and cheerfulness. Do you think that your father has less need o' you now than he has ay had? And do you think it is because o' you that George is so set on taking his wife to the High-street? I see no great change that has come to you or your work, and though it is like giving up your brother in a sense, yet you are glad to do it. What has happened to you, my dear? Would it ease your heart to tell it to me?"

Jean had changed colour many times while her aunt was speaking, and now she sat with her eyes turned away to the sea, as if she were considering whether it would be well to speak. Miss Jean kept silence. She needed no words to tell her the girl's trouble. She had guessed the cause of the weariness and restlessness that Jean could not hide from her, though she could keep a cheerful face before the rest of her world. But she thought it possible that after so long a silence it might do her heart good to speak, if it were only a word, and so she waited silently. But on the whole she was not sorry when Jean rose and took her hat in her hand to go.

"No, Auntie Jean, I have nothing to tell you, positively nothing. I am 'ower weel off,' as Tibbie Cairnie says. That is what ails me, I dare say."

"You'll ha'e May and her bairns through the summer, and plenty to do, and there is nothing better than that to put away—"

"Discontent," said Jean, as her aunt hesitated for a word. "My dear, ye should ha'e gone with your father and George. It would ha'e done you good."

"Well, perhaps it might. But it is too late now. Did I tell you that May wrote that Sir Percy Harefield was at the wedding?"

"No, ye didna tell me."

"May thinks he asked my father to invite him, and my father seems to be as much taken up with him as ever. He is coming north again, she says."

"And has his new tide changed him any, and his new possessions, does your sister say?"

"He has grown fat—more portly, May calls it," said Jean laughing. "She says he is going to Parliament."

"He'll do little ill there, it's likely."

"And as little good, ye think, auntie. It will keep him out of mischief, as he used to say. And after all, I dare say he will do as well as most of them. He is a gentleman anyway, and that is ay something."

And then she went away, and while Miss Jean mused on the cause of Jean's discontent, she could not forget what she called the Englishman's constancy, and she heartily wished that something might happen to keep him from coming north for a while.

"And I canna help thinking that if Jean had gone to her brother's marriage, something might have happened to set her heart at rest."

But that was not Jean's thought. She had not said until the last moment that she was not going, partly because she wished to avoid discussion, and partly because of something else. The many good reasons by which she had succeeded in convincing her father that it was best for her to stay at home, were none of them the reason why she did not go. That could be told to no one. It was only with pain and something like a sense of shame—though she told herself angrily that there was no cause for shame—that she acknowledged to herself the reason.

"I care for him still, though he has forgotten me. I ay cared for him. And he loved me once, I know well. But if he loved me still, he would come and tell me. I could not go and meet him now—and his mother's eyes would be on me—and yet, oh! how I long to see his face after all these years!"

After all these years she might well say. For since May's marriage day, when her heart fell low as Marion told her that her brother had gone away, she had never seen him. He had come north once with George when she was away from home, and he had been in England more than once while she was visiting his sister, but he had never come to see her.

It had hurt her, but she had comforted herself, saying it was because of her father or perhaps also because of his own mother that he did not come. But since Marion was coming home to them, that could be no reason now if he cared, and almost up to the last moment she had waited, hoping that he might come. And then she told herself it was impossible that she should go to meet him, caring for him still.

"And the best thing I can do now is to put it all out of my mind forever."

If she only could have done so, and she did her best to try. May came home with her father; and she and her pretty boys and her baby daughter were with them all the summer. And by and by George brought home his wife, and it was a gay and busy time with them all.

May, who saw most things that were passing, noticed that in some ways her sister was different from what she used to be. She was not the leader in all the gay doings, but left the young visitors at the house to amuse themselves in their own way. She was intent on household matters, as was right, and she took more time to herself in the quiet of her own room than she used to do. But she was merry enough with the children, and indeed gave much of her leisure to them, going about in the house and the garden with baby Mary in her arms, and the little brothers following in their train for many a pleasant hour.

George brought his wife home to the High-street. Even Mr Dawson after a while acknowledged that they had been wise to secure for themselves the quiet of a house of their own. Not that they began in these first days by living to themselves. There was enough to do. There were gay doings in many homes in honour of the bride, and the honour intended was generally accepted none the less gratefully or gracefully, that the gay doings could have been happily dispensed with by them both.

They had pleasures and occupations of another kind also, for Marion was too well-known to the poor folk of Portie to make her coming among them as young Mrs Dawson an intrusion or a trouble. So the young husband and wife went in and out together, "the very sicht o' them," as even Mrs Cairnie owned, "doing a body gude as they passed."

And on the comings and goings of these happy young people, on the honour paid them, on their kindly words and deeds, and heartsome ways with rich and poor, with old friends and new, Mr Dawson looked and pondered with a constant, silent delight which few besides the two Jeans saw or suspected. Even they could not but wonder sometimes at the unceasing interest he found in them and their doings at home and abroad.

He wondered at it himself sometimes. It was like a new sweet spring of life to him to see them, and to hear about them, and to know that all things went well with them; and though few out of his own household could have seen any change in him, it was clear in many ways to those who saw him in his own house day by day.

"God leads His ain by many ways to Himself," thought Miss Jean in her solitary musings over it all. "They that think they ken a' the secrets o' nature tell us that the flowing waters and the changing seasons, bringing whiles the frost and whiles the sunshine, have made from the rocks that look so unchangeable, much o' the soil out of which comes bread to us all. And who kens but God's gender dealings, coming after sore trouble, may prepare his heart for the richer springing o' the good seed, till it bring forth a hundred-fold to His honour and glory. I ay kenned that the Lord had a richt hold o' him through all, and that He would show him His face at last. Blessed be His name?"

"It whiles does folk gude to get their ain way about things, though that's no' the belief o' gude folk generally, and nae in the Bible, as they would gar us believe," said Mrs Cairnie, who never kept her opinions to herself if she could get any one to listen to them. "George Dawson is growing an auld failed man—and nae won'er considerin' how lang he has been toilin' and moilin', gi'ein' himsel' neither nicht's rest nor day's ease. But auld and failed though he be, there's a satisfied look on his face that naebody has seen there since the days he used to come in to the kirk wi' his wife and a' his bairns followin' after him,—langer ago than ye'll mind, Maggie, my woman. And for that matter naebody saw it then. It was satisfaction o' anither kind that he had in those days, I'm thinkin'."

"But, grannie," said Maggie Saugster, giving her the name that the old woman liked best, though she would not acknowledge it, "is it about young Mr and Mrs Dawson you are thinkin', or is it about May and her bairns? Because I mind ye once said to my mother and me that you doubted the old man wasna weel pleased when Mr George brought Marion Calderwood home."

"Oh! ay. Ye're gude at mindin' things that's nae speired at you whiles. He's gotten his will about mair things than that of late, and what I say is, that it has done him gude, as trouble never did."

"Maybe his satisfaction comes from giving up his ain will, rather than from getting it. I ken the look ye mean, mother," said her daughter gently.

"Weel, it may be. A thing seems to ha'e taken a turn sin' I was young. But it's nae the look his face used to wear when man or woman countered him in the old days."

"Ay. But it would be different when the Lord took him in hand."

"The Lord has been lang about it, if it's only the day that He's takin' him in hand. But what I'm sayin' is this, that it does folk gude to get their ain will about things whiles, and I only wish that the Lord would try it on me, and set me strong on my ain twa feet again," said Mrs Cairnie, taking up her crutch with a sigh.

"Or satisfy you with His will instead. That would do as well, mother."

"Weel, weel! That's your way o' it, and if I'm allowed to tak' the wrang gait, it winna be for want o' tellin'," said the old woman, moving slowly down to the corner of the street which was almost the length of her tether now. The eyes of the others followed her pitifully.

"She's nae that sharp now—nae that soon angered, I mean," said Maggie, with some hesitation, meaning to say something kind, but not quite sure how far her sister-in-law might accept her sympathy.

"No," said the other after a pause. "And I whiles think that the Lord is getting His will o' her too, though she hardly kens it hersel' yet."

"Ay. As Miss Jean says, the Lord has many ways," said Maggie reverently.

Chapter Twenty Five.

Suspense.

And so the summer wore over, and May went home with all her children, though Jean would fain have kept one boy with her. But her mother feared the bleak east winds for the rather delicate Georgie who was the favourite at Saughleas, and she had reasons that satisfied herself for taking little Keith home also, but she promised to send them both back again as soon as the winter was over.

The summer ended, and autumn days grew short, and a quiet time came that reminded Jean of the days when May had gone to London "to meet her fate," and she was waiting for the coming home of the "John Seaton." There was the same long dreaming in the gloaming, before her father came in, the same listening to the woeful voices of the winds and the sea, and the same shadow on Jean's face and in her wistful eyes that her father had seen in those days—now so long ago. He sometimes surprised it now, but, if this happened, it went hard with Jean if she did not make him forget it before he slept.

About the new year Mrs Calderwood's old friend died, and when her will was read, to her surprise Mrs Calderwood found that she had left her money enough to enable her to live henceforth free from the cares which accompany the task of making too little do the work of enough, as had been her lot during the greater part of her life of widowhood.

George, who had gone to London to be with her at that time, insisted on bringing her back to Scotland with him. She had exhausted herself in attendance on her old friend, and she needed a change. Later she was to return and make all necessary arrangements, but in the mean time it would have been neither wise nor kind he thought to leave her there alone.

For this George had a better reason than he gave to her. News had come of terrible storms that had passed over Southern seas. Already rumours of disaster and loss had reached England, and the owners of Captain Calderwood's ship, the "Ben Nevis," were beginning to feel some anxiety with regard to her.

Another ship, the "Swallow," had arrived from Melbourne, bringing word that the "Ben Nevis" was to have sailed three days after the time she had put to sea. The voyage had been a long one, though happily the "Swallow" had passed beyond the latitudes where the storms had raged most fiercely before the danger had arisen. The "Ben Nevis" was the swifter vessel of the two, and by rights, she ought to have reached England before her. And when ten days passed, and then ten more, there was good reason for fear for her safety.

Happily Captain Calderwood's outward voyage and his stay in Melbourne had been shorter than his mother had calculated upon, so that as yet no thought of anxiety had come to disturb her, and she was glad to go with George, believing that she could pay a few weeks in Scotland with her daughter, and still be in London in time to receive her son when he should return.

It was Mrs Calderwood's first visit after an absence of several years, to a place which had been her home during the greater part of her life. There were many to welcome her, and there was much to see and hear, and she was greatly occupied. But George wondered sometimes that she should live on from day to day, showing no misgivings, even no surprise, at the continued absence of her son.

He need not have wondered. She had been a sailor's daughter, and a sailor's wife, and she had lived the greater part of her life among sailors' wives and widows, and had learned the necessity of giving no unwise indulgence to fancies and fears, and to keep quiet and face them when fears and fancies had to give place at last to a knowledge of disaster and loss.

She had had anxious thoughts doubtless while she awaited the expected summons to meet her son, when the ship should be heard from, but outwardly she was calm and even cheerful. It was wise for her own sake not to dwell on her fears—which indeed were hardly fears as yet, but only a vague movement of surprise and impatience that she should have to wait so long. And it was wise also for the sake of her daughter, who was not so strong as usual. So she kept herself cheerful and seemed to be taking so little thought of what might be awaiting her, that George questioned at last whether it might not be both kind and wise to prepare her for the shock which he began to fear must come soon. This painful task did not fall to him however, and Mrs Calderwood was already better prepared for it than he knew.

It was drawing near the end of February by this time, and it was a milder season than Portie often sees. There were weeks of bleak weather to come yet, for this eastern coast rarely escapes a full share of that sooner or later. But in the mean time the days were fair and calm, and looking over a pale grey sea, bright now and then with a blink of sunshine, thoughts of storm and danger did not come so readily, as with a wild and angry sea they might have done. But even Marion was beginning to wonder that her mother said nothing of what might be keeping the "Ben Nevis" so long.

And then a single word came to break the silence between them, and they knew that the mother's quietness had cost her something. But she was quiet still when doubts and fears and even despair were busy at her heart.

They were still sitting at breakfast one fair morning when Jean came in. She was just as usual, they all thought at the moment, but afterwards each remembered the look on her face as she opened the door. The air had brought a colour to her cheeks, so she was not pale, but there was a startled look in her eyes as she turned them from one to another before she uttered a word. It changed as she marked the unmoved face of each.

She kissed Marion, and then, strangely enough, she kissed Mrs Calderwood, and laid two pale primroses, the first of the season, on a book which she held in her hand.

They were friendly, these two, and even more than friendly, but there was always a touch of shyness and reserve between them, even when they were most friendly. Marion, who so dearly loved them both, saw it and wondered at it often, but she smiled now as Jean stooped and touched her lips to her mother's cheek. Mrs Calderwood grew a shade paler, and a question came into her eyes as she met Jean's look. But Jean had no answer for it.

"I found them in a sheltered nook in the wood when I was out this morning. They are come earlier than usual, and there will soon be more of them."

Jean did not meet her look as she thanked her, but turned to George who was preparing to go out, nor would she sit down.

"I only looked in as I passed, to see if all was well with you. I have many things to do, but I will come in again before I go home, unless I should be detained longer than I expect in the town." So in a little she and her brother went out together. "Are you taking the paper with you, George?" said Mrs Calderwood following them to the door.

"Not if you wish to see it. I will send for it by and by when I want it."

"You have seen it, George?" said Jean as they went on. "If you mean the paragraph about the 'Ben Nevis,' yes, I have seen it. It does not say much beyond the usual, 'Fears are entertained for the safety, etc.'"

"And now she will see it."

"Yes, I think it is as well. It will help to prepare her for what she may have to hear later."

"George," said Jean in a little, "does that mean that you are afraid?"

"There is cause for anxiety. There was that before we left London. I only wonder that Mrs Calderwood has said so little about it."

"And you left London more than six weeks ago." George told her of the succession of terrible storms that had swept over the Southern seas about the close of the year, in latitudes where possibly the "Ben Nevis" had been at that time, acknowledging that there would be reason to fear for the fate of the ship unless she were heard from soon. His anxiety had been greater than he knew, and he had kept it to himself so long that to speak was a relief, which led him to say more to his sister than he would otherwise have done. His words were less hopeful than he meant them to be, until Jean said, "Do you mean that you give them up?"

"By no means. I do not even give up the ship. I know Willie Calderwood and what he can do too well to do that yet a white. And even if they had to forsake the ship, the chances are in favour of safety for the men. All that depends on circumstances of which we can know nothing. But I by no means give up the ship even yet."

"But, George, should you not have stayed to tell Mrs Calderwood so?"

"No, I think not. There will be time enough for that, and she is of a nature to meet the first pain best alone."

"But Marion?"

"She will not speak to Marion at once. And, Jean, it is as well that the awful possibility of loss should be admitted. But my hopes are stronger than my fears."

"The awful possibility of loss?" Jean repeated the words with white lips, not knowing that she did so. They had lengthened their walk, passing Miss Jean's house and going on to the pier. They turned now and came back in silence. At Miss Jean's door they paused.

"It will be as well to say nothing as yet," said George.

"Not to Aunt Jean?"

"Oh! yes. I have spoken to her already. I mean to people generally. And, Jean, go and see Marion and her mother again before you go home."

But Jean said nothing to her aunt about what she had heard. She stayed her usual time, and discussed certain purchases that were to be made of material for the summer outfit of some of her aunt's "puir bodies," and went into matters of detail as to quantity, and needles and thread, and as to the help that each would need in the making of her gown. And then she went away and did all else that she meant to do when she left home, and lingered over it, till it was too late, she told herself, to go to the High-street again.

Three days passed before she went there, and the like had seldom happened since Marion came home. She did not know how she could speak to the mother of the anguish and suspense that lay before her, and she shrank from a betrayal of her own pain.

But when she went in on the fourth day it struck her with surprise to see that they were just the same as usual. No change of grief or terror had passed upon them. Mrs Calderwood was grave and pale, but she spoke about various matters cheerfully enough, though she made no allusion to the fears for her son.

Marion spoke of her brother, and said how hopeful George was about him, and how the old sailors about the pier were saying to one another, that Captain Calderwood was not the man to be caught unprepared for a storm, and being prepared, with plenty of sea room, what was there to fear? He would bring his ship home all right. There was no fear of that.

But the next news that came made even the old sailors shake their heads when the ship was spoken of. A boat had been picked up by a South American vessel, filled with men from the wreck of the "Ben Nevis" and from the Southern port to which these had been carried came the tidings.

They had encountered a succession of storms, which had so strained and shattered the good ship "Ben Nevis," that there seemed a fairer chance of escaping with life by betaking themselves to the boats than by remaining with the ship. There were not many passengers on board, only seventeen all told. Nine of these, with four sailors, were in the boat which the American had saved when they had been five days away from the wreck.

They could say nothing of those whom they had left on board, though they had still seen the ship afloat in the distance on the second day. There was no familiar name in the list of the rescued, but it was said that the weather had moderated while they were in the vicinity of the ship, and there seemed no reason to doubt that the rest of the passengers and crew had been able to save themselves.

Captain Calderwood's name was mentioned in terms that brought tears of pride and sorrow to the eyes of those who loved him. His courage and kindness and patience had never failed through all the terrible days of storm. Discipline had been maintained through all, as perfectly as during the summer calm that preceded those awful days; and the last sight which the rescued saw as they drew off from the ship, to await the manning of the other boats, was their captain standing on the deck encouraging them with hand and voice.

And that was all. But that was much, and now they could wait for further tidings with patience. On the whole they kept in good heart for a while. But as time went on, the suspense and anxiety of the days that went before, seemed to pass into each new day as it came. For they knew that each passing day without tidings mocked the hope they had so long cherished.

Through all the mother waited quietly. Never quite without hope that she would see her son again, but after a while the poor pretence of cheerfulness for which she had striven, because of Marion, failed beyond her power to help it. The silent patience which had been the habit of her life under other troubles, stood her in good stead now. And when this failed her, and the restlessness, of a slowly dying hope came upon her, she would go away by herself till she could hide all tokens of her pain again.

Sometimes she went to Miss Jean's for comfort, but often when her daughter believed her to be there, she was walking up and down the wet sands, or sitting in some sheltered nook among the rocks, striving for calmness to bear to the end. She had gone through it all before, and now she seemed to be waiting again and longing and fearing for his father, while she waited for her only son. When other eyes were upon her she was calm enough, and troubled no one with her trouble, but she needed the rest which solitude gave her to carry her through the lengthening days.

Marion bore the long suspense well, they all said. She was young, and it was her nature to look for brightness rather than gloom, and no such trouble had come upon her as had darkened the life of her mother. There were only hopeful views expressed in her presence, and though she knew that cheerfulness was encouraged and often assumed for her sake, she had the sense and courage to respond to the efforts of those who loved her, and to keep herself quiet and patient for their sakes.

One good came to Mrs Calderwood out of the trouble of those days. She had forgiven Mr Dawson the hard words and unreasonable anger of the old days, or she believed that she had, but even to herself she could not say that she had forgotten them. She was never quite at her ease in his presence. It was not so much that she disliked him, as that she could not convince herself that he did not dislike her. The sight of her could only, she thought, recall to him much that he could not but wish to forget; and if she could do so, without remark, she generally chose to be out of the way during his frequent visits to the house.

But whatever he might feel towards her, there could be no doubt as to the esteem in which he held her son, or as to the anxiety which he shared with them all. He was not, as a general thing, ready with words of sympathy, but she had seen tears in his eyes more than once as he spoke her son's name, and her heart could not but soften towards him, and a real friendliness, which in other circumstances might have come but slowly, grew up in this troubled time between them.

There was no lack of sympathy. Not a man or woman in Portie, but felt deeply for the trouble of Willie Calderwood's mother and sister, though they were for the most part shy as to any expression of it. Indeed Mrs Calderwood kept out of the way of words. George guarded his wife from the hearing of any thing that would move her out of her usual quiet, and when he was not at hand, Jean guarded her as carefully for his sake.

To Jean, as to the rest, the days passed slowly and heavily. To the eyes of even her aunt she was just as usual, no graver nor sadder than was natural since a friend, and one who was more than a friend to those she loved, was in danger. But no one ever heard her speak of the anxiety that oppressed them all. She listened in silence when, as is the way at such times, the causes for hope or fear were gone over, and over, and over again, or she went away and did not listen, but she never put in her word with the rest.

It was only as a friend that she had a right to grieve for Willie Calderwood, she told herself. They had never been lovers. They had cared for one another long ago—oh! so long ago now. But they had not seen one another for years, because he had not cared to see her, and it was all past now. She had been angry at first, and then sorry. Yes, she had suffered sharply for a while, she acknowledged. But she was neither sorry nor angry now. She was anxious for his safety, and she longed for his return, as all his friends did. And her heart ached for his mother and his sister, and for George, to whom he was both brother and friend. And that was all.

But a day came when her heart spoke, nay, cried out as the heart of no mere friend could cry. She was sitting one day in Miss Jean's parlour, when her brother came in. There were tears in his eyes and a strange, uncertain smile on his lips, and he laid his hand on her shoulder as she stood by the window, pausing a moment before he spoke, as if he were not sure of his voice.

"Jean," he said, "there is news at last."

Jean grew very white.

"Well?" said she sitting down.

"Is it good news, George, man?" said his aunt hastily.

"It is just such news as one would expect to hear from Willie Calderwood. Yes, I call it good news, whatever may come next."

And then he told them how another of the "Ben Nevis"' boats had been heard from. After much suffering from anxiety and exhaustion, they who left the ship in it had landed somewhere on the West African coast, and had, after some delay, been taken from thence in a Portuguese vessel to Lisbon. And now some of them at least had reached England. And this was the news they brought.

When those who were to go in the second boat were about to take their places in it, Captain Calderwood had, to their utter amazement, declared his intention of remaining with the ship for that night at least. The vessel was new and strongly built, and within the hour he had seen some tokens that led him to believe that, during the storm, it had not gone so hardly with her as had been at first feared.

The cargo was a valuable one, and his duty to his employers demanded that, while there was a chance of saving it and the ship, he should remain on board. At the same time he acknowledged, that as far as could now be judged, there was but a chance in ten, that he could do this, while by taking to the boats at once, there was a fair prospect of their being picked up by one of the many homeward bound vessels which at that season followed the course which they had taken.

Then he called for volunteers to remain with him. Not a man among the sailors but would have stayed at his bidding. But an able crew was placed in the departing boat, and he was left with just men enough to work the ship, among them three passengers, should all go well. Should they find when the night was over, that chances were against saving the ship, they also were to take to the boat and do what might be done to escape with the rest.

They who were in the second boat had stayed in the vicinity of the ship that night and the next day and night, but when the second morning dawned she was no longer to be seen. Whether she had sunk or whether she had sailed away out of their sight they had no means of knowing, nor could they form any conjecture as to the fate of those who remained on board. They might have betaken themselves to the boat at the last moment, or they might have gone down with the ship.

But whatever had happened this was sure—No braver man or better sailor than Captain Calderwood had ever commanded a ship. This was all that was to be told about the "Ben Nevis."

"And what do you gather from it all?" said Miss Jean in a little. "Ye dinna give up all hope?"

"We can only wait patiently a little longer. If the bringing home of the disabled ship was a thing to be done, Captain Calderwood was the man to do it. No, I by no means give up hope. He may come any day now."

They had said this many times before, and now none of them had the courage to say that he should have been home long ago if all had been well.

"I fear it was an unwise courage that led him to undertake an impossible work," said Miss Jean sadly.

"No, aunt. You must not say that. He must have seen more than a possibility, or he would never have risked life. It was his simple duty as he saw it, neither more nor less. We may be sure of that, knowing him as we do."

"But, oh! George, what is a ship's cargo, or even the ship itself, in comparison with a young strong life like his?"

"Ay, aunt. But duty is the first thought with a true man like Captain Calderwood. And he has all the resources that strength and patience and skill and courage can give to a man, and I cannot but hope that he'll come safe home yet."

"He is in God's hands," said Miss Jean.

"Ay, is he. And God bless him wherever he is," said George with a break in his voice.

Jean had sat in silence, turning her eyes from one to the other as each had spoken.

"Have you told his mother?" said Miss Jean.

"Yes, she has heard all. It seems two of the sailors have reported themselves to the owners in London, and she thinks she must see them, though I fear it will do little good."

"It will give her something to do anyway," said Miss Jean. "But she is quite worn out with anxiety, though she has said so little about it, and I doubt she ought not to go alone."

"No, I shall go with her," said George. "It would make Marion miserable to think of her mother with her sore heart solitary in London. We need not stay long."

"And after a day or two she will think of her daughter's need of her, and come home. If only the suspense were over one way or another—"

"No, aunt, don't say that. We have hope yet—strong hope of seeing him again. If you only heard the tales I hear on the pier about the wonderful escapes that skill and courage have won. Hope! Yes, I have hope."

"My dear, I have heard all that could be told before you were born. But all the same there has many a ship gone down since then, and many a sore heart has waited and hoped in vain. But I'm no' goin' to say all that to Willie Calderwood's mother, true though it be."

"And, George," said Jean speaking for the first time, "you may be quite at peace about Marion."

"Yes. I leave her with you. She will keep herself quiet."

"We will take her to Saughleas. That will please my father."

And so it was settled, and the long days went on. Jean busied herself with her father and her sister, and went out and in just as usual, giving no time when other eyes were upon her to her own thoughts. But she welcomed the night. Sitting in the darkness, with only the grey gleam of the sea for her eyes to rest upon, she gave herself up to thoughts of her friend.

She called him her friend, but she knew that he was more than a friend to her; and she had at least this comfort now, that she was no longer angry or ashamed to care for him still, although he had forgotten her. He would always be her friend now, whether he lived or died. She might grieve for those who loved him, and whom he loved, and for the young strong life lost to the world which needed such as he to do its best work, but he would still be hers in memory, and more in death than in life.

And yet she had a vague dread of the dreariness and emptiness of a world in which he no longer lived and moved, and doubted her power to adapt herself to its strangeness. She knew, or she tried to believe, that good would come out of it all even to her, and when she came to this she always remembered her aunt.

It had been by "kissing the rod" under such discipline as this that her aunt, after long, patient years, had grown to be the best, the most unselfish woman that she knew; yes, and the wisest with the highest wisdom.

Sometimes she had said to herself and to others, that she meant to grow to be such a woman as her aunt, and so take up her work in the world when it should be time for her to lay it down. And now, perhaps, the Lord was taking her at her word, and was about to prepare her for His own work, in His own way, which must be best; and she tried to be glad that it should be so. But when she looked on to the life that lay before her, her heart sank at the length of the way.

"I am not like Aunt Jean. I am not good enough to get her work to do, and to take pleasure in it. Maybe after long years I might be able to do it. If I only had the heart to care for any thing any more!

"But I must be patient. The pain is new and sore yet, but time heals most wounds, and as auntie says, 'The Lord is ay kind.'"

This was her last thought most nights; but there were times when she could not get beyond the darkness, and lay lost and helpless till the morning. Then she put aside her own pain, and grew cheerful and hopeful for the sake of others. If she came to the task with white cheeks and heavy eyes, as happened now and then, no one wondered, or indeed noticed it much, for she was none the less ready with cheerful words and kindly deeds for the comfort of them all.

Chapter Twenty Six.

Safety.

And so the nights passed and the long days, and even Jean's heart sprang up to meet the next news that came.

The ship "Ben Nevis," Captain Calderwood, supposed to be lost, had been spoken at sea by a vessel homeward bound. Her latitude and longitude were given, and it was said that considering her condition, she had made good progress since the time her boats had left her. She lay low in the water and laboured heavily, but her captain and crew were in good heart, and with fair wind and such weather as they might hope for now, they were sure soon to reach an English harbour.

So hopes were raised and courage renewed. Mrs Calderwood would fain have remained in London to meet her son when he came; but the time of his coming was uncertain, and he might even put in to some nearer port, and her daughter needed her. So she returned home to Portie with George again.

And when they came it was to find Marion the joyful mother of a son. The news had been duly telegraphed to London as soon as possible after the event, but they had left before that time. It was Mr Dawson himself who met them at the station with the news, and passing by George without a word, it was to Mrs Calderwood that he told it with a trembling but triumphant voice. There were tears in the eyes that she had always thought so cold and hard, and these tears washed away the last touch of pained and angry feeling from the heart of the mother of poor dead Elsie.

If any thing could have added to the old man's pride and delight in his grandson, the fact that he had drawn his first breath in Saughleas would have done so. Not that either his pride or his delight was made very evident to the world in general. He answered inquiries and accepted congratulations with as much composure as was compatible with the satisfaction that the occasion warranted, it was thought, and perhaps with rather more. But even the world in general began to acknowledge that he was growing to have gender and more kindly ways than he had once had, and folk agreed with Mrs Cairnie, that it had done him good to get his own will.

As for George, he took his new happiness soberly enough to all outward appearance. There was still so much anxiety as to the fate of the "Ben Nevis" as to temper the joy of the young father and mother over their firstborn, and to make them quiet and grave in the midst of it. But their hopes for their brother and those who had stayed with him were stronger than their fears, and even Mrs Calderwood took heart and did not shrink from the hearing of her son's name. Her care for her daughter and her grandson left her little time to brood over her fears, and she felt that to do so, would be "to sin against her mercies," since her daughter had been spared to her and was growing stronger every day.

As Marion grew strong, and Mrs Calderwood devoted herself to her, Jean had more time for herself, spent much of it in the wood or on the shore, or in her aunt's parlour, which, during those days, she found to be as good a place as either the wood or the shore for the indulgence of her own thoughts. For Miss Jean troubled her with few words; but sat silent, seeing without seeming to see, that all was not well with her niece.

It was a rest for Jean to sit there in the quiet room, and it is not to be wondered at that there were times when she forgot to keep guard over her face, as even before her aunt she had done of late. At such times her aunt regarded her anxiously. She had become thin and white, and her eyes had grown large and wistful; as her mother's eyes had been, before she had resigned herself to the knowledge that she must leave them all.

"A word or two might do her good, if I could ken the right word to say," thought Miss Jean, as she sat one day watching the stooping figure and averted face. The suspense about the "Ben Nevis" would soon be over, but Miss Jean's thought was that the ending of this suspense would not be the ending of her bairn's troubles. However her first words turned that way.

"It canna be long ere we hear now."

"No. It canna be long," said Jean, recalling her thoughts and taking up her work again.

"And they all seem to be in good heart about the ship. They may come any day. It has been a long time of suspense to his mother, and to us all."

"Yes. It has been a long time."

"It will soon be over now in one way or another. And even if he should never come, it will only be like a longer voyage, that will be sure to have a happy ending in a peaceful haven, where the mother and son are sure to meet."

"And she will have him for her own at last."

Neither spoke for a long time after this. Jean's head drooped lower, and though her eyes were on the sea, it was not the harbour of Portie that she saw, but a wide waste of ocean with a labouring ship, making for her desired haven, it might be, but bringing no one home to her. She rose and moved restlessly about the room.

"I wish you were able to go for a little walk, auntie. Dinna ye think it might do ye good to take a turn or two up and down by the sea?"

"No' the day, my dear. But if ye would like to go out, never heed me. I think myself that a walk would do you good, or a fine long seam, such as your mother used to give you to do, when your restlessness was ower muckle for yourself and others. But the walk would be more to your mind, I dare say." Jean laughed.

"But then, I have the long seam ready to my hands," said she, sitting down again and taking up her work resolutely. By and by, when she forgot it and her face was turned seaward again, her aunt laid down hers also and said softly, with a certain hesitation,—

"Jean, my dear, did you and Willie Calderwood part friends?"

Jean sat absolutely motionless for a minute or two. "Yes, aunt, we were friends always. As to parting—"

"Weel—as to parting?"

"We had no parting. He went away without a word."

"That was hardly like a friend on his part," said Miss Jean gravely, and then in a little she added,—

"And, Jean, love, were ye never mair than friends?" Then Jean rose, and turning looked straight in her aunt's face.

"No. Never more than friends. You surely havena been thinking ill thoughts of Willie, auntie?"

"That's nae likely. But whiles I ha'e wondered—and now that he is coming hame—" Jean stood a moment irresolute, and then coming forward she sat down on a hassock at her aunt's feet, as she often did, and leaned her head upon her hand.

"Jean, my dear, have ye nothing to say to me?"

"No, aunt. There is nothing. I have no more right to grieve or to be glad for Willie Calderwood than any one of his many friends in Portie."

"Grief or gladness is whiles no' a question o' rights," said Miss Jean gently.

Jean said nothing. She was too weary and spent to be very angry with herself for the weakness which had betrayed her secret. But she had strength and courage to shut her lips on the words that rose to them. And before her aunt had time for another word they heard Mrs Calderwood speaking to Nannie at the door. Except for a sudden bright colour that had risen to her cheeks, Jean was just as usual when she came in.

"There's nae news?" said Miss Jean.

This had long been her first salutation to any one coming in.

"No, there is nothing more," said Mrs Calderwood.

"Weel, we maun just have patience."

Jean brought forward an easy chair for her aunt's friend, and carried out some tea for Nannie to make a cup to refresh her after her walk. But she did not sit down again.

"I'll go now. I have something to get in the town. Shall I come round this way again, Mrs Calderwood, so that we may walk home together? or will it be too long for you to wait?"

It would not be too long. There was no haste, Mrs Calderwood said. George had gone home already and was to take Marion out for a little while, and they might come round this way to get a sight of Miss Jean. So Jean promised to return, and then she went out, not quite knowing where she was to go, or what she was to do. But it was settled for her. For as she turned into the High-street she met her father.

"I was going to your aunt's to say that I am going to John Stott's. I canna say just when I may be home, and you are not to wait for me."

"Is John worse, papa? Let me go with you. I needna go into the house."

"I doubt he is near as bad as he can be, and be living. I doubt it is ower far."

"Ower far! No' for me, if it's no' ower far for you. And I have nothing to do that canna be put off. And it is a long time since we have had a walk together."

So, well pleased, they set out John Stott was a labourer who had long been in Mr Dawson's employment. He had been for days ill with fever, and was now supposed to be dying. They spoke of him a little, and of the helpless family he would leave, and of the best manner of helping them without making their help seem like alms. For John had long been a faithful servant, and Mr Dawson meant to set his heart at rest about those, he was leaving; indeed this was the reason of his visit at this time.

Then after a little he spoke, not quite so hopefully as usual about the "Ben Nevis," saying they must hear soon now, or they would have to give her up altogether. Then he went on to say how well it was that Marion had grown so strong before any particular excitement either of joy or pain had come to disturb her.

"She is very well," said Jean. "George is going to take her out in the pony carriage this afternoon, her mother told us. I left her at Aunt Jean's."

"I doubt that is venturesome of him. I hope he'll take the best of the afternoon to it. And that is near over already. He'll be thinking of taking her back to the High-street again, I suppose," said he discontentedly, "unless we can persuade them to bide at Saughleas altogether."

Jean was silent a minute or two.

"There are just two things that would be likely to prevent them," said she.

"Weel, let us hear of them."

"One is that except for a while, Mrs Calderwood would not easily be persuaded to think of Saughleas as her home; and both George and Marion wish her to remain with them."

"Which is but right. George is no' a man to let himself be vexed with his mother-in-law, even were she a more difficult person. But why should she not live with them at Saughleas?"

But as he asked the question he saw that such a thing would seem impossible to Mrs Calderwood. It was not a matter for discussion, however.

"And what is the other reason?"

"It is not a very good reason. Both George and Marion think that I should be the mistress of Saughleas, while I am there. They think, and other folk think, that I would not like to—to be set aside. And I might not like it. But if it were the best way for all, my not liking it would be a small matter."

Mr Dawson muttered impatiently,—

"Ay. It's ay said that twa women canna agree in the same house. But I think, Jean, ye might show them something else. I'm sure Marion wouldna be ill to live with."

"It is not a matter of agreement or disagreement, papa. There cannot be two mistresses in any house with comfort to, any one concerned. And there need not be two if Marion were willing. And if I were not there she would fall naturally into her right place. I might go away for a little while, papa, and when I came back I might fall into the second place, and make no work about it. Or I might bide with Auntie Jean."

"Nonsense! Bide with Auntie Jean, indeed! If you were going to a house of your ain, it might do. But good and dear as Marion is, I could ill bear to see you put out of your place in your father's house, even for her."

"Yes, if I cared, papa. I might once when I was younger. But I dinna think that I could care much now."

Mr Dawson looked at her curiously, but Jean's eyes were turned away to the sea.

"But even if that were the best way—which I am far from thinking—there is ay Mrs Calderwood and her wishes to be considered. I doubt we'll just need to let them go."

"But I think—and Aunt Jean thinks—which is more to the purpose—that Mrs Calderwood would hardly content herself in her daughter's house wherever it was, for a continuance. I mean that she would rather be in a home of her own. That might be got over."

There was silence between them for some time, and then Jean said with more earnestness than she had shown yet,—

"Papa, will you let me tell you just what I would like? I would like you to give me the house in the High-street for a present—as a part of my portion—just as if I were to be married, ye ken. And then I would persuade my aunt and Mrs Calderwood to live there together. And by and by when I grow old—and have not you any longer, I could live there myself."

Mr Dawson listened to her with mingled feelings, but he said quietly, "What would two women folk, seeing little company, do with a big house like that? And you could never persuade them."

"But they would see company more or less, and have folk coming for the summer. And the house is not so very big, and none too good for the 'auld laird's' sister, and the 'young laird's' mother. And I think I could persuade them. And if this were all settled George would be content to bide with you at Saughleas. And I could—come and go."

"Jean," said her father gravely, "why do you ay speak as if you were never to have a house of your own? I'm no' pleased to hear you."

"But, papa, I never do. That is what I am wanting—a house of my own—sometime—not just yet."

"But I am not thinking of such a home as ye could make to yourself in the house in the High-street, but of something quite different." Jean laughed. "I canna help it, papa."

"But ye might have helped it."

"No, papa, I never could yet."

"Weel! weel! We'll say nae mair about it. It's nae ower late yet. We maun ha'e patience, I suppose."

Though Jean laughed her face grew strangely grave and sad, her father thought, as they went on in silence together.

"You might think about it, papa, and speak to Aunt Jean about it. I should never feel safe or happy to be long away from Portie, unless there were some one ay with Aunt Jean. And I think that she and Marion's mother would suit one another as no one else would suit either of them. They would be busy and happy together, and I should feel safe about my aunt wherever I might be."

"But why should you speak as if you were not to be here? Why should you go away?"

"Only for a little while, papa. And then George and Marion would stay. And it is not for that altogether. I would like to go a while for my own sake. I think I need a change."

"Are ye no' weel?" said her father in some surprise.

"Oh! I am well enough; but I would like to go away for a little. I am tired, I think. We have been anxious, you know, especially when George and Mrs Calderwood were away. And I think I am wearying for a sight of May and the bairns. I know a change would be good for me, for a little, I mean."

She spoke with some difficulty, and the colour was coming and going on her cheek. Her father's surprise changed to anxiety as he regarded her. He saw as her aunt had seen, that she had grown thin and pale, and that her eyes looked large and anxious, like eyes that had slept little of late.

"What ails ye, my lassie? Ye're surely no' weel. If it's only May and her bairns that ye're wanting, ye can easy get them. Only," continued Mr Dawson after a little, "it might hardly look kind to go away now, till the 'Ben Nevis' has been heard from again."

"No, I suppose not."

"And if we shouldna hear—ye'll be needed all the more. Willie Calderwood will be a hero to the seafaring folk o' Portie when he does come. And I dare say ye'll like to see him as well as the rest."

"Yes. It is long since I saw him."

"If he brings the 'Ben Nevis' safe to an English port, his reputation will be established, and his fortune will be made. That is as far as a mere sea captain can be said to be able to make a fortune by his profession. He must be a man of great courage and strength of character, as George says, even to have made the attempt to bring the ship home. They may weel be proud of him,—his sister and his mother, and we must do nothing that would seem to lichtlify him—neither you nor me."

Jean looked at her father in a strangely moved way which he remembered afterwards, but she said nothing.

"I mind ye were ay fond o' sea-heroes; and all his friends will need to make much o' him when he wins safe home."

They were drawing near the cottage by this time. Mr Dawson would not let Jean go in because of the fever, and she sat down on the dyke at the house end. But her father did not keep her waiting long. John had fallen into a sleep which might be the saving of him yet, and must not be disturbed, and promising, if it were possible, to see him to-morrow, he came quickly out to Jean.

They had little to say to each other as they turned homewards. Jean acknowledged herself tired with her walk, and when she said she had promised to go back again to her aunt's to walk home with Mrs Calderwood, her father bade her wait there, and the pony carriage, when George and Marion returned, should be sent for them both.

Mr Dawson pursued his homeward way alone, but he had not gone very far before he met a messenger and turned back again.

"Good news! good news!" shouted young Robbie Saugster as soon as he was within hearing distance. "The 'Ben Nevis' is safe in port, and Captain Calderwood is here in Portie, I saw him mysel' at the station, and I told him that his mother was at Miss Jean's, and then I ran on to Saughleas with the news; but there was naebody there to hear it but Phemie and Ann. And I'm glad to see you, sir, anyway."

"Good news!" That it was, well worth the half crown which Mr Dawson put into the hand of the astonished laddie. He had heard no news so good for many a day, he said, as he turned toward the town again. But when he came to his sister's house, and went softly in, he was not so sure of its being the best of news to him.

For the first sight he saw was his daughter Jean lying on her aunt's sofa with a face as white as death, and her bright hair tossed and wet falling down to the floor. Leaning over her, but not touching so much as a finger, was a sailor in rough sea clothes; and though he neither moved nor spoke, there was no mistaking the tale told by his working face and his eager eyes. Mrs Calderwood stood beside him with her hand on his shoulder.

"Willie," she entreated, "you must come away. She must not see you when she comes to herself. She was startled, and you have no right—"

"No, mother. I know I have no right—except that I have loved her all my life—"

"But you must come away. It is not fair to her. And think of her father."

"Yes. I have ay thought of him. Yes, mother, I will go with you," and he stooped and touched, not with his fingers, but with his lips, the shining braid of hair that hung down to the floor, and then he turned and went out.

It was hard on Mr Dawson. He had been more than anxious for the sailor's return for his mother's sake and his sister's, as well as for his own, and he had meant to give him the best of friendly welcomes. But now what was this he saw?

Astonishment was his first feeling. He had never once thought of these two in this way, at least he had not for a long time. Then he was angry. Had Jean been deceiving him all this time. But his anger was only momentary. He knew his daughter too well to believe that possible. He knew not what to think, except that his welcome to the sailor was not so ready as it would have been an hour ago.

Fortunately it was not called for at the moment, for Captain Calderwood turned into Nannie's kitchen and went out the other way without seeing him.

Seldom in his life had the old man been so startled. Instead of going into the house, he turned down to the pier to consider the matter. He had not much comfort in that. As he turned again into the High-street, he heard the sound of voices far up in the square, and as he went on, he caught sight of his own low carriage standing in the midst of what seemed a crowd of people, not waiting there quietly, but eager and excited, over something which had pleased them well.

And could it be possible? In the carriage sat his daughter-in-law with his grandson on her lap. He knew that he was angry then, and he pushed his way forward intending to say so plainly, and to put an end to all this, at least as far as she was concerned.

But when he drew nearer, and Marion, with the tears running over her smiling face, stretched out both hands to him over her son, claiming his sympathy in the great joy that had come to her, somehow he forgot his anger and shook her hands kindly and joyfully; yes, and kissed her there before all the folk, to their intense amazement and delight.

It had not been at Marion that he had been angry. And he had not even the excuse of danger for his anger, for young Robbie Saugster had placed himself at the heads of the ponies, and there was not the slightest danger of their running away.

And when he had time to look about him, there was half the folk in Portie assembled to welcome the returned sailor, and in the midst of them stood George, with his arm laid across the shoulders of his friend. It was something to see these two faces—the one fair, smiling, noble,—the other no less noble, but brown and weatherbeaten, and with a cloud upon it, notwithstanding all the joy of home coming. They were brothers in heart, he saw that, whatever might befall. Before he could make up his mind to push his way toward them, a hush fell on the crowd. Captain Calderwood was making a speech.

It was not much of a speech that Captain Calderwood made, however.

He had only done his duty, he said, as nobody knew better than the seafaring folk of Portie, every one of whom would have done the same in his place, if they had seen the same reason. He was glad to be safe home again with his ship and cargo, and not a life lost, and he was proud of the welcome they were giving him—for there was no place like Portie to him, and no folk like the folk of Portie whom he had known all his life.

That was all. But George made a speech, and said just enough and no more—"as he ay does," his proud father thought as he listened.

Still standing with his hand on his friend's shoulder he said a few words about what Captain Calderwood had done. He could not tell them the story, because he had heard nothing as yet, more than the rest. But he knew as well as if he had been told, how all things had been ordered on board of the "Ben Nevis," both before the storm and after it, because he knew Captain Calderwood.

He had done his duty. That was all. But he need not tell the men of Portie—the Saugsters and the Cairnies, the Smiths and the Watts, the Bruces and the Barnets, who had had sailors among their kin longer ago than the oldest of them could mind—what duty meant to a sailor.

It meant to him, whiles, what heroism meant to other folk. It meant courage to face danger, patience undying through want and weariness and waiting, cheerful endurance through wakeful nights and toilsome days, and long banishment from friends and home.

It meant to the master, a power to command himself, as well as his men; it meant skill and will, and wisdom to act, and strength to bear up under the terrible responsibility of holding in his hand other men's lives, no one but him coming between them and God.

To the men it meant obedience, entire and unquestioning, sometimes, alas! to unreasonable commands—to tyranny to which, in the hands of evil men, unrestrained power might easily degenerate. It meant to all and each—to master and to man—a taking his life in his hand—a daily and nightly facing of death—ay, and of suffering death. It might mean that to some of their own, now far away. It might have meant that to Captain Calderwood, for instead of coming home with ship and cargo safe and with not a life lost, he might have given his own life in doing his duty, as his father had done before him, and his grandfather, as all the men of Portie knew.

"And is he less a hero to us to-day because he has only done his duty? And if instead of having him here among us to-day—to fill with joy and pride every sailor's heart in Portie—there had come to us from the sea, first a vague and awful rumour of danger and loss, and then one or other of the tokens that have come to some here—a spar, a broken piece of the ship, a word or two written beneath the very eyes and touch of death—would he not have been a hero to us then? And all the more, that having no thought of what men's eyes might see in his deeds, or men's tongues tell of them, he had lived through the violence of the tempest, and through the lingering days of peril that followed, only to do his duty?"

It was here that George's speech ought to have come to an end. It was at this point that his father thought he had said "just enough and no more." And it was here also that Willie shrugged his shoulders under the hand that still rested lovingly on them as he muttered,—

"Hoot, man, Geordie! Cut it short." But the folk—who had listened in a silence so absolute that the "click, click" of Mrs Cairnie's crutch could be heard on the stone causeway—stirred a little and murmured, and then waited for more. And George had more to give them.

"And now, men of Portie—sailors and fishers—ay, and sutors and saddlers, masons and merchants—every man among you, I have just one word more to say to you all—but chiefly to you sailors. Willie here has whispered two words in my ear, and one of them I'll give you.

"Never through all that terrible storm that beat upon them, nor after it, when the bitter thought that the ship must be forsaken was forced upon them, nor during the long doubtful days—harder to bear—that followed, when in the morning none could say whether hope or fear was to win the day, or at night whether there was to be another day to them—through all that time, I say, not a man among them looked to the devil for courage to dare his fate, or deaden his fears. There passed not the lips of a man among them a drop of that which has lost more ships, and broken more hearts, and beguiled more sailors from their duty, than you and I, and all here could count in a day."

"Is that so, Willie?" cried a voice from the crowd. "Ay, is it. And no man here needs me to point the moral."

Willie had had enough of it by this time. He would not be beguiled into answering questions or telling tales. So he slipped his shoulder from under George's hand and withdrew a little from him.

But George did not move. He stood with glad eyes looking down on the familiar faces of his townsfolk and with a sweet and kindly gravity which was better to see than a smile, and when he lifted his hand, the movement in the crowd and the murmur of talk that had risen were hushed.

The last word had been from his friend. This was from himself. It was only a word. It was not about the courage or skill or immovable patience of the young commander that he spoke; but of something that lay behind all these, and rose above them—the living belief in an eye that saw him, in a hand that held him, in a will that controlled and guided and kept him through all, and in a love and care that could avail in shipwreck and loss; ay, in death itself.

It was this living belief in the Lord above as a living Lord that had stood him in such stead in those terrible days.

"Was Willie *feared*, think ye?" said George, coming back to their common speech in his earnestness. "Some o' ye ha'e come through, and mair than aince, the terrors o' storm and threatened shipwreck, and ye ha'e seen how strength and courage, and common humanity itself, whiles fails before the blackness and darkness and tempest; and it's ilka ane for himsel', be he master or man.

"But, with this belief in a living Lord who has called Himself and proved Himself friend and brother in one, was there danger of this to Captain Calderwood and those whom he commanded?

"Belief, said I? Nay, lads, who of us can doubt that the Lord Himself stood by him, as He stood by Paul His servant at such another time, giving him promise of life to them who saw only death waiting them.

"Was Captain Calderwood afraid? Look ye at his clear eye, and take a grip o' his steady hand, and hearken to what his men may have to say of him, and ye'll ken that he came out of it all by other help and a better strength than his own—a help and a strength that we a' need, on land and sea, and that we can get for the seeking—as some o' ye ken better than I can tell you—and may it be baith yours and mine when our time of trouble shall come—" said George ending rather abruptly at last.

Chapter Twenty Seven.

At Last!

"Grandpapa," whispered Marion, as her husband and her brother drew near, "do you think there ever was so glad and proud a woman as I am to-night?"

He had not time to answer her, but he shook her brother's hand cordially.

"God bless ye, Willie, man. Welcome home." And for the moment he quite forgot the shock which the first sight of the young man had given him. It was only for a moment, however, and the remembrance of it brought a cloud to his brow, and sharpened his voice as he said,—

"George, man, I think ye have been forgetting your wife with your speech-making."

George laughed.

"She will forgive the first offence in that way, for the sake of the occasion."

"Weel, weel! haste ye home now for it's mair than time baith for her and the bairn. No, ye'll go with her yourself I have sent Robbie Saugster with the inn fly to your aunt's, and they'll all come out in it. And I'm going to walk. I have a word to say to Captain Calderwood. Not go?" added the old man sharply as a look of hesitation and doubt passed over Willie's face. "Where on earth should you go but to your ain sister's house? It's hers while she's in it, and so it's yours, to say nothing o' George there, who surely is your friend and brother, whatever ye may ca' me."

And as Captain Calderwood had something to say to him also, they set off together. But they walked half the distance before either uttered a word. Willie waited for Mr Dawson to speak, and he, remembering that no one bad seen him at his sister's house, was at a loss how to begin. But when they came in sight of Saughleas, Captain Calderwood paused.

"Mr Dawson, I must say a word to you now, or I shall be taking a welcome from you under false pretences. I love your daughter. I have loved her all my life."

Here was an opening with a vengeance!

"And what says she to that?" asked Mr Dawson grimly.

"I have never spoken a word to her. May I speak to her now?"

"And how was that—since it's been all your life?" said Mr Dawson ignoring the question.

"There were reasons enough. I was only the mate of the 'John Seaton,' and she was the young lady of Saughleas. And I had promised my mother that I would never even look my love without your sanction. Afterwards there were other reasons as well."

"I dare say ye may have a guess as to what her answer might be?"

"Mr Dawson, give me your leave to ask her. I have not seen her for years. Yes, I have seen her—but she has not seen me, and we have not spoken a word to each other, since the day before May's marriage."

"And I mind ye left in a hurry. Did she send ye awa'?"

"No. I did not speak to her; but if I had stayed I must have spoken. And what would you have thought of my pretensions beside those of Captain Harefield? And indeed, I knew well that, except for my love of her, I wasna her equal. So I said, I will forget her and I went away?"

"That's a long time since. And ye have never seen her again?"

"Yes. I have seen her. I saw her once in the Park riding with her brother and Captain Harefield, and I saw her looking at the pictures among all the great folk, and I used to see her whiles, playing in the garden with her sister's bairns."

"And that was the way ye took to forget her?" said Mr Dawson dryly.

"No. I had given that up as impossible. That was the way I took to teach myself the folly of remembering her."

"And what has happened to make it less like folly now?"

"Well," said Captain Calderwood after a pause, "the first gleam of hope I got was when Sir Percy Harefield proposed to take ship with me on the 'Ben Nevis.' He has gotten his answer, I thought. And I vowed that if ever I came home again I would speak to you—"

"Jean is of age, and in a sense her own mistress. She could do as she pleased, even if I were to refuse you."

"I shall never speak to her unless I have your full and free consent."

It was queer, Mr Dawson thought George had said the same to him about Marion, and had meant it too, as possibly this young man meant it also. He cast a sidelong glance at the strong, grave face beside him. It had grown white through all its healthy brown.

"Curious!" thought Mr Dawson. "Now, I dare say that didna happen in the very face o' the tempest. Surely a love that has lasted all his life must be a good thing for any woman to have."

But all the same he wished with all his heart that he could refuse to let him speak. Not that he had any special fear of Jean. She would surely have given some token during all these years, if her fancy had turned to Willie Calderwood. But he had returned a hero—"in a small way," as Mr Dawson put it, and young lassies are so open to impressions of that kind. And the lad was every inch a man, that could not be denied.

"I ken well she might look higher. Who is worthy of her?" said Willie humbly.

"It teems to me ye can ken little about her," said Mr Dawson irritably. "There's George now, what says he? He kens all this, doubtless?"

"He kens, doubtless," repeated Willie gravely. "But his sister's name has never been named between us—in that way."

So the father had not even that excuse for vexation. He had no excuse. The young man was acting honourably in the matter, and he told himself that he was not afraid about Jean's answer. And yet in his secret heart he was a little afraid. They had come to the gate by this time.

"Mr Dawson, do you bid me come into your house, after what I have told you?"

"Bid ye come in! And your sister waiting for you at the door, and your friend and brother as weel! I would hardly venture in myself without you. And indeed I welcome you heartily to my house, for your own sake as well as theirs. And as to—that other matter—we'll say nae mair about that the nicht."

With this the young man was obliged to content himself George's eyes were full of questions, but his lips uttered not one as he took him to his room, to supply all that had been left in the bag forgotten in the town. Before they came down again the fly had crept up to the door, but there was no one waiting for them in the hall except Miss Jean, and she was ready with a second welcome.

"It is good to see ye here, Willie," said she as they went into the parlour together.

Jean had gone straight to the dining-room, and her father heard her there giving orders to Phemie in her usual voice. By and by she came out, carrying her head high—"the young lady of Saughleas" indeed; and Mr Dawson smiled at his fears as she came slowly toward him. She went up the long room in the same stately way, holding out her hand and saying gravely,—

"You are welcome home, Captain Calderwood."

But when they looked into each other's faces—these two who had been strangers so long—how it all happened cannot be told. Did he clasp her to him? or did she lay her head upon his breast?

It was only amazement that the father felt at first. No one knew less than he did himself whether he was glad or sorry at the sight. And then Miss Jean came over to him with slow soft steps, and they went out together.

"George," said she gently, "I think I might say that I have nothing else to wish for here, if I were sure that this didna trouble you."

"It canna be helpit, it seems, whether or no," said he, but he let her take his hand, and his eyes looked soft and kindly.

George and Marion came in at the moment and made a diversion.

"Are ye no' ower weary to be down again, my dear?" said Mr Dawson. "Ye ha'e had an afternoon of exertion and excitement, and ye maun mind that ye ha'e anither dependin' on ye now."

"Tired! Do I look tired?" said Marion.

Certainly there was no sign of fatigue in the bright face of the young mother as she came smiling toward him.

"Weel, then, George, ye'll bring in your aunt and Mrs Calderwood. The dinner has waited long, and it shall wait no longer." And he gave his arm to Marion as he spoke.

"My dear," said he, leading her to Jean's place at the head of the table, "sit ye here, for I doubt Jean will want little dinner the day." And it was Marion's seat ever after.

"Has any thing happened to Jean?" said Marion. "Nothing is wrong, I hope."

"Nothing that can be helpit, I doubt. Ye'll hear in time, I dare say." And then he nodded to Mrs Calderwood who had grown very white.

"Ay, it's the old way. I doubt your Willie is thinking as little of you as my Jean is of me at this moment. But we'll take our dinner anyway."

Mrs Calderwood sat down without a word. It was an awkward hour for every one of them, though Miss Jean and her nephew did what they could to keep up conversation for them all. It was all the more so for Mr Dawson, that he was not sure what his own feelings were or ought to be. He sat hardly hearing what was said, though he put in a word now and then, but all the time he was thinking,—

"If any one had said to me four years since that the widow Calderwood's daughter would be sitting at the head of my table, and that I should be glad to see her there, would I have believed it? And her mother too, the very sight o' whose widow's cap used to anger me in the kirk itself. As for Jean, my sister, I ay ken when she's pleased, though she says nothing. And George too, though I dare say he's sorry for me, and will say no word to his friend, till I give him leave—as I maun do now, I suppose, whether I'm pleased or no'."

But Mr Dawson was less displeased than he supposed himself to be. He had been taken utterly by surprise, which was never agreeable to him, even when the surprise was a pleasant one. And it came to him with a feeling of comfort that neither his sister nor his son was likely to make a mistake, and be glad for the wrong thing where Jean was concerned. But it was a long hour to him, and when it was over he went away as his custom was for a while's peace to his own peculiar domain.

And here after a little Jean found him. She went in, feeling very much as she used to feel long ago, when some piece of girlish mischief more than usually serious, made her conscious of meriting a rebuke from her father.

She had been upstairs since she came home, and now wore one of her prettiest gowns, as befitted the occasion, and she had put a rose in her hair, which had not happened for a long time; and when her father turned at the sound of her voice, he saw as fair and sweet a daughter as ever gladdened a father's heart.

She had always been fair and sweet, but there was a new look in her face to-day. Her eyes fell before his; but he knew it was rather to veil the happiness that shone in them, than to hide the shyness which made it not easy for her to look up. His heart could not but grow soft as he looked.

"Were you wanting me, papa?" said Jean, feeling more and more like the childish culprit that was to be chidden first and then forgiven. Mr Dawson himself thought of those days, when his hardest words to Jean were sure to end gently, as he bade her be a good lassie and go to her mother. But he did not let the softness pass into his look or his voice as he said,—

"What is this that I have been hearing of you, Jean?"

"Are ye very angry, papa? I couldna help it."

"Dinna ye think I have a right to be angry, hearing such a tale after all these years?"

"But, papa, I didna ken. I thought he had forgotten me, and whiles I wasna sore that he had ever cared; and, papa, nothing has been said even yet." Mr Dawson laughed.

"And ye wouldna have broken your heart, even if this confident sailor had never come home?"

"No, papa. I don't think it. There is always plenty of work in the world, and I would have tried to do my share, as Auntie Jean has done. I should not have broken my heart, but—you are not very angry, papa?"

"My dear, my anger is neither here nor there. Ye are your ain mistress now, and can do as you please without asking my leave."

Jean went white as she listened, and sat suddenly down, gazing at him with wide, startled eyes. She had expected her father to be disappointed, perhaps angry, but she had expected nothing so terrible as this.

"Papa," she said, rising and coming a step nearer, "nothing can happen without your full and free consent. If you cannot give it, you must send— Captain Calderwood away—"

"They have all said that," said Mr Dawson to himself. Aloud he said with a dubious smile, "And ye'll promise no' to break your heart about him yet?" But his eyes softened wonderfully as he looked at her. "Papa," said Jean laying her hand on his shoulder as she stood a little behind him, "we love one another dearly. And you ay liked Willie, papa, and so did— mamma."

"My dear, I like him well. But have you thought of all you will have to bear as a sailor's wife?—the anxiety and suspense, the long, long waiting, and—"

"But, papa, I should have that anyway. I *have* had it, though—"

"My dear, ye little ken. And it might have been so different with you?"

"No, papa. It never could have been different. I wouldna have broken my heart, but I could never have cared for any one else."

A knock at the door prevented any thing more, and in answer to Mr Dawson's voice Captain Calderwood entered.

"I beg your pardon, Mr Dawson. I thought you were alone," said he in some embarrassment.

"Come awa' in," said Mr Dawson. "I thought, my lad, there was nothing more to be said the nicht?"

"And so did I. And indeed there has been little said as yet."

Mr Dawson laughed uneasily. No one was less fitted to act the part of the mollified father at the last moment, and he felt quite as little at his ease as either of them. But he could not but look with pride and pleasure on the handsome pair.

"I doubt there is little more that need be said."

"Only a single word from you, sir. I know as well as you that I am not worthy of her, but man and boy I have loved her all my life."

Mr Dawson had risen and Jean's face was hidden on his shoulder. He raised her face and kissed her, saying softly,—

"I doubt the word is with Jean now."

It is possible that even now Mr Dawson might have resented a triumphant claiming of Jean on her lover's part. But he only smiled, well pleased when the young man bowed his handsome head and kissed her hand as if it had been the hand of a royal princess. And then he sent them away to be congratulated by Aunt Jean and the rest.

"And if they are any of them more surprised at my consent than I am myself, it will be strange," said he to himself as he sat down again, not sure even yet that he was not displeased, or at least disappointed still. But by the time he heard the slow unequal steps of his sister coming, as was her custom when any thing more than usual was going on, for a word or two with him before she went to her bed, he was able to receive her softly spoken congratulations cheerfully enough.

She did not use many words; for she had an intuitive knowledge that some of her brother's thoughts about this matter had better not be uttered. But there was no mistaking the grave gladness of her face, and it came into her brother's mind that his sister's thoughts about most things were such as usually commended themselves to him in the end.

As for the others to whom Captain Calderwood after a little conducted his promised wife, none of them except Marion confessed to surprise, and none of them seemed to share the old man's doubt as to whether it was matter for rejoicing or no. Jean's first glance at Mrs Calderwood was a little wistful and beseeching, as though she were not quite sure of a daughter's welcome. But two or three low spoken words set that at rest forever. Captain Calderwood's doubtful looks were cast on Miss Jean.

"I ken weel I'm no worthy of her, auntie," he said.

"Ah! weel!—if she thinks it—that is the main thing," said Miss Jean.

"My friend, and twice my brother," was all George said to him. And to Jean he said softly, "Happy woman?" and that was all.

Not a soul in Portie but had something to say about them on the occasion. Every body was surprised at the first announcement of the news, though afterwards there were two or three who had had, they said, an inkling of it all along. There was a whisper among the fine folk in the High-street which implied that Miss Dawson might have laid herself open to the suspicion of having "passed through the wood to find a crooked stick at the last." But even in the High-street no one ventured to say it aloud. For the handsome sailor, though he was not a rich man, was as good as the best of them, even in their own partial opinion.

It was a grand ending to Captain Calderwood's romance of the sea in the opinion of all the seafaring folk of the town. The hand of the best and bonniest lass in Portie was a suitable reward for the hero. And when it was whispered that they "had ay cared for one another since they were bairns together" the tokens of the general approbation were given with enthusiasm.

"And that is an end o' the twa Miss Jeans. But it's o' George Dawson himsel' that I'm ay thinkin'," said Mrs Cairnie to all who would listen to her. "As for auld Miss Jean—her consent was what ye would expect. She was ay soft-hearted, and she has had an experience o' her ain. But as for auld George!—"

But even Mrs Cairnie owned that if he was not satisfied with the prospects of his daughter, "ye wouldna ken it by him." And Mr James Petrie, who watched him closely, and had better opportunities, said the same, and so did Portie generally.

One token of his satisfaction was of a kind that all Portie could appreciate, though those chiefly concerned would gladly have dispensed with it. He insisted on a grand wedding, and as Captain Calderwood's time was limited, the wedding had to be hastened, and there was some dismay at Saughleas at the thought of it. But May, who agreed with her father heartily on this point, came down, and took the matter into her own hands, and distinguished herself on the occasion.

It was a grand wedding. There were many guests and many gifts, and it must be confessed many opinions entertained, though not expressed, as to the wisdom of the marriage. But no one ventured to hint that the wedding itself was not a splendid success.

Strangely enough, Sir Percy Harefield was there and his sister. They were visitors at Blackford again. Mrs Eastwood looked with silent and rather scornful amazement on the girl who had slighted all that her brother had to offer, and who was now giving herself to this—sailor.

Even Mrs Eastwood could not look at Captain Calderwood on his wedding morning and join any contemptuous term to his name. He was like a young sea king among them all, she acknowledged; and he was a hero, it seemed, to these quaint northern folk that made his world. With a dim remembrance of her own youthful dreams, she acknowledged that perhaps, after all, Miss Dawson's choice was not so surprising; and even her love and admiration for her brother could not make her blind to the contrast which the two men made. But she was scornful of Jean's choice all the same.

Sir Percy was scornful of no one, but friendly and admiring, though a little heavy and dull, among so many gay folk. But he presented the bride with an elegant bracelet and bore no malice. He offered his congratulations to both bridegroom and bride with sufficient heartiness, and not even his sister could tell whether any painful sense of regret touched his heart that day.

One good thing came out of the grand wedding. There were guests from far and near, and among the rest—as one of the bridesmaids—came pretty Emily Corbett. Not the slip of a lassie who had clambered over the rocks and run about the sands with her little brother and sister and the rest of the bairns that happy summer long ago, but a stately young Englishwoman, tall and fair and wise.

In her presence Mr James Petrie forgot several things, and among the rest, his father's pawky hints about Miss Langrigs and her tocher, which were to be had for the asking, as he thought. And despite many prophecies to the contrary, James married for love a portionless bride, and was made a man of by the doing it.

The "young sea king" and his bride had a few days among the Highland hills, and a few days more among the English lakes. But the real "wedding journey" was made in the "Ben Nevis." They sailed away together into a new summer beneath Southern skies, and Jean got a glimpse of a new world full of wonders to her untravelled eyes.

Happily both voyages were as peaceful and pleasant as the last had been tempestuous, and nothing happened to darken a single hour of that happy time. Through the quiet of the soft sunny days, and the glory of nights made beautiful by the light of unfamiliar stars, these two young people, who had been for the last five years almost as strangers to each other, renewed their acquaintance, and indeed grew into a truer and deeper knowledge of each other than years of common life might have brought them, and before the happy outward voyage was over, there mingled with Jean's love for her husband the reverence which no true heart can withhold from the man "who is good before God."

It was not a full experience of sea life which his wife had got, Captain Calderwood owned, but this was less to be regretted, that she looked forward to many another voyage in the years that were before them. In the mean time she came home to her own house in the High-street where Miss Jean and Mrs Calderwood had been living together all this time. It was her home and theirs for many a happy year, and other homes in Portie were made happier through the happiness of theirs.

Jean had much work laid to her hand in her own home as the years went on, and she found also something to do beyond it. She was her father's almoner to many a widow and orphan child in Portie; and she helped her brother with higher work than her father's almsgiving.

Through her Miss Jean enjoyed in her last days, that which had made the happiness of her life for many years—the ministry of love to the "stranger," the "naked," the "sick, and in prison," for His sake who said, "Inasmuch as ye did it to the least of these, ye did it unto me."

And her experience as a sailor's wife and the mother of children, did not make her less fit for this work, but more. It made her wise to understand, and strong to help other sailors' wives in their time of need, and firm as well as tender in her dealings with many a child whom the cruel sea made fatherless.

And to many "puir auld bodies," who had forgotten the events of yesterday, and last year, and of many a long year besides; and had come in their second childhood to live over the days of their youth again, the help and comfort which made their days of waiting a quiet rest, before the last "flitting," still came to their belief as help and comfort used to come through "The Twa Miss Jeans."

The End.